A SOCIAL HISTORY
EDUCATIONAL STU____
AND RESEARCH

A Social History of Educational Studies and Research examines the development of the study of education in the UK in its broader educational, social and political context since its early beginnings in the first part of the twentieth century. By providing a historical analysis of the contested growth of the field, this book examines the significant contribution that has been made by institutions of higher education, journals, textbooks, conferences, centres and academic societies. It discusses the problems and opportunities of the field, as well as its prospects for survival and adaptation to current changes in the decades ahead. The work draws on documentary sources, social network analysis and interviews with leading figures from across the field.

This book highlights international influences on the development of educational studies and research in the UK, its role in the growing internationalisation of the field as a whole and also comparisons and contrasts with the nature of the field elsewhere. It relates the development to the wider social, political and economic changes affecting higher education in general and educational studies and research in particular. It addresses the historical development of disciplines in higher education institutions and the nature, extent and limitations of interdisciplinarity.

A Social History of Educational Studies and Research discusses the problems and opportunities facing the study of education today and its prospects of adapting to changes in the decades ahead. It is a distinctive and original analysis of educational studies and research that provides the first comprehensive study of its type.

Gary McCulloch is Brian Simon Professor of the History of Education at the UCL Institute of Education, University College London, UK.

Steven Cowan is a researcher in the history of education.

Foundations and Futures of Education

Peter Aggleton, *UNSW Australia*
Sally Power, *Cardiff University, UK*
Michael Reiss, *UCL Institute of Education, UK*

Foundations and Futures of Education focuses on key emerging issues in education as well as continuing debates within the field. The series is interdisciplinary and includes historical, philosophical, sociological, psychological and comparative perspectives on three major themes: the purposes and nature of education; increasing interdisciplinarity within the subject; and the theory-practice divide.

A full list of titles in this series is available at: **www.routledge.com/Foundations-and-Futures-of-Education/book-series/FFE.**

A SOCIAL HISTORY OF EDUCATIONAL STUDIES AND RESEARCH

Gary McCulloch and Steven Cowan

Routledge
Taylor & Francis Group

LONDON AND NEW YORK

First published 2018 by Routledge

2 Park Square, Milton Park, Abingdon, Oxfordshire OX14 4RN
52 Vanderbilt Avenue, New York, NY 10017

Routledge is an imprint of the Taylor & Francis Group, an informa business

First issued in paperback 2018

British Library Cataloguing-in-Publication Data
A catalogue record for this book is available from the British Library

Library of Congress Cataloging-in-Publication Data
Names: McCulloch, Gary, author. | Cowan, Steven, author.
Title: A social history of educational studies and research / Gary McCulloch
   and Steven Cowan.
Description: Abingdon, Oxon ; New York, NY : Routledge, 2017. |
   Series: Foundations and futures of education | Includes bibliographical
   references.
Identifiers: LCCN 2017005710 | ISBN 9781138898073 (hbk) |
   ISBN 9781315708775 (ebk)
Subjects: LCSH: Education—Study and teaching (Higher)—Great
   Britain. | Education—Research—Great Britain.
Classification: LCC LA637 .M3545 2017 | DDC 370.71/10941—dc23
LC record available at https://lccn.loc.gov/2017005710

ISBN: 978-1-138-89807-3 (hbk)
ISBN: 978-0-367-22058-7 (pbk)

Typeset in Bembo
by Apex CoVantage, LLC

CONTENTS

FIGURES

APPENDICES

ABBREVIATIONS

AERA	American Educational Research Association
AERS	Applied Educational Research Scheme
ATCDE	Association of Teachers in Colleges and Departments of Education
BAAS	British Association for the Advancement of Science
BBC	British Broadcasting Corporation
B.Ed.	bachelor of education (degree)
BERA	British Educational Research Association
BERJ	*British Educational Research Journal*
BJEP	*British Journal of Educational Psychology*
BJES	*British Journal of Educational Studies*
BJSE	*British Journal of Sociology of Education*
BPS	British Psychological Society
BSA	British Sociological Association
CACE	Central Advisory Council for Education (England)
CARE	Centre for Applied Research in Education
CATE	Council for the Accreditation of Teacher Education
CERI	Centre for Educational Research and Innovation
CCCS	Centre for Contemporary Cultural Studies
DCS	Department of Curriculum Studies
DBRA	Danish Business Research Academy
DES	Department of Education and Science
DFBE	Danish Forum for Business Education
DfES	Department for Education and Skills
EARLI	European Association for Research in Learning and Instruction
ECER	European Conference on Educational Research
EEC	European Economic Community
EEF	Education Endowment Foundation

EERA	European Educational Research Association
EERJ	*European Educational Research Journal*
ESRC	Economic and Social Research Council
GNP	gross national product
HEA	Higher Education Academy
HEFCE	Higher Education Funding Council for England
HES	History of Education Society
HOCD	House of Commons Debates
HoE	*History of Education* (journal)
HTML	Hypertext Markup Language
IOE	Institute of Education (London)
IIEP	International Institute for Educational Planning
ISCHE	International Standing Conference for the History of Education
JEP	*Journal of Education Policy*
JEXP	*Journal of Experimental Pedagogy*
JPE	*Journal of Philosophy of Education*
JSTOR	Journal Storage (Web-based source)
KCL	King's College London
LCC	London County Council
LDA	latent dirichet allocation
LDTC	London Day Training College
LEA	Local Education Authority
LSE	London School of Economics
MACOS	Man: A Course of Study
NERF	National Education Research Forum
NF	Nuffield Foundation
NFER	National Foundation for Educational Research
NSSE	National Society for the Study of Education
OECD	Organisation for Economic Co-operation and Development
ORE	*Oxford Review of Education*
PESGB	Philosophy of Education Society of Great Britain
PISA	Programme of International Student Assessment
PPE	philosophy, politics and economics
PSC	Parliamentary and Scientific Committee
RAE	Research Assessment Exercise
REF	Research Excellence Framework
SCER	Standing Committee on Educational Research
SCRE	Scottish Council for Research in Education
SCSE	Standing Conference on Studies in Education
SERA	Scottish Educational Research Association
SES	Society for Educational Studies
SRHE	Society for Research into Higher Education
SSRC	Social Science Research Council
SUCSE	Scottish Universities Council for Studies in Education

TCA	Training College Association
TLRP	Teaching and Learning Research Programme
TTA	Teacher Training Agency
UDE	University Department of Education
UFC	University Funding Council
UKRI	UK Research and Innovation
UNESCO	United Nations Educational, Scientific and Cultural Organisation

ACKNOWLEDGEMENTS

We wish to acknowledge the generous support of the Society for Educational Studies (SES), which funded the national project, The Social Organisation of Educational Studies – Past, Present and Future, on which the current work is based.

Professor Gary McCulloch took the lead in preparing and writing the work as a whole. He is currently president-elect of the British Educational Research Association (BERA) and editor of the *British Journal of Educational Studies* but writes here as an independent researcher, and neither BERA nor SES is responsible for the contents of the work.

Dr Steven Cowan (the research associate on the project) took the lead on chapter 6 and contributed to the authorship of the work as a whole.

We would also like to acknowledge Professor James Thomas, a member of the project team, who led the research work on network analysis of journals and is primarily responsible for chapter 5, and the significant contribution of Professor Gemma Moss, who was also a member of the project team and led the planning of the interviews with senior education academics.

We are also most grateful to the senior academics who gave their time to be interviewed for the present study, and to Logan Moss for his advice on international archives relating to the Carnegie Foundation.

Thanks to the members of all the seminars and conferences where aspects of the present work were rehearsed and discussed, to the series editors who have provided invaluable advice and to the publishers for their support and patience.

Gary McCulloch and Steven Cowan take joint responsibility for the work as a whole and for any shortcomings and errors.

Gary McCulloch
Steven Cowan

1

INTRODUCTION

Over the past century, education has become recognised as a prime investment for the future in order to pass on the cultural heritage to the next generation, to improve society, to organise production and industry. It is also a key to the organisation of society, to patterns of opportunity, status, hierarchy and power. With the accelerating growth of interest in the nature and impact of education, there has emerged in modern universities a comparatively new field of study: the study of education itself, based principally in departments of education. Such departments were created in many countries from the late nineteenth century onwards, originally with the main purpose of training teachers for the new national systems of education, but increasingly during the twentieth century to support the development of a deeper understanding of the phenomenon of education through concerted study and research. In Europe, this new field has often been framed in terms of the 'educational sciences' (Hofstetter 2012). In the UK, it has usually been described as 'educational studies' or more specifically in research terms as 'educational research' or 'education research'. This book will seek to examine the historical development of educational studies and research in UK universities – the academy. It will also assess how this broad and diverse field has developed in a changing social and political context into the knowledge formation that it has become in the twenty-first century.

There has been increasing international interest in the history of educational studies and research over the past decade. In the United States, the most important work has no doubt been Ellen Condliffe Lagemann's *An Elusive Science*, which traced the 'troubling history' of education research through the twentieth century, highlighting its variety and range, defining itself as a 'discipline history' in the sense that it sought to investigate 'the changing ecology of knowledge and the politics that has been part of that' (Lagemann 2001, p. xiv; see also Lagemann 1997).

David Labaree, also in the US, has valuably examined the low status of schools and departments of education within the academy, commenting:

> The ed school is the butt of jokes in the university, where professors portray it as an intellectual wasteland; it is the object of scorn in schools, where teachers decry its programs as impractical and its research as irrelevant; and it is a convenient scapegoat in the world of educational policy, where policymakers portray it as a root cause of bad teaching and inadequate learning.
>
> *(Labaree 2006, pp. 2–3)*

Labaree explains this poor reputation in terms of the historical association of schools of education with teacher education.

In Western Europe, Hofstetter and Schneuwly have analysed the institutionalisation of educational science in terms of the number of academic chairs, textbooks, institutions and posts that supported educational research, publications in specialised journals and public discourses in education (Hofstetter and Schneuwly 2004). Other recent European work has begun to chart the development of the educational sciences in different European countries since the Second World War (Laot and Rogers 2015). In the Baltic states, too, there has been a growth of interest in this theme, for example with the publication of two edited collections on the development of the educational sciences in Baltic countries during the twentieth century (Baltic Association of Historians of Pedagogy 2009, 2010). In Western Australia, a comparative history of five different departments of education in universities across the state has also been produced (Gardiner et al. 2011).

Such studies have been slower to develop in relation to the UK and have until recently tended to focus more upon developments in Scotland rather than in the rest of the country. As H.M. Knox pointed out in 1951, the study of education was treated in the later nineteenth century as an academic and cultural subject in Scotland, whereas in England the main focus was the professional preparation of teachers (Knox 1951, p. 34). The earliest academic chairs in education in Scotland were established at Edinburgh (Laurie) and St Andrews (Meiklejohn) in 1876. From 1892, education was a recognised arts subject for the master of arts degree in Scotland, and Scottish universities were also pioneers in creating an honours degree in education with the bachelor of education (B.Ed.) degree approved at Edinburgh in 1916 (Knox 1951; see also Simon 1990). The academic study of the theory and history of education was thus separated from teacher training, which was confined to training colleges (Bell 1983). In the interwar years, the Scottish Council for Research in Education (SCRE) was established (in 1928), and an independent and distinctive research tradition was created (see for example Lawn et al. 2010). This faded after the Second World War, although the creation of the Scottish Educational Research Association (SERA) in the 1970s was a significant initiative to revive and develop a distinct approach in a changing context.

There has until now been relatively little written on educational studies and research in the UK as a whole. John Nisbet, the first president of the British

Educational Research Association (BERA), was something of a pioneer in this respect with a number of reflective essays on the early origins of the field and also one on its development in the 1960s (Nisbet 2000, 2002, 2005, 2009). William Richardson has produced an extended article on the history of educational studies in the four nations of the UK from 1940 to 2002 (Richardson 2002). Peter Gordon edited four volumes of inaugural lectures by professors of education since the late nineteenth century, constituting a running commentary on the development of the field over the course of more than a century and the issues that have arisen during that time (Gordon 1980a, 1980b, 1988, 1995). J.B. Thomas has contributed a useful edited collection on the history of teacher education in universities, as well as a number of institutional histories (Thomas 1990, 1992).

A number of studies have considered the development of particular disciplines applied to education, for example a collection edited by Furlong and Lawn on the 'disciplines of education' (Furlong and Lawn 2011; see also Furlong and Lawn 2007). This focused on the state of the key disciplines of sociology, psychology, philosophy, history, economics, comparative and international education, and geography in relation to educational research and argued that, although they were all confident about their own roles and importance, they were becoming increasingly small and isolated. This view differed markedly from that of J.W. Tibble forty years before, who in 1966 had edited a widely noted work, *The Study of Education*, which framed the study of education fundamentally around the 'foundation disciplines' of philosophy, history, psychology and sociology (Tibble 1966; see also McCulloch 2002). Another significant recent work is John Furlong's 'anatomy of the discipline' of education (Furlong 2013a). Furlong's work seeks first to consider the history of the study of education in UK universities and then to understand the current situation of education in relation to teaching and research.

A particular concern of the current work is to consider the extent and nature of interdisciplinary approaches in educational studies and research, as well as the contributions made by the different disciplines in relation to these, with particular reference to the historical experience of the UK. It relates these to the broader emergence of interdisciplinarity as a strategy to define common problems in a changing educational, social and political context. Interdisciplinarity is currently a theme that is attracting general academic debate, represented for example in the publication of the report *Crossing Paths* in 2016 (British Academy 2016), and this book seeks to make a contribution to this broad discussion. These aims raise significant prior issues of definition about what we mean by disciplinarity and interdisciplinarity and also about the social construction of educational studies and research. They have a great deal of potential for enhancing our understanding of this field – its past, its present and indeed its future – and for promoting its contribution to education and the wider society (see also McCulloch 2012a). Within this overall picture, the field has always been in flux, never stable, and tensions between different interests across this broad and diverse coalition have been constant.

In the 1920s, the philosopher R.G. Collingwood published a book entitled *Speculum Mentis*, by which he meant the 'map of knowledge' (Collingwood 1924/2013).

Collingwood argued that unlike in the medieval world, when there had been an overarching unity of mind, the Renaissance had unleashed separation, difference and conflict in understandings of the world. Despite the growing complexity of modernity, Collingwood sought a mental map or general theory by which to understand the state of human knowledge. This has been an aim of many philosophers and theorists through the ages, witnessed for example in the Enlightenment of the eighteenth century in the *Cyclopedie* and in the early twenty-first century in the Internet (Burke 2012). A number of theorists and philosophers have proposed a general map of knowledge for the domain of education, for example the philosopher Louis Arnaud Reid and the historian W.H.G. Armytage in the 1950s (Armytage 1954/1980; Reid 1952). Increasingly, however, educators have resorted to focusing instead on dividing and categorising different parts of a complex and expanding map. Different phases of education have become established, from early childhood and primary through secondary and tertiary through further, higher, adult and third age education, as well as education designed for different groups of the population from the masses to the elite, according to location, family, religion, vocation, gender and ethnicity. Approaches to learning have multiplied, and teaching has also become diverse and multifaceted. The content or curriculum of education has extended and become divergent. As education has grown, it has become more complex; as it has expanded, it has differentiated.

At the same time, there have been interdisciplinary visions and initiatives at regular intervals over the past eighty years, episodes that have punctuated and also helped to shape the making of the field during this time. These include for example the Standing Conference on Studies in Education (SCSE) (founded in 1951), the *British Journal of Educational Studies* (*BJES*) (1952), the Centre for Contemporary Cultural Studies (CCCS) (1964) and the British Educational Research Association (BERA) (1974). Conferences have been a key site for such activity. The SCSE, founded originally with a broadly interdisciplinary mission, became for some years an elite vessel for discussion through its annual conferences, mainly for professors of education (McCulloch 2012b). Annual conferences have become a significant focus for societies and associations such as BERA, on a mass membership basis, and such societies have again witnessed tensions between disciplinary and interdisciplinary approaches. Societies have also organised the publication of journals on particular topics, which themselves represent the field in a particular way. The SCSE for example was responsible for the *BJES*, while BERA organised the development of the *British Educational Research Journal* (*BERJ*). Centres have similarly fostered study on a larger scale and with wider groups than has often been possible through university departments. CCCS is an interesting example of a university-based centre that promoted an interdisciplinary approach to issues closely related to education. The Teaching and Learning Research Programme (TLRP), in the late 1990s and the subsequent decade, also gave rise to a large number of large research projects across departments and universities designed to address broad problems.

Taking account of these activities, this book argues that this past and ongoing set of relationships between academic disciplines and interdisciplinarity is best understood in relation to an extended university project. That is, it occupies not only the departmental and faculty structures of the university but also its many accompanying projects, developed and promoted by practising academics, such as journals, societies, centres and conferences. This is what Smeyers and Depaepe have recently referred to as 'institutional spaces' that mediate intellectual space but also provide a wide range of places within which to conduct academic work (Smeyers and Depaepe 2013). Schriewer and Keiner have also usefully discussed the communication patterns and intellectual traditions of the educational sciences in France and Germany that represent a recognised body of knowledge (Schriewer and Keiner 1992).

It is important to understand the changing and contested nature of a discipline or of a field in relation to its history, that is, in the context of its long-term formation over a number of decades, often reaching back to the development of modern research universities in the nineteenth century. This is demonstrated compellingly by Lagemann in the US, who proposes that her 'discipline history of the scholarship of education' is intended directly to address her belief 'that many of the most difficult educational problems that exist in the United States today are related to the ways in which the study of education has been organised and perceived within universities' (Lagemann 2001, p. xv). In historical terms, Lagemann also insists that her notion of discipline history is not a rarified history of ideas, but is concerned with politics and society and is indeed a contribution to social history. The historian of literacy Harvey J. Graff, in his book *Undisciplining Knowledge* (Graff 2015), a comparative and critical history of interdisciplinary initiatives in the modern university, also makes a strong case for understanding knowledge formations from a perspective grounded in social history (see also McCulloch 2011 on the contributions of social histories of education). The present work therefore attempts to approach these issues around educational studies and research in terms of a social history, as an attempt to establish a deeper historical understanding than has previously been attained in the UK.

It is vital also to recognise the changing context within which these developments have taken place over the longer term. These include for example the growing role of the State in higher education since the Second World War and especially since the 1970s. The character of higher education has itself changed fundamentally, from a narrow social and academic elite to a diverse mass formation. Financial resources provide a further key variable, in the case of educational studies and research most clearly from a very small base in the 1940s through growth in the 1960s, to significant injections of finance associated with specific initiatives such as the TLRP in the 1990s. The four jurisdictions of the UK itself have also changed internally and in relation to one another over the past century. The processes of internationalisation and transnationalism, insidious on an everyday level and powerful both institutionally and structurally, have also increasingly impinged on local and national concerns.

In examining these issues, a number of methods have been deployed, in particular historical documentary methods including archives, text-mining of relevant journals and interviews with a cross-section of education academics. The combination of this unique set of data over several decades provides significant insights into a range of areas. Archival sources are particularly helpful over the period from the 1930s to the 1980s. The social networks of journals tell us a great deal about the nature of the field from the origins of the *BJES* in 1952 up to the present day. Interviews with academics highlight the issues as perceived by individual academics over the past two decades, in some cases reaching back further into the 1960s and even the 1950s. Overall, we are able to trace both institutional issues affecting national societies, journals, centres, conferences and departments, and the ways in which these also impinged on key individuals in the field.

Historical documentary methods have been used in the present study to trace the development of a number of key institutions, including archive-based documents where possible. There is no single large archive on which to base such a work in relation to educational studies and research in the UK, with the possible exception of the archive of the Institute of Education (IOE) itself, unlike many other fields and disciplines. This in itself reflects the general lack of historical memory in this area of study. However, there are several relatively small collections of primary source material that together help to shed light on the role of particular institutions and individuals. These include records from the National Archives, as well as from institutional archives of BERA (in the Modern Records Centre at Warwick University) and the IOE and from the personal papers of figures such as the historian of education Brian Simon (also based at the IOE archive). The many published texts in the field especially since the Second World War provide another useful set of evidence for the current study. McCulloch (2004a) discusses the use and analysis of such sources in a historical study of education, and this informs the present work.

This work also makes innovative use of text-mining as a way to assess the kinds of social networks represented by the academic journals in this field, most notably the *BJES*. As the US researcher Brian Carolan has affirmed, patterns of academic journal articles can tell us a great deal about what he describes as the structure of scholarly knowledge: 'As a cultural object, the journal article is intimately connected to both producers and consumers of scholarly knowledge. Whether using citations or collaborations there is much to be gleaned about the interworkings of a research community through this artefact' (Carolan 2008, p. 20). We focus especially on the oldest generic journal of the field in the UK, the *BJES* (founded in 1952), and also compare this with later broad-based journals such as *British Educational Research Journal* (*BERJ*) (1974) and the *Oxford Review of Education* (*ORE*) (1976), as well as the disciplinary journals *Journal of Philosophy of Education* (1965) and *History of Education* (1972).

A further source especially on the development of the field over the last thirty years is interview evidence from a broad range of senior academics who have worked in this field over that time. We selected forty academics from across the field, some of them associated with particular disciplines and others with a more generalist outlook, to discuss their views and experiences through semi-structured interviews in the academic year 2012–13 (40 anonymised semi-structured interviews in

2012–2013). Nearly all of these are anonymised and are given fictitious names here (consistent with their genders). Richard Johnson of the University of Birmingham is named as a respondent with his permission because his testimony bears in a unique way on the development of CCCS, with which he was closely involved. Interviewees were not in general asked about their memories of particular events, such as would be usual for an oral history interview, but rather for their approach to the issues around disciplinarity and interdisciplinarity and examples of these from their own careers.

In the next chapter, we critically assess the characteristics of modern disciplines and of multidisciplinarity and interdisciplinarity before considering the emergence of educational studies and research in the UK. Chapter 3 examines the case of the Institute of Education (IOE) in London and the extent to which it provided a model for other departments in the field. The IOE has been the largest university education department in the UK over the past century, a unique specialist institution in its own right and a leader in the field of educational studies and research both nationally and internationally. The IOE was founded originally as the London Day Training College in 1902 and assumed the title of the IOE in the 1930s when it became part of the University of London. Its size and scope have meant that it has been a key site for debates around disciplines of education and also interdisciplinarity, from the work of Fred Clarke as its director in the 1930s and 1940s, through its focus on the separate disciplines in the 1960s. Chapter 4 charts the growth of a national infrastructure for the field, first at an elite level through the SCSE in the 1950s and then on a mass basis with the emergence of BERA and SERA in the 1970s, in each case attempting but largely failing to foster an interdisciplinary approach. In Chapter 5, attention is given to the many journals in the field, including the *BJES*, and their influence on the construction of the field. Chapter 6 considers the various ways that have been developed for mapping the field as a whole, through textual and graphical representations of the field, including initiatives such as the Students Library of Education in the 1960s. In Chapter 7, the career of CCCS is examined in depth as an interesting example of an interdisciplinary project in an area closely related to education, cultural studies, and the advantages and problems that arose from this project. Chapter 8 focuses on the career patterns of academics in educational studies and research in order to analyse the nature of their interactions in the field. Chapter 9 assesses the changing nature of educational studies in the twenty-first century, as well as the opportunities and challenges that face the field in the future. Chapter 10 offers some final reflections by way of conclusion.

2

INTERDISCIPLINES AND THE MODERN UNIVERSITY

Historian of literacy Harvey J. Graff has demonstrated the importance of a historical perspective in tracing interdisciplinarity in the United States through the twentieth century and across several case studies in the university curriculum (Graff 2015). Graff argues that disciplinarity and interdisciplinarity have been closely linked and dependent on each other and should be understood in relation to each other. According to Graff, the tension between them has been played out in different ways from one discipline to another, often resulting in what he calls 'interdisciplines'. Both disciplines and interdisciplines, he suggests, are products of the modern research university, with their origins in the nineteenth century. He points out also that established disciplines may combine to form new disciplines, or 'interdisciplines', for example in the new social history and social science history that developed from the 1960s onwards (Graff 2015, chapter 4). This chapter will investigate the character of disciplines as they emerged and developed, as well as the idea of interdisciplinarity, in the British context. Educational studies and research have been powerfully shaped by the disciplines in interesting and distinctive ways over the longer term.

Theories of interdisciplinarity

Theoretical debates over the role of the disciplines and the nature of interdisciplinarity have been current since the 1960s. Differentiating between multidisciplinarity and interdisciplinarity has occupied much of this activity. Hugh Petrie, professor of the philosophy of education at the University of Illinois at Urbana-Champaign, defined the key difference between these approaches in 1976:

> The line is not hard and fast, but roughly it is that multidisciplinary projects simply require everyone to do his or her own thing with little or no necessity

for any one participant to be aware of any other participant's work. Perhaps a project director or manager is needed to glue the final product together, but the pieces are fairly clearly of disciplinary size and shape. Interdisciplinary efforts, on the other hand, require more or less integration and even modification of the disciplinary subcontributions while the inquiry is proceeding. Different participants need to take into account the contributions of their colleagues in order to make their own contribution.

(Petrie 1976, p. 9)

More recent analyses have largely maintained this basic distinction. For example, one of the leading theorists in this area is the US scholar Julie Thompson Klein, whose 1990 volume *Interdisciplinarity: History, Theory and Practice* (Klein 1990) set the tone for much detailed work. According to Klein, a subtle restructuring of knowledge has produced new divisions of intellectual labour, collaborative research, team teaching, hybrid fields, comparative studies, increased borrowing across disciplines and new pressures on the traditional divisions of knowledge. All of these trends, she argues, have encouraged a trend towards unity, synthesis and convergence, and the growth of 'interdisciplinarity'.

Klein has also produced a general model or taxonomy of interdisciplinarity that serves to highlight the key distinctions between multidisciplinarity, interdisciplinarity and transdisciplinarity (Klein 2010). In this model, multidisciplinarity is about juxtaposing, sequencing or coordinating different disciplines, in which they complement each other in a common endeavour leading to a partial integration of work. Interdisciplinarity is a more radical, shared enterprise in which the disciplines integrate, interact, link, focus and ultimately blend together. Transdisciplinarity is more radical still, conceived as an activity connected with the university but moving beyond the academy with the aim of transcending, transgressing and transforming boundaries in society as a whole (Klein 2010, p. 16). While 'conventional taxonomies' should not be jettisoned, she affirmed, 'they need to develop open, dynamic, and transactional approaches capable of depicting research in a network representation that is more aligned with changing configurations of knowledge and education' (Klein 2010, p. 28).

Beyond these fairly abstract distinctions, Klein also identifies the traits that she associates with what she terms the 'interdisciplinary individual'. She argues that these career patterns are usually well established among senior academics who have the confidence and experience to be able to step out of line and engage in interdisciplinary activities (Klein 1990, p. 182). On the other hand, she claims, the enthusiasm and creativity of many new scholars may also lead them in this direction, regardless of the conventional obstacles and restraints of the modern university. She also proposes a number of character traits of the interdisciplinary individual, including reliability, flexibility, patience, resilience, sensitivity to others, risk taking, a thick skin and a preference for diversity and new social roles (Klein 1990, p. 183). Also, certain abilities might be linked with such individuals, including a capacity to look at issues from different perspectives, and also skills such as differentiating, comparing, contrasting, relating, clarifying, reconciling and synthesising (Klein 1990, p. 183). Appraising the work of such individuals through their careers and biographies, she suggests, might be an effective means of highlighting their contributions to interdisciplinarity.

An idealised theorisation of a trend towards new forms of knowledge production was Gibbons et al.'s *The New Production of Knowledge* (1994). According to Gibbons et al., 'a new form of knowledge production is emerging alongside the traditional, familiar one' (Gibbons et al. 1994, p. vii). The older form, they proposed, could be characterised as 'Mode 1': disciplinary, hierarchical, institutionalised. The new knowledge production, Mode 2 knowledge, was by contrast transdisciplinary, non-hierarchical and non-institutional. It would be diffused more evenly and efficiently throughout society to help guide problem-solving efforts. This work attributed the structural shift towards Mode 2 knowledge to the expansion of higher education since the 1940s, the increasing number of institutions, a vast expansion in the supply of knowledge and increasing internationalisation and globalisation, which encouraged both collaboration and competition across nations. Overall, they contended:

> In transdisciplinary contexts, disciplinary boundaries, distinctions between pure and applied research, and institutional differences between, say, universities and industry, seem to be less and less relevant. Instead, attention is focused primarily on the problem area, or the hot topic, preference given to collaborative rather than individual performance and excellence judged by the ability of individuals to make a sustained contribution in open, flexible types of organisation in which they may only work temporarily.
>
> *(Gibbons et al. 1994, p. 30)*

This was a confident vision of the future that emphasised social benefits and improvements rather than the potential problems and complexities of new forms of knowledge production.

The British political scientist Wyn Grant has also analysed this general development. He explores the intellectual and practical challenges involved in working across disciplines, especially in teams and in 'thick' interdisciplinary work across the social and natural sciences, but points out the potential rewards in terms of understanding and responding to the large urgent problems of today, such as the environment and climate change (Greaves and Grant 2010). Both Klein and Grant emphasise, moreover, that interdisciplinarity does not necessarily replace the disciplines but indeed depends on disciplinary knowledge for its further development. This is also a key point for Peter Weingart, who insists that disciplines and their derivatives, specialities and research fields remain 'the principal organisational unity for the production and diffusion of knowledge'. At the same time, Weingart comments, boundaries between the disciplines are softened, and new interdisciplinary fields emerge, allowing cross-boundary research activities. Even if social and political interests were to promote interdisciplinary approaches, according to Weingart, this would be unlikely to lead to a system based exclusively on interdisciplinarity, and therefore he concludes that 'traditional disciplines and inter-, multi-, and trans-disciplinary research fields will exist side by side' (Weingart 2010, p. 13).

Further discussions have assessed the nature of boundary work around and across the disciplines. Klein has suggested that impermeable boundaries are associated with tightly knit, convergent communities, indicating the stability and coherence of intellectual fields such as the physical sciences and economics, while permeable boundaries are more characteristic of loosely knit, divergent academic groups, signalling a more fragmented, less stable, comparatively open-ended structure like sociology. She also points out that some fields of knowledge are hybrid in nature, including child development, cognitive science, women's studies, biopolitics and criminology (Klein 1993). The potential for interaction between and among the disciplines is frequently emphasised. For example, Jan Parker suggests that higher education curricula in the humanities need to build on both core disciplinary and supra-disciplinary texts, as well as 'texts which both inculcate and question inter-disciplinarity, preparing students to work in interdisciplinary collaborations' (Parker 2008, p. 264). The sociologist Neil Smelser insists, moreover, that '[t]he boundaries of most disciplines have become so permeable and indistinct, and so much exportation and importation has occurred that if one ranges widely in his or her discipline, one is being in effect interdisciplinary' (Smelser 2003, p. 653). These ideas are taken further in new work by Richard Thaler on the making of behavioural economics, a combination of psychology and economics, over the past half-century, highlighting the vagaries of individual decision making (Mullainathan and Thaler 2000; Thaler 2015).

Departments and disciplines

The academic disciplines and the departments that housed them assumed their modern form in universities in the nineteenth century, remaining highly resilient to change in the century that followed (Anderson and Valente 2002). This is an issue that is also taken up by the cultural historian Peter Burke (Burke 2012, especially chapter 6), who points out that Auguste Comte coined the term 'specialisation' in the mid-nineteenth century, while a new wave of specialised learned journals in the late nineteenth century accompanied the separation of disciplines and departments.

A 'discipline' might be defined, following King and Brownell (1966, p. 68), not solely as an area of study or of knowledge but as a community of scholars who share a domain of intellectual enquiry or discourse. This commonly involves a shared heritage and tradition, a specialised language or other system of shared symbols, a set of shared concepts, an infrastructure of books, articles and research reports, a system of communication among the membership and a means of instruction and initiation. It is therefore concerned with teaching as well as research and with a specific audience or constituency. It is also a dynamic as opposed to a static group that may often be a coalition of contested views and priorities (see also for example Goodson 1983 on 'subject coalitions'). According to Allen Repko, 'Disciplines are scholarly communications that define which problems should be studied, advance certain concepts and organising theories, embrace certain methods of investigation, provide forums for sharing research and insights, and offer career paths for scholars' (Repko 2008, p. 1). On this general basis, we may emphasise the nature of the books, articles and reports that have been published in each area. Nevertheless, it is also fundamental to such a study to note the kinds of extended community that each of the disciplines has generated, especially in the form of societies, journals and conferences. They thus make it possible to discuss the history of the disciplines not simply in terms of intellectual nor even of institutional history but also as a form of social history.

As Andrew Abbott has argued, the disciplines were themselves social structures, based on the organisational form of university departments, that have withstood assault for many years. Thus, he notes, the departmental structure in the US was largely unchanged between 1890 and 1910, and especially in the humanities and social sciences, the departmental structure showed only marginal change during the twentieth century (Abbott 2002, p. 206). They provide models, images and social practices of coherent discourses in academia. Indeed, according to Abbott, 'Every academic knows the experience of reading work from outside his or her discipline and knows the unsettling feeling it induces. Disciplines in fact provide a core element of the identity of most intellectuals in modern America' (Abbott 2002, p. 210). They also, he suggests, prevent knowledge from becoming too abstract or overwhelming and thus provide a specific tradition or heritage that can be built on (Abbott 2002). For these reasons, Abbott contends, in fifty years there will probably remain 'a disciplinary system recognisably descended from the present one' (Abbott 2002, p. 227).

In the UK, Becher and Parry have also emphasised the endurance of the disciplines. They argue that a discipline has both a cognitive and a social aspect. Social factors include incorporation in a typical academic organisation with the provision of courses from the undergraduate stage to an advanced level, a shared set of cultural values and recognition by the academy at large. Indeed, they insist, 'Only when a scholarly community is deemed intellectually acceptable by its peers, is it qualified to achieve disciplinary status' (Becher and Parry 2005, p. 134). They concur with Abbott that the established disciplines will continue to survive, 'even if only as unacknowledged partners to academic communities of practice' (Becher and Parry 2005, p. 142). Nevertheless, disciplines themselves are not stable or unchanging entities but are in constant flux. Christie and Maton have complained that the disciplines, despite their longevity and familiarity, are unappreciated for their enduring value and too little understood in terms of their theoretical and sociological characteristics (Christie and Maton 2011; see also Jacobs 2013).

Until the mid-nineteenth century, the social organisation of knowledge was developed through broadly based societies and journals. Major scholarly journals emerged in different parts of Europe from the 1660s, including the *Journal des Savants* in Paris (1665), the Royal Society of London's *Philosophical Transactions* (1666) and the *Giornale de Letterati* in Rome (1668) (Ruegg 2003). In the nineteenth century, however, Germany and the US were pioneers in the institutionalisation of disciplines in the form of separate university faculties, institutes or departments. For example, the University of Berlin, founded in 1810, was initially organised into only four faculties – philosophy, theology, law and medicine – but gradually diversified into institutes in different subjects (Burke 2012, p. 168). The key period was 1868–1914, a phase of keen competition between the new disciplines for academic recognition and status within the academy. Specialist journals and societies were also founded in rapid succession in Germany: in 1852 in forensic medicine, 1864 in opthalmology, 1868 in chemistry, 1872 in surgery, 1883 in botany, 1886 in gynaecology, 1889 in dermatology, 1892 in internal medicine, 1892 in dendrology, 1895 in otology and 1898 in pathology (Ruegg 2003). In the US, departments began to proliferate in the new universities that were being established. Daniel Coit Gilman, the first president of Johns Hopkins University, founded as the first research university in the United States in 1876, announced at his inauguration that the criterion for choosing professors would be their devotion to a particular line of study and their eminence in that speciality. Johns Hopkins and Chicago (1892) followed German models and themselves became models for other US universities such as Harvard and York (Burke 2012, p. 169).

In the UK, there were few new universities until the civic universities of Leeds, Sheffield and Manchester became established at the end of the nineteenth century, but specialised academic subjects became institutionalised even at the most traditional university. Philosophy had been entrenched in the traditional universities curriculum for centuries, and in the twentieth century was represented in new chairs and in the British Institute of Philosophical Studies (later the Royal Institute of Philosophy) in 1925. History became established as a separate academic discipline in the second half of the nineteenth century, although always in close connection with other subjects across the arts and sciences. The Royal Historical Society was founded in 1868 and the *English Historical Review* first published in 1886, the first journal of historical scholarship to be published in the English-speaking world. A School of Modern History was created at the University of Oxford in 1850. By the end of the century, modern history was overtaking the classical school of *litterae humaniores*, or 'Greats', in terms of student numbers. After 1901, the Honours School of History at Oxford produced more graduates than any other degree course, and their numbers continued to grow (Soffer 1987). At the University of Cambridge, Charles Kingsley, a novelist with broad interests, became Regius Professor of History in 1860, followed in 1869 by John Seeley who was particularly interested in political science (Briggs 2004, p. 469). After a separate history tripos was created under Seeley, by 1914 history was the largest single course at Cambridge also. In the University of London, too, there was rapid development, with the Institute of Historical Research founded in 1903. Thomas Tout was appointed to a chair of history at Owen's College in Manchester in 1890, with the University of Manchester becoming widely recognised as a centre for historical studies in the early decades of the twentieth century.

At the same time, there was innovation in higher education across the social sciences. The London School of Economics (LSE) was established in 1895, responsible not only for economics but also for geography, politics, administration and law, among others. The following year, the British Library of Political Science was founded with a similarly broad remit. Sociology also began to emerge, initially influenced by Comte and Durkheim in France. The *American Journal of Sociology* was founded in 1895 and Durkheim's *L'Annee Sociologique* the following year. In Britain, the Sociological Society of London was founded in 1904 and the first professor of sociology, Leonard Hobhouse, appointed at the LSE in 1907 (Briggs 2004, p. 485).

Another social science, psychology, was institutionalised as a university discipline, framed as an experimental science to be housed in dedicated departments and laboratories. In 1897, W.H.R. Rivers was made a lecturer in experimental psychology and the physiology of the senses at the University of Cambridge, with a room in the physiology department. Psychology departments were also established in London at University College, Bedford College and King's College. In Scotland, too, and also in the universities in the north of England, experimental psychology became widespread. The British Psychological Society (BPS) was formed in 1901, taking over the *British Journal of Psychology*, which was first established in 1904, as of 1914. The British Association for the Advancement of Science (BAAS) was also a significant forum for psychological debates, especially after a special subsection of Section I (Physiology) was set up for psychology in 1913 and then a separate section (Section J) for psychology on its own as of 1921 (see also Hearnshaw 1964 for a more detailed account).

Redrawing the map of learning?

Since the 1940s, there has been a general growth of interest in the idea and practice of interdisciplinarity. The earliest uses of the term itself have been traced to the late 1930s (Repko 2008). The Second World War and the establishment of national science policies in different countries encouraged systematic efforts to coordinate strategy across designated lines of work. In the 1950s, the success of the Soviet Union in sending the Sputnik satellite into orbit around the Earth prompted a determined response by the United States and Western allies to mobilise stronger outputs from higher education and higher levels of investment in areas of strategic importance (Wang 2009). This was the precursor to the rise of 'big science' more generally. Robert Siedel, tracing the origins of the Lawrence Berkeley Laboratory in the United States, observes:

> If the lines between science and technology blurred, so did those between the disciplines, as chemists, biologists, and physicians joined to exploit new radioactive substances, high voltage X-rays, and neutron beams against disease. The result was a new interdisciplinary enterprise: nuclear science, which combined radiochemistry, radiobiology, nuclear physics, and nuclear medicine.
>
> *(Seidel 1992, p. 36)*

Other researchers, for example, adapted the tools of bioinformatics and pharmaceuticals to study and interpret data on the interplay between diet and genetics

(Larsen 2010). In the social sciences too, large projects tackling global themes such as disease, climate and environment were increasingly based on expensive budgets and extended cross-institutional interdisciplinary teams (Aronova 2014, p. 393).

In the UK at this time, higher education underwent a fundamental shift from a relatively few institutions catering for a small elite group to become a larger and more diverse mass system. Student numbers grew from less than 50,000 in 1946 to over 180,000 in 1965 and over 280,000 by 1975. The *Robbins Report on Higher Education* in 1963 endorsed the further expansion of the system and the creation of new universities (Committee on Higher Education 1963). These new institutions aimed to attract a wider social group, less restricted in terms of social class and gender and more attuned to scientific and technological change than that of the older universities, Oxford and Cambridge, and the departmental institutions created in the late nineteenth century. This led a number of them to offer a different kind of organisation and curriculum.

Already, in 1950, the new University of Keele (initially the University College of North Staffordshire) under A.D. Lindsay began what was known as the 'Keele experiment', with four-year degree courses including a common curriculum in the foundational first year and studies that included at least one science and one arts subject for a joint degree course that avoided subject specialisation (Gallie 1960; Whyte 2015, p. 223). Lindsay, a prominent philosopher with many years of experience in higher education, developed plans for a broad and integrated course covering different disciplines (Korbert 2000). All students followed a four-year course leading to a joint honours degree in two subjects or else in international relations (economics, history and politics) or PPE (philosophy, politics and economics) (Holloway 1977).

In 1961, the University of Sussex opened, with ambitious plans, as its later vice chancellor, the leading historian Asa Briggs, tellingly described them, of 'redrawing the map of learning' (Briggs 1986). The university was organised through so-called Schools of Studies rather than in departments. The first four Schools were in Social Studies, European Studies, English Studies (later including American Studies) and Physical Sciences. A School of African and Asian Studies followed, with a School of Educational Studies (which became a School of Cultural and Community Studies in 1970), and then Molecular Sciences, Biological Sciences and Applied Sciences. It also housed interdisciplinary centres and institutes such as the Institute of Development Studies from 1965, the Centre for Contemporary European Studies and later the Science Policy Research Unit (Briggs 1986). According to another senior colleague, Professor Brian Smith, Briggs recognised that populating each school with staff who came from different disciplines would stimulate interdisciplinary research and create alternative models for teaching. Smith notes that the key appointments were 'highly respected academics, but they were also intellectual risk-takers', such as David Daiches from Cambridge, who became dean of English and American studies, the philosopher Patrick Corbett from Oxford who became Sussex's first senior tutor, and the theoretical physicist Roger Blin-Stoyle, also from Oxford, who joined Sussex to lead science (Smith 2001). Another senior colleague, Margaret McGowan, later recalled the advantages of schools of studies for areas of study such as the humanities in encouraging interactions among disciplines, often creating new disciplines: 'Such novel academic possibilities have been noticed and the interdisciplinary venture represented by a School of Studies has grown less unusual as time has passed, since it has provided a model for organising the arts now used in several other university institutions' (McGowan 1986, p. 67).

Alongside these new developments in higher education and encouraging them further, unprecedented national support was being provided for curriculum development in the schools. The Nuffield Foundation Science Teaching Project, launched in 1962, promoted a new approach to science education, including (eventually) integrated science, that was based on collaboration between the universities, schools, government and a leading charity (see for example McCulloch et al. 1985). The Schools Council for Curriculum and Examinations, a national consortium established in 1964, supported many curriculum projects, including some that directly challenged the established academic disciplines. For example, the Humanities Curriculum Project, led by Lawrence Stenhouse, was set up in 1967 to extend the range of choice open to teachers working in the humanities with pupils of average and lower than average ability. A US project, Man: A Course of Study (MACOS), established by the National Science Foundation, was disseminated in the UK by the Centre for Applied Research in Education (CARE) at the University of East Anglia (see also Stenhouse 1980).

Under the Labour government of 1964–70, further attention was given to the expansion of higher education that again supported the idea of interdisciplinarity. A new group of higher education institutions was created, described as polytechnics rather than as universities, aiming to encourage applied rather than pure or narrowly academic approaches to higher education. An influential supporter of the new polytechnics, Eric Robinson, rejected subject departmentalism as it was practised in both the established and new universities and called for a broader range of study (Robinson 1968). Meanwhile, other new universities were set up including in 1969 the Open University, pioneering distance education through the medium of television and promoting innovation in teaching through teamwork, the use of textbooks for a large but dispersed student population and laboratory experience through new technologies.

The innovatory climate of the 1960s fostered wider recognition of the possibilities of interdisciplinarity not only at a national level but also internationally through agencies developed through European cooperation under the European Economic Community and more broadly. In 1966, a report under the auspices of the Organisation of Economic Co-operation and Development (OECD) highlighted the disciplinary and departmental structure of the European university as an obsolete division of labour among different fields, tending to encourage rigidity, conservatism, economic weaknesses and fragmentation (Martinotti 1997, p. 155). In 1972, the Centre for Educational Research and Innovation (CERI), on behalf of its parent organisation the OECD, produced a significant report entitled *Interdisciplinarity: Problems of Teaching and Research in Universities* (CERI 1972). This was the published outcome of a seminar held in September 1970 on the theme of interdisciplinarity in universities, organised by CERI in collaboration with the French Ministry of Education at the University of Nice in France. The organising group included Professor Asa Briggs, who was now the vice chancellor of the University of Sussex, and Professor Guy Berger of the University of Paris.

The report acknowledged that the academic disciplines were the foundations for the organisation of knowledge in universities not only as a convenient breakdown of knowledge into its component parts, but as 'the basis of the organisation of the university into its autonomous fiefs, and of the professions engaged in teaching and research' (CERI 1972, preface). Indeed, it observed that 'to meddle with the disciplines is to meddle with the social structure of the university in its entirety' (CERI 1972, p. 9). It went on to define key distinctions among a range of approaches to disciplinarity, including multidisciplinarity, pluridisciplinarity and transdisciplinarity, as well as interdisciplinarity, and provided a detailed survey of interdisciplinary teaching and research in universities in different countries. Interdisciplinarity, it announced, should be understood as 'the *integration* of concepts and methods' in disciplines (CERI 1972, p. 12).

While it stressed the difficulty involved in 'meddling' with the disciplines, the CERI report pointed out that there was an emerging set of imperatives and incentives working in favour of interdisciplinary work. The impact of knowledge on action, it commented, forced interaction between the disciplines and also generated new disciplines. Moreover, it argued, creative change in university education and research increasingly called for an interdisciplinary approach not to demolish the disciplines themselves but to encourage dynamic relationships with other disciplines and with the problems of society.

Only a few years later, in 1975, the Nuffield Foundation (NF) also produced a substantial volume reporting on the idea and practice of interdisciplinarity (NF 1975a). The Foundation's group for research and innovation in higher education, which was responsible for preparing this report, based it on a number of visits to higher education institutions, during which it had encountered what it described as interdisciplinary practices in its study of undergraduate teaching. It found that many familiar disciplines, such as modern history and English, remained strong at university level: 'Disciplines have thus a certain historicity, and current changes must be seen against a historical perspective of continual evolution' (NF 1975a, p. 38). Moreover, like CERI before it, the NF identified obstacles to interdisciplinary work that were social, professional and organisational no less than they were conceptual or academic in nature.

First, it advised that university departments, which usually represented particular disciplines, were not simply academic or curricular units but should be recognised as 'a social unit, a research grouping, a welfare centre, a territory, an administrative entity, and a symbol for both staff and students' (NF 1975a, p. 11). It was therefore difficult to abolish departments. At the same time, it noted, there were many examples of interdisciplinary courses based in departmental institutions. Interdepartmental courses tended to be in a difficult position because bilateral treaties between departments were usually unstable and temporary, often dependent on personal relationships between the individuals involved. Instead of these approaches, the NF favoured the development of schools of studies such as those that had developed in several institutions such as the University of Sussex and a number of polytechnics in the 1960s, arguing that 'the school of studies seems to provide the best structure for a cluster of overlapping interdisciplinary courses – say, grouped around biological and environmental studies, or urban and regional studies' (NF 1975a, p. 22).

Secondly, the NF report warned of a 'professional risk' for the staff who were involved in interdisciplinary work. It suggested that '[o]nce one moves out of the shared domain of the single discipline, one is forced to communicate in a new way: forced to develop a "mediating language" in which to discuss the relationship between disciplines' (NF 1975a, p. 28). Such an approach usually entailed additional work and the stress created by being a member of a teaching course team. On the other hand, some types of interdisciplinary work were less difficult than others. For example, 'bridge-building' between complete and stable disciplines was quite common, while 'restructuring', or taking elements from several disciplines to form a new coherent whole, was more radical and critical. These two approaches in fact summed up the difference between multidisciplinarity, in the case of the former, and interdisciplinarity, provided in the latter type. Another conference, organised in September 1975 by the Society for Research into Higher Education (SRHE), held at the City University, London, and supported by the Council of Europe, was addressed by Guy Berger who had been involved in the earlier CERI study. Berger took the opportunity to affirm that 'interdisciplinarity is a marvellous starting point to approach the fundamental problems of the university' (Berger 1977, p. 7). Examples of interesting interdisciplinary initiatives were identified in the study of politics at the university of York, a BA social science modular degree started at the Polytechnic of Central London from 1974, and elsewhere (NF 1975b).

European networks continued to encourage the notion of interdisciplinarity, supported by the new possibilities raised by information technology at the end of the century. For example, Guido Martinotti, an urban sociologist based at the Milan-Biccocci University in Milan, Italy, argued at a conference on interdisciplinarity and the organisation of knowledge in Europe, organised by the Academia Europaea and held in Cambridge in September 1997, that 'the main pressures towards interdisciplinarity come from the creation of "European Society", the profound reorganisation of knowledge caused by the new information technologies, and, connected to this last point, the growing mass of common data for scientific research' (Martinotti 1997, p. 162). Indeed, according to Martinotti, 'the use of a computer itself is interdisciplinary ... increasingly the day-to-day experience of the researcher is based on dealings with digitised data and tools, which provide at least an array of common languages and tools' (Martinotti 1997, p. 176).

The case of education

The study of education, or educational studies, has its own distinctive history so far as the tensions between the disciplines and interdisciplinarity are concerned. Until the Second World War, except in Scotland, it struggled to develop as a recognisable university subject. As J.W. Tibble noted, its position had always been 'ambiguous and peripheral' (Tibble 1966b, p. 1). Very little time was allowed for future teachers to study broad educational issues, and so the courses were regarded as being superficial. The schools, for their part, tended to regard them as being irrelevant to their practical needs and too remote from the classroom (Tibble 1966b, p. 1). Overall, they suffered from very low status and esteem within universities.

As early as 1877, the famous essay on 'Education as a Science' by Alexander Bain insisted that the scope of the study of education should be confined to its psychological dimensions, that is, 'the means of building up the acquired powers of human beings' (Bain 1877, p. 6), thus leaving its environmental aspects for other departments to pursue. An emphasis on psychology over other potential approaches to the study of education continued well into the twentieth century. Educational psychology was an established subject of study by the 1920s, fostered for example by Cyril Burt, appointed to the London County Council in 1913 as the first educational psychologist (Tibble 1966b, p. 10).

Day training colleges for the training of elementary school teachers in connection with local universities or university colleges were established in the 1890s under the Education Department's Code for 1890, following the recommendations of the Cross Report of 1888. The first day training colleges were set up at King's College London, Manchester, Durham, Sheffield, Birmingham, Nottingham and Cardiff, and the first chair of education in England, Mark Robinson Wright, at Durham in 1895 (Gordon 1980c, pp. xi–xii). These included study of the theory, history and psychology of education and increasingly catered for the training of secondary school teachers. Nevertheless, they were designed on the whole for teacher training purposes rather than for the academic study of education.

Several notable figures were given the title of professor of education in leading institutions around the UK between the 1870s and the Second World War, an achievement that Hofstetter and Schneuwly have described as a key indicator in the institutionalisation of a field (Hofstetter and Schneuwly 2002). From the earliest chairs awarded in Scotland, to the first in Wales (Aberystwyth, 1893) and England (Durham, 1895), to others in the first four decades of the twentieth century at Belfast, Birmingham, Bristol, Cambridge, Exeter, Hull, Leeds, Liverpool, London, Manchester, Newcastle, Nottingham, Reading and Sheffield, these academic pioneers sought to shape the study of education as a whole while identifying its key attributes and approaches. They were often given only limited academic status even within their own institutions and responded by attempting to balance a claim to academic respectability with a declaration of professional relevance (see also Gordon 1990).

The first professors of education in Scotland, for example, clearly worked under difficulties. Laurie at Edinburgh and Meikeljohn at St Andrews were both appointed in 1876 to chairs endowed by trustees of Andrew Bell, an advocate of the Madras system of monitorial pedagogy, but the government delayed in supporting the endowments, and Edinburgh's support was only limited. Ultimately, the new professors' basic salaries were fixed well below those of their colleagues, many of whom distrusted the idea of pedagogical studies on ideological grounds. Their courses were not included in the regular degree programme, nor did they have a clear connection with teacher training. It was not until the 1890s that education was made a full qualifying subject for the Master of Arts programme at all four universities in Scotland, although Glasgow and Aberdeen still avoided appointing professors in the subject. From 1906, there was a formal separation between teacher training in teacher training colleges and the study of education as an academic subject in universities, although as R.E. Bell remarks, 'Usually opposition to the university departments manifested itself after 1906 in the wish that "all this business", by which was meant both teacher training and educational research, should be "left to the colleges" . . . as a suitable dumping ground for a not very respectable and embarrassing academic discipline' (Bell 1983, p. 164).

Meikeljohn's chair at St Andrews was founded for the teaching of the theory, history and practice of education, and, as he suggested in his inaugural address, these three aspects mapped out his future work. He proposed that 'though it is impossible for one man to occupy more than a small portion of the field, yet he is bound to survey the whole of it, and to invite and urge others to co-operate with him in the cultivation of the whole' (Meikeljohn 1876/1980, p. 4). Thus began a long-running debate within the UK on whether professors of education should seek to cater for education in general or specialise in a particular area of it. At the same time, he aligned himself with the idea of education as a science, based on observation and experiment, in which the psychology of the growing mind was 'a chapter in science which still remains to be written' (Meikeljohn 1876/1980, p. 4). He looked forward to the science of education progressing just as the science of medicine had done over the previous forty years, benefiting from 'a preliminary and thorough-going examination of the nature and development of the growing mind' (Meikeljohn 1876/1980, p. 7).

The University of Manchester agreed to establish a professorship in the art, theory and practice of education in 1899, with the new chair being entitled the Sarah Fielden Chair from 1901 after Mrs Fielden, an educational philanthropist, gave an initial donation. The first appointee, Harry Livington Withers, took up the chair in January 1900 but died three years later at the age of 38. His successor, Joseph John Findlay, was appointed in 1903 together with another professor, Michael Sadler, the first professor in England in the history and administration of education. Sadler was formerly a senior figure in the Board of Education and a leading expert in comparative education systems, going on to become vice chancellor at the University of Leeds in 1911. A four-year course was begun that same year with most of the work in education in the fourth year, and a faculty of education was established in 1914 with 250 students, the first faculty of education in the country with a higher degree in education. As Alex Robertson comments, based on his detailed studies of the Manchester department, 'In so hierarchical and traditionalist a world as the early Twentieth Century university the existence of the Faculty, the Education degree and two Chairs of Education in the leading civic university must have contributed substantially to a reappraisal of the state of Education in a university setting' (Robertson 1990, p. 30). It appeared that Manchester was to be one of the more successful centres for educational studies.

Other notable professors of education at Manchester in the early decades of the twentieth century included Henry Bompas Smith, who was appointed in 1913 to succeed Findlay and was director of the department for the next twenty years. His inaugural address underlined the importance of education as a science, a development, as he averred, 'which bids fair to revolutionise our whole educational procedure' (Smith 1913/1980, p. 76). This address developed the idea of education as the training of personality, and his involvement helped to consolidate Manchester's position as a leading centre of educational psychology. This was also the case with Richard Oliver, who became the Sarah Fielden Professor of Education at Manchester in 1938 and continued in this position until 1970. Oliver had received his doctorate in educational psychology at the University of Edinburgh in 1932, in preparation for which he spent two years in East Africa developing an intelligence test for use in the native schools and also two years at Stanford University in the United States (Pearson 1989). At the same time, Oliver was not narrowly academic nor simply a specialist in educational psychology. He supported demands for a democratic new order in education including common schools and day continuation schools. He also spent many years as the Manchester University representative on the Joint Matriculation Board, chairing this body from 1952, and he developed a course on general studies, resisting tendencies towards specialisation in the school curriculum (Pearson et al. 1989, Introduction).

Professor John Alfred Green, professor of education at the University of Sheffield from 1906 until his early death in 1922, similarly cultivated particular strengths in educational psychology, being responsible for the training of secondary school teachers and for instruction in advanced psychology and education. His early work was on the ideas of the Continental educational reformer J.H. Pestalozzi, but his interests turned increasingly to new developments in educational psychology on the Continent. He became a prominent member of the British Psychological Society, was for many years the editor of the *Journal of Experimental Pedagogy* and was one of the earliest supporters in Britain of the Binet-Simon scheme of psychological tests. Like Oliver, he also had other interests that can be described as applied and professional in nature and indeed assumed diverse responsibilities as the dean of the Faculty of Arts at Sheffield. He was a leading figure in the Sheffield Workers' Educational Association and a member of Sheffield Education Committee where he also championed educational reforms such as the principle of free secondary education for all (McCulloch 2004b; Mathers 2005, pp. 58–59).

Another leading centre with particularly strong credentials in educational psychology during the early part of the century was the University of Edinburgh, with Godfrey Thomson the Bell professor of education and head of Moray House teachers' college from 1925 until 1951. Thomson had previously been the professor of education at the University of Newcastle and stayed at Columbia University School of Education in 1923–24, where he was strongly influenced by the psychologist E.L. Thorndike. Lawn and Deary have argued that Edinburgh under Thomson represented the 'new model' school of education, and it is certainly true that it combined in a very creative way a university department, teachers' college, research laboratory and advanced research degree (Lawn and Deary 2014). In another sense, though, Edinburgh was the most advanced incarnation of an established model in which education was inspired by models of psychology and the ideal of education as a science (see also Vernon 1962). It was another institution based in London that was to become the largest and in many ways the most distinctive centre for educational studies and research in the UK in the twentieth century. This was originally established in October 1902, unusually by a local authority, the London County Council, rather than by an institution of higher education. There had been earlier attempts within the sprawling University of London to establish training colleges. King's College began a training department for men in 1890, while a similar initiative at University College was attempted in 1891 but ended three years later (Aldrich 2002, p. 7). A Board of Studies of Pedagogy was set up in 1900, which was renamed in 1934 as the Board of Studies in Education (Aldrich 2002, p. 7). The new London Day Training College (LDTC) was approved by the Senate of the University of London and would be led by its first professor of the theory, history and practice of education at a salary of £800 per year, who would also be the principal of the training college (Aldrich 2002, p. 10).

John Adams was appointed as the LDTC's first professor of education. His inaugural address, 'The Training of Teachers', pointed out that the key issue was no longer whether teachers should be trained but how they should be trained (Adams 1902/1980, p. 43). He argued that this should be pursued as a postgraduate study (see also Rusk 1961). Adams was succeeded in 1922 by Percy Nunn, who had eclectic interests in education, as reflected in his key generalist text *Education: Its Data and First Principles* (Nunn 1920).

Clearly there was no representative body, nor was there a journal that fully represented educational studies in general. So far as organisations were concerned, the Training College Association (TCA) was formed in 1891 but confined itself mainly to teacher training issues. Debate around new legislation, especially the Education Acts of 1902 and 1918, and an awareness of the need for broad social reform following the Boer War and the First World War, helped to stimulate reforming activities. The North of England Education Conference was established in 1902 as an annual event organised by Local Education Authorities (LEAs) to discuss current educational issues (Gosden 1992). The Education Reform Council, formed in 1916, stressed the need for great organisation (Brehaut 1973, p. 5). At the same time, new initiatives were often led by other disciplinary groups. One interesting development, for example, was the creation in 1901 of Section L, Educational Science, under the auspices of the British Association for the Advancement of Science (BAAS). This became a forum for the discussion of a wide range of educational issues, as well as a means of promoting enquiry into the institutions, practices and outcomes of education (Collins 1979, p. 241; Layton 1981, p. 188). Its principal founder, the science educator H.E. Armstrong, hoped that for the first time, 'the scattered forces of the educational army are about to be organised' (van Praagh 1973, p. 92). Meanwhile the British Psychological Society (BPS), established in 1901, gave approval to the introduction of a Psychology of Education Section in 1919, and this section created a Standing Committee on Educational Research in 1923.

Some journals were also created during this period. A short-lived *Training College Record*, begun by the TCA in 1908, gave way to the *Journal of Experimental Pedagogy* (*JEP*) in 1911. The *JEP* had a strongly psychological emphasis in its articles, with a large number of papers on experimental and statistical approaches to education but also a substantial minority on general and philosophical issues. Both of these journals were edited by Professor J.A. Green of the University of Sheffield until his untimely death in 1923 (Thomas 1982). After Green's death the journal was renamed the *Forum of Education*, edited by C.W. Valentine, professor of education at Birmingham University. This journal attempted to develop a broader approach and to be less dominated by psychology, but in 1930 it was taken over by the British Psychological Society and renamed the *British Journal of Educational Psychology* (*BJEP*), although still with Valentine as its editor.

The development of the *BJEP* underlined the anomalies of this alliance between a self-styled scientific subdiscipline, educational psychology and its audience of training college lecturers. As before, the journal would be under the joint control of the TCA and the BPS, and about 200 members of each society subscribed to the journal, but the practical difficulties of the arrangement soon became evident. Valentine explained in an editorial that the journal would be devoted to educational psychology but that this would be 'broadly interpreted'. Psychology would be the means of understanding all educational issues, 'as nearly all problems of education have a psychological aspect, so that papers dealing with researches on almost every aspect of education may be included, and, in particular, papers dealing with Method from a psychological point of view' (Valentine 1930, p. 161). Just seven years later, Valentine felt obliged to spell out to the directors of the journal and the Council of the BPS the compromises that this involved in practice. In future, he advised, no articles would be published in the journal in which a substantial part was devoted to a discussion of the validity of statistical methods. This was simply because most of the journal's readers would not understand them. As Valentine observed, 'The great majority of our readers would be incompetent to judge the merits of such discussions even if they tried to read them' (Valentine 1941). If statistical or mathematical discussions seemed essential, he proposed, they should be relegated largely to appendices or footnotes, and they should not exceed about one-tenth of the whole paper.

Valentine also regretted that there were not more articles of a general or readable kind to be published in the *BJEP*, despite his own efforts in seeking such contributions from a number of leading educational psychologists. He concluded that the journal should 'go slow' in educating its readers to a certain standard to appreciate statistical articles. As he noted, indeed:

> It is well to bear in mind that many members of both Societies are hardly familiar even with the elements of statistical method. Our readers include, for example, some lecturers and teachers in such subjects as English, and Art,

some concerned with infant work, and lecturers in Domestic Science Colleges, who in some cases seem hardly to understand even what is meant by a co-efficient of correlation. To make highly statistical articles a prominent item of the Journal would, I think, tend to frighten off readers from other articles involving a certain amount of statistics, which would gradually lead them to a better knowledge of statistical procedure – an end which I think is extremely important, and which I have constantly had in mind.

(Valentine 1941)

For the time being, at least, Valentine favoured a pragmatic approach to retaining a readership of limited expertise and understanding of relevant topics.

Valentine's dilemma as editor of the *BJEP* highlighted the basic quandary of the study of education. Approaching education through the medium of psychology involved yoking together a group of training college lecturers, with widely disparate interests and very little expertise in psychology, with a group of psychologists of uncertain academic status. This represented a unidisciplinary approach to the study of education with a very limited base in terms of a clientele or market. The wider implications of this situation were still more problematic. Such a subject with this kind of disparate following, for all its claims to scientific standing, was hardly likely to gain any respect or status alongside other subjects in universities.

The emerging field of educational studies and research was therefore shot through with contradictions and had little prospect of improving its academic status when based on such an approach. It lacked the expertise and common language of an academic discipline and also failed to draw on the related perspectives from cognate disciplines in the humanities and social sciences that might generate multidisciplinary or even interdisciplinary insights on education. The solution that presented itself was to broaden the focus of the field to include a range of disciplines, while also deepening the expertise that was available for these. As this chapter has already shown, in the decades that followed the Second World War, interdisciplinary approaches were to become increasingly common, and the university sector was strongly encouraged to 'redraw the map of learning'. To what extent would educational studies and research contribute to this trend as the field became more established? The initial responsibility for this fell particularly to the specialist institution that was taken under the wing of the University of London in the 1930s – the Institute of Education.

3

THE INSTITUTE OF EDUCATION LONDON

All the gates of knowledge thrown open?

The London Day Training College (LDTC), founded in 1902, was transformed in the 1930s into the Institute of Education (IOE), which was now fully part of the University of London, led initially by Percy Nunn and then Fred Clarke. It changed significantly in other ways also, as a new model of educational studies that began to move away from psychology, became increasingly multifaceted, and yet also had an ultimate sense of education as a unity, of a map of educational knowledge that it took as its main *raison d'etre* as a university department rather than the training of teachers *per se*. It was instrumental in helping to shape the sociology of education as a subdiscipline within this broader field, continually in flux and in tension, yet by the 1950s and 1960s was beginning to inform a more fully developed and coherent contribution to educational studies as a whole.

It was Nunn who began to plan for the full entry of the LDTC into the University of London, which took place in 1932, with the LDTC being renamed the Institute of Education (Aldrich 2002, pp. 84–87). He argued that the Institute should transcend its earlier focus on teacher training to become instead 'a centre of educational thought, inquiry and training' and more specifically 'a centre for educational research' (Nunn 1930). Yet it was not Nunn but his successor as the director of the IOE, Fred Clarke, who was to be the driving force in establishing the IOE as both a national and international base for educational studies and research. In so doing, Clarke aimed to transform the position of professors of education – from the largely isolated and often low-status individuals, usually psychologists and always male, who had characterised such positions until the 1930s, to specialists in a range of different areas who could claim some respect from their academic peers in other departments.

Interdisciplinarity and internationalisation

Fred Clarke succeeded Nunn in 1936, having previously had a wide range of international experience, especially during his time as professor of education at the University of Cape Town, South Africa, from 1911 to 1929 and at McGill University, Montreal, in Canada from 1929 to 1934. Clarke himself had a British background. Born in 1880, he became a pupil teacher at what was then known as St Ebbe's Boys School. He went on to Oxford Day Training College, then to the University of Oxford as a non-collegiate student in 1899, where he studied modern history under the tutorship of Ernest Barker. He was appointed to a teaching post at St John's Diocesan Training College in York and at the very early age of 26 then became professor of education at Hartley College, Southampton, in 1906 (Clarke 2006; see also Mitchell 1967).

After moving to the University of Cape Town as its first professor of education, Clarke became active both nationally within South Africa and internationally. By 1920, he was the president of the South African Teachers' Association. He already harboured grand ambitions for the study of education and outlined these in an address delivered at the University of Cape Town as early as August 1918. The university study of education, he argued in this address, as a subject of university study worthy of a professorship was 'still so new as to be very imperfectly understood, even, it may be, by the occupants of Chairs of Education themselves' (Clarke 1918/1923, p. 132). He insisted that the inclusion of education among university studies could be justified only on the grounds that it could be based on 'scientific methods of investigation and exposition' (Clarke 1918/1923, p. 133). Indeed, he asserted:

> if the processes of education are what our methods of training teachers in the past have made them appear to be, namely, a series of didactic tricks and devices picked up from observation and assimilated by persistent practice, then the University might just as well institute courses in dancing, conjuring and – shall we say? – golf.
>
> *(Clarke 1918/1923, p. 133)*

This scientific study was the true *raison d'etre* of university departments of education, with the training of teachers a secondary although direct consequence: 'A University Department of Education is not justified merely as a Training College incorporated with a University; rather it can train teachers because of the special character that belongs to it, or should belong to it, as an organisation for the scientific study of education' (Clarke 1918/1923, pp. 133–134).

Clarke proposed J.F. Herbart through his work at Königsberg and Göttingen as 'the real founder of educational science as a modern University study' (Clarke 1918/1923, p. 134). In England, on the other hand, the establishment of training colleges, as he scathingly observed, undermined this fundamental purpose, 'diverting them from their real function as centres for the study of education and degrading them into drill-squads under a professor-sargeant' (Clarke 1918/1923, p. 136). Yet now, Clarke insisted, had arrived the time to affirm anew the true purpose of a university department of education. First, it should be an experimental school, with an experimental attitude, keeping its work under close observation and recording and checking the results. Second, it should be able to study all features of education, 'good, bad or indifferent', including what he boldly labelled 'the stigmata of a common school disease of ours which may be called *syllabitis*, as well as those of that equally common one, *rigor inspectoris*' (Clarke 1918/1923, p. 140). Third, he argued, the university department of education should be a central bureau for receiving and collating information about educational developments, especially in its own country, as well as a centre to provide help and guidance to all who were pursuing their own investigations. There was enormous potential for a field of study such as this in South Africa, Clarke contended, with its wide diversity of social problems and conditions that had hardly even begun to be studied properly and that required detailed examination from one centre, such as Cape Town (Clarke 1918/1923, p. 140).

This outline of what a university department of education should be carried with it significant implications for the nature of its staffing. Education must be a study with a number of specialisations: 'No man can dream of professing the whole subject' (Clarke 1918/1923, p. 140). For this reason, the department should be split into at least three divisions: first, history and organisation; second, methods of instruction and training; and third, philosophy and psychology of education. There would also need to be scope for teachers of school hygiene, for the demonstration school and for the technical needs of training students. Such a department would be more like a school of medicine or agriculture than of a single university department, although he conceded that for a long time ahead, 'we shall have to do what we can with very incomplete and defective equipment' (Clarke 1918/1923, p. 140). Under the influence of such tutors, he concluded, the training of teachers would also be greatly elevated and improved, with access to 'all the gates of knowledge thrown open' (Clarke 1918/1923, p. 144).

This was a powerful vision of the future of university education departments and the nature of educational studies, and Clarke reinforced it with a potent critique of the current situation. He complained that 'the ship of education, now that it has come to be officered very largely by Professors of Education, may get itself stuck in academic flats and shallows, and be lost in the quicksands of statistics or on the sunken reefs of experimental psychology' (Clarke 1923, p. ix). He accepted the necessity for detailed investigation of particular matters but hoped that 'when they are near completion, the ship will head once more for the wide waters of the open sea' (Clarke 1923, p. ix). There would be plenty of work for all in the vast and mysterious open sea, Clarke concluded, and professors of education, as he put it, 'need constant renewal from its tingling air and its vast spaces' (Clarke 1923, p. x).

The general philosophy that Clarke was beginning to develop was around the tension between the unity of thought and the organisation of ideas, interdisciplinarity and disciplinarity, or what Collingwood was already describing as the *speculum mentis*. Like Collingwood, Clarke was opposed to the specialisation that characterised the modern age. According to Clarke, 'in education as in every other department of life and thought, disintegration and parcelling out have proceeded so far that without some deliberate attempt at a synthesis the whole effort may pass into aimlessness and meaninglessness' (Clarke 1923, p. 1). The challenge that he posed was to reconcile 'some conception of the unity which can give meaning to all forms of educational effort' with 'that bewildering conflict of aims and ideals and necessities of life which in all educational work we have to face' (Clarke 1923, p. 1). His own strong religious beliefs underpinned this emerging philosophy. His was a belief in an ultimate meaning of life that was still vulnerable to failure unless a 'synthesis' could be reached and adopted as a basis for practice (Clarke 1923, p. 2).

Clarke represented the clash between unity and disintegration as one between the beginnings of a new synthesis of educational ideas and the decay of older methods and aims, which was currently creating what he viewed as 'a state of lost bewilderment which is reflected strongly in the comparative aimlessness and want of strong, clear *meaning*, which now characterise so much of our education' (Clarke 1923, p. 5). Individualism provided one kind of synthesis for the future, but he was sharply critical of this approach, including the representation of this put forward in Percy Nunn's recent tome, *Education: Its Data and First Principles* (Clarke 1923, p. 8). Against this, Clarke insisted on the need for 'a whole, which, while being concrete and diversified, is also a unity' (Clarke 1923, p. 11). This was in contrast both with individualism, which provided 'the concreteness and the diversity without the unity', and with science, which gave 'the unity without the concreteness and diversity' (Clarke 1923, p. 11).

Clarke was especially critical of individualism in psychology – 'the very science which, it is claimed, is the basic science for education' (Clarke 1923, p. 12). He was emphatic in his counterclaim: 'If there *is* any controlling Science for Education at all there is good reason for maintaining that it is neither Psychology nor Biology, but Sociology' (Clarke 1923, p. 13). The key concept, according to Clarke, was not 'Instinct' but 'Civilisation', 'Idealist' in philosophical terms and for the ordinary person religious in nature. He drew on the ideas of Emile Durkheim and Friedrich Fröbel in developing this argument, seeking to show how they both reconciled opposite tendencies to create a full synthesis or unity.

Such were the philosophical underpinnings of Clarke's ideas about the future of the study of education. They provided the basis for an interdisciplinary outlook but one that was organised around disciplinary strengths. These strengths he saw as moving decisively from individualist psychology towards sociology and history. Moreover, he identified the key purpose of university education departments as being to study the foundations of education, with the training of teachers becoming a secondary concern. Finally, he perceived a shift being drawn from local and national concerns towards international and global connections.

Fred Clarke and the Institute of Education

Over the next decade, Clarke was able to find the means to put these ideas into practice. First, in 1929 he moved to become the first professor of education at McGill University in Montreal, Canada. This provided easy access to key centres and contacts on the eastern seaboard of the United States. Two in particular were to be highly relevant to establishing an international network for the support of educational studies and research. The first was the Carnegie Corporation of New York, led by Frederick Keppel; the other was the Teachers College, Columbia University, also in New York, with its professor of education Isaac Kandel. Second, he established himself as an intermediary, soon a confidant, between Keppel, Kandel and the LDTC, in the throes of becoming the Institute of Education in London.

The principal of the University of London, Edwin Deller, recognised that although the LDTC was already the most important and largest centre in England for advanced study and research in education, its position outside the university had 'stood in the way of its development as an imperial and international centre for higher study and research, which is emphatically the business of a university though not of a municipality to promote and encourage' (Deller 1931). Kandel noted with interest that the establishment of such a centre for the advanced study of education in England would be a highly positive development internationally, 'first, because it will give the subject itself a position which it has not hitherto enjoyed, and, secondly, because it may make the English articulate about the strength of their system and contribute to the progress of education generally' (Kandel 1932). Yet such a development would have financial repercussions for the university in the midst of a financial crisis that in 1931–32 had already become recognised both in Britain and in the United States as an economic depression of an unprecedented scale. If it were to achieve its potential as an investment for the future, the transformation of the LDTC to the IOE would also entail attracting suitable students and staff to London from around the world. The Carnegie Corporation was in a strategic position as an established philanthropic organisation that had already provided large-scale funding to support new ventures in education around the world. In the early 1920s, its funds had helped to establish a National Bureau of Economic Research and an American Law Institute. Frederick Keppel took over as president of the Corporation in 1924 with a mission to promote cultural philanthropy of international dimensions, and he continued to distribute largesse even after the Wall Street stock market crash of 1929 led to a historic level of social, political and economic dislocation (see Lagemann 1989).

Thus, the Carnegie Corporation was a prospective sponsor for the new IOE, and Deller took care to spell out the situation in correspondence with Keppel at the end of 1931. As he explained, the LDTC was the property of the London County Council (LCC), which also appointed its teachers, but it was for academic purposes a branch of the University, with two of its main teachers (Percy Nunn and Cyril Burt) being university professors and two others university readers in education. The LCC had now agreed to hand over the LDTC to the University and to pay for its rebuilding on the University's site in Bloomsbury in central London. As Deller noted, after the transfer, it was intended 'to create out of the College an Institute of Education which, while continuing at any rate for the present its work of training teachers, should be developed as a great centre of research and higher study and especially for students from overseas' (Deller 1931). The emphasis on research, higher study and internationalisation as opposed to teacher training is significant here, as is the clear hint that its teacher training role might only be temporary. However, Deller continued, the whole project was dependent on the national Board of Education and the Treasury recognising the IOE as a university department, which would involve a charge on the State of £12,000–£13,000 per year. This had not until recently appeared to be a serious obstacle, according to Deller, because all were convinced of the potential of the project, but because of the financial crisis it would now come under rigorous scrutiny from the Treasury. Deller now finally came to the real point of his approach to Carnegie: in these circumstances, the University wished to be able to stress the importance of providing facilities for carefully selected students from the Dominions and elsewhere who were capable of doing advanced work. Reassurances had already been received from a number of centres that there were students who would wish to take advantage of this, and so Deller asked Keppel whether Carnegie would be able to allocate a scholarship scheme from its funds for this purpose (Deller 1931).

From this point, Clarke was closely involved in negotiations behind the scenes and made his preferences clear. For example, in a private meeting with Keppel and a few other key contacts in early 1933, Clarke strongly favoured the development of the new IOE and the approach being taken by Nunn as its director. At the same time, he argued that Britain was too dominant in current international relations and that there should be a fuller 'exchange of ideas' in which the United States should have a role – no doubt music to the ears of Carnegie Corporation officials. He supported the idea of sponsoring travelling scholarships, but proposed that these should be 'not for boys [sic] just out of the University, but for men [sic] of some experience'. This might enable further professors to be appointed in key areas, which he identified as being in comparative education and modern educational history (Carnegie Corporation 1933). In Clarke's view, a key means of promoting these objectives was the internationalisation of educational studies and research. Through mutual influence in different countries around the world, Clarke aimed to heighten the ideals and develop the practices of educational studies and research in a number of ways. He hoped that at least some of the traditions of education in England might be adapted for use in other countries. At the same time, he argued that the educational ideas of other countries might also have a significant bearing on the changes that were taking place in the English context, and also that there should be an international market of students and staff to help to build up an enlarged role for educational studies and research in England as well as elsewhere. In all of these developments, Clarke saw the IOE as potentially having a crucial and leading role to play (see also McCulloch 2014a).

In 1934, Nunn secured a substantial grant from the Carnegie Corporation with the aim of developing what he called 'the imperial and international, as distinguished from the domestic, side of the Institute' (Nunn 1934). Nunn therefore proposed to introduce a 'Department of Overseas Students', which would attract in particular students from the Dominions and colonial dependencies (Nunn 1934). The key feature of this new department, Nunn continued, would be the appointment of a director of professorial rank who would be entitled the Adviser to Oversea Students. This should be ideally a 'man of high standing in the educational world of one of the Dominions', who would be based at the Institute for at least one year and preferably for three years and who would be brought into 'close intellectual contact with our best British students as well as those from oversea, and with the numerous leaders in educational work who for one reason or another resort to the Institute' (Nunn 1934). As Nunn was already well aware, Clarke was admirably suited to such a role and took his opportunity with vigour.

Two key projects that Clarke took forward, then, were outcomes of the agenda that Nunn had initiated and that, with the support of the Carnegie Corporation, he was able to bring to fruition. The first was what he described as his 'World Tour', in practice restricted in 1935 to western Canada, Australia and New Zealand, which was also made possible through substantial financial assistance from the Carnegie Corporation for his travelling expenses and those of his daughter Mary who accompanied him. The second was his role as Adviser to Oversea Students, to which Nunn appointed him in 1934. Clarke's World Tour, through a succession of journeys by ship and train, lasted for 16 weeks from May to September 1935. He considered that he already had sufficient experience of South Africa and eastern Canada, so concentrated his effort on western Canada, New Zealand and Australia. His initial purpose was to identify how the IOE could support students from the dominions (Clarke 1935a) and also to develop personal contacts with key individuals such as C.E. Beeby in New Zealand and Frank Tate in Australia (Clarke 1935b). During his tour, Clarke interviewed the authorities of state departments of education, universities, teachers, leading citizens and others interested in education. He also made public addresses in Winnipeg, Auckland, Wellington, Christchurch, Dunedin, Brisbane, Melbourne, Adelaide and Perth, had discussions with informed groups in almost every centre that he visited, and gave interviews to newspapers in nearly every town along his route. He concluded in his formal report on the tour that there was an agreed need for considerable development of facilities in London for 'advanced' cooperative studies and also that priority should be given to mid-career men and women who showed promise to shape educational policy. He considered that the number of advanced students should be kept at a small size at present, while at the same time the IOE should appoint a few men as professors with outstanding attainment and reputation in selected specialised areas, in particular educational philosophy, comparative education, history of education and the economics of education (Clarke 1935c).

Clarke's ultimate purpose was certainly not, as he told Keppel, a 'glorified Training College', especially since 'Training Colleges excite no enthusiasm in England: for many that puts it mildly!' Clarke's vision was of 'something analogous to the [London] School of Economics', which would be 'a place concerned with fundamental studies in the conduct and apparatus of statecraft' (Clarke 1935d). He acknowledged, with a Biblical flourish, that this was akin to washing in the clean waters of Abana and Pharpar rather than in 'lowly and despised Jordan' but hoped still to make progress in this way (Clarke 1935d). Realisation of this general vision in itself depended on a clear linkage being made between the creation of an international pool of researchers and fellows in educational studies and the formation of an approach to the field as a whole that could draw on specialist expertise in a wide range of disciplines. Indeed, in private, Clarke made this precise point when writing to Frank Tate in Australia, emphasising the importance of first creating two or three chairs for key people and, second, of increasing and tightening permanent bonds with people overseas. He continued:

> It is the second of these which troubles me most at the moment. If there is not very strong evidence of a demand from oversea for the most advanced studies, it will not be easy to move conservative English and London opinion to the point where it will consider the appointment of additional chairs. . . . If my point no. 2 does not come off, then my point no. 1 has less chance.
>
> *(Clarke 1936)*

Building up an international field was therefore seen as a prerequisite to developing more advanced study in specialist areas based on the disciplines such as history, philosophy and sociology. At the same time, he argued that, although the staff at the Institute should include individuals from around the world, it should not be selected on a territorial basis, 'a sort of Joseph's coat, to include a patch for each land concerned in the scheme', but rather should be 'constituted to represent diverse interests in education in general, different lines of approach to the problems' (Clarke 1934).

Clarke was appointed to succeed Nunn as the director of the Institute of Education with effect from September 1936. There were some differences between Clarke and his predecessor in recruiting and organising a number of professors with the requisite specialist knowledge and expertise in their own areas. Nunn argued privately at the start of 1937 that his priorities would be a chair in comparative education and a half-time chair for Susan Isaacs, the head of the Child Development department. Another senior colleague, Francis Cavenagh, who had expertise in the history of educational thought, was a potential professor in this area, and Nunn recognised this. Nonetheless, he explained to Clarke, 'If I had my way I should be inclined to make him professor of Education *sans phrase*, and let him give himself partly to history and partly to principles'. His view was that Cavenagh's experience in schools was so strong that it would be 'very valuable to the Institute as a whole'. At the same time, he added, if Cavenagh was to be designated wholly to history, it needed to be on the assumption that 'a clear delimitation of the frontiers of that subject and comparative education is desirable and possible'. On the other hand, if a 'good man' [sic] to head the principles course was the most pressing issue, Cavenagh lacked training in formal philosophy, although Max Black and Joseph Laurewys, two other promising colleagues, both possessed this (Nunn 1937). Here was an explicit set of calculations around the depth and quality that could result from specialisation in the disciplines and a more flexible and general support for a range of areas that would be associated with the allocation of broadly based responsibilities.

Internationalisation was clearly a key theme for Clarke, and he made use of his wide range of international experience and expertise to provide the basis for the emergence of a new IOE located in London, comparable in its international stature and reputation to the Teachers College in Columbia University and the International Bureau of Education in Geneva. These are the historical origins of the Institute of Education's long-term strategy for internationalisation that was maintained and developed into the twenty-first century. Moreover, the international market in advanced studies in education that Clarke helped to foster, including students, fellows and professors, also provided a base for the growth of educational studies in England more generally, as well as a model for the international field. This featured a growing emphasis on specialisation in particular areas such as the philosophy, history and sociology of education and comparative education.

Institutionalising the sociology of education

Clarke's new position at the IOE led him by the end of the 1930s to put his views on the study of education into practice, while also demonstrating his awareness of the broader public issues of the time. This was in the context of a growing international crisis that culminated in the Second World War. He continued as director of the IOE, now relocated to Nottingham in the English Midlands, and spent much time in public discussions about the need for educational reform, leading eventually to the Education Act of 1944 (see McCulloch 1994; Ku 2013). His ideas about society were influenced by Karl Mannheim, a Hungarian-born sociologist forced out of Germany in 1933 with the rise to power of Adolf Hitler. Mannheim was a lecturer in sociology at the LSE but came into contact informally with Clarke through groups such as the Moot, which discussed possibilities for post-war planning. Mannheim was appointed as professor of education at the IOE in succession to Clarke when Clarke retired as director in 1945 to chair the newly formed Central Advisory Council for Education (CACE). The subsequent development of the sociology of education at the IOE in the post-war years provided a significant test for Clarke's initial vision for the field.

At the start of the War, Clarke made what was to become probably his best known contribution to educational studies through a short book entitled *Education and Social Change: An English Interpretation* (Clarke 1940). In this work, he laid out his ideas on how English society had a massive bearing on the character of education, both its institutions and values and the social inequalities that persisted between different kinds of schools. It was a powerful critique that helped to inspire a generation of sociological writing on education, but it was significant no less for its interpretation of history than for its sociological insights. It highlighted the 'obstinately resistant' effects of England's historical development (Clarke 1940, p. 32) and reflected on whether the new circumstances of the War would lead the English educational tradition to adapt itself to the demands of a changed social and international order.

Three years later, newly knighted for his public services to education, Clarke returned to develop his ideas further in another short work, *The Study of Education in England* (Clarke 1943). In this, he proposed that post-war society would require a completely new approach to the study of education than had been dominant in the interwar years. The necessary studies would require in his view a sociological dimension, 'revising rather drastically our conceptions of social purpose as well as our ideas of educational technique and school organisation' (Clarke 1943, p. 6). Yet new ideas and practices would also need to range widely, for example into the learning of English as a foreign language. There was also an urgent need to provide detailed explanations of the connections between English education on the one hand and English social structure and institutions on the other, setting this into a historical perspective. Further work on comparative education was also necessary in his view, conceived as an aspect of comparative history and sociology (Clarke 1943, p. 13).

These were broad, synoptic ideas about the study of education, even though they were underpinned by the disciplines of sociology and history. They were accompanied by a perception of the effects of a lack of serious study of education that was uncompromisingly critical:

> The conviction has formed itself that if we conducted our medical and engineering services and our industrial production with the same slipshod carelessness, the same disregard for precision of thought and language, the same wild and reckless policy of sentimentality or class prejudice or material interest masquerading as principle, with which we carry on our public discussions about education, most patients would die, most bridges would fall down, and most manufacturing concerns would go bankrupt.
>
> *(Clarke 1943, p. ii)*

He attributed this neglect to the low status with which education continued to struggle. In part, he suggested, this was because everyone saw themselves as an expert on education: 'We all feel so competent to write to *The Times* about education and are so sure that it is our sacred duty to do so, whereas it would never enter our heads to dogmatize in the same way about medicine or engineering or the techniques of central heating' (Clarke 1943, p. iii). He also continued to point out the low status of training colleges and university-based educational studies, expressing a fear that 'it may be doubted whether Professors of Education have even yet received full recognition as being academically respectable' (Clarke 1943, p. 17). Indeed, according to Clarke, 'Some of them still know what it is to be greeted by that sceptical and characteristically British smile when they are introduced as such' (Clarke 1943, p. 18).

Karl Mannheim offered something different. He was theoretically rigorous, could hold his own with his academic peers at the LSE and possessed the mystique of international experience. For Clarke, too, there was another cause for attraction. While Mannheim unmistakably possessed formidable intellectual depth, he also covered a wide range of academic territory and moreover had a broad synoptic vision to bring the whole together. As W.A.C. Stewart has argued:

> Education was, from his point of view, a social science. It was a synoptic study for pursuing which data could be collected and collated from many different fields. Just as the Modern Greats School at Oxford had to work out the content and relationship of the studies involved, so too Education, from the sociological point of view, would have to show how aspects of history, philosophy, psychology, anthropology, economics, political theory, aesthetics and pedagogy could be brought into some synthesis, or, in another fashionable word, could form some discipline.
>
> *(Stewart 1952, p. 112)*

Mannheim and Clarke found intellectual affinity at meetings of the discussion group the Moot, where they exchanged papers on 'Planning for Freedom' (Mannheim 1939). After succeeding Clarke at the IOE as professor of education, Mannheim's title was changed to professor of the sociology of education, the first to be designated as such in the UK. This was a significant step forward for the IOE itself in terms of academic respectability alongside the LSE. Yet it was fated to be brief, for within a year Mannheim was dead, in January 1947, at the age of 53.

The immediate post-war years were a heady period of rapid development for sociology in the UK. There was still only one professor of sociology in the whole country, David Glass at the LSE, a demographer who was appointed in 1948 in succession to a number of distinguished figures such as Hobhouse and Ginsberg who cultivated a strongly empirical basis and tradition for British sociology. Nevertheless, the prominence of social reconstruction as an issue under the Labour government was a powerful stimulus for sociological studies. The *British Journal of Sociology* was founded by staff at the LSE in 1949, followed in 1951 by the establishment of the British Sociological Association (BSA) (see Platt 2003). At the same time, the sociology of education remained a fragile plant, and no natural successor could be found for Mannheim at the IOE. The person appointed to the sociology of education chair, W.O. Lester Smith, was an administrator, having been the chief education officer in Manchester for eighteen years from 1931 until 1949. Already over sixty years old, his was a stopgap appointment made in the hope that new figures would emerge within a few years to take his place, and also he was a 'natural deputy' for the new director, George Jeffery (Aldrich 2002, p. 136). Lester Smith also represented a different tradition from that of Mannheim, rooted in the applied and professional origins of the LDTC at a local level, supporting a growing national education service, rather than in its new aspirations as a social science with academic respectability and an international profile. His inaugural lecture delivered in October 1950, 'The Teacher and the Community', with its reminiscences of life as a CEO, had very little in common with Mannheim's sociology (Lester Smith 1950).

No less telling was the debate that ensued over who should be Lester Smith's successor when he retired from his position in 1953. By now, the IOE had six professors representing different constituencies or disciplines within the field: Lester Smith himself in sociology, Joseph Lauwerys (1947) in comparative education, Louis Arnaud Reid (1947) in philosophy, Bruce Pattison (1948) in English as a foreign language, Margaret Read (1949) for the colonial department and Philip Vernon (1949) in psychology. The history of education was catered for at King's College London (KCL), at this time through Professor A.V. Judges. Yet sociology still posed a problem, and Jeffery frankly admitted his dilemma to Sir Alexander Carr-Saunders, director of the LSE since 1937. He reflected that his policy with regard to chairs at the IOE had been based on the view that '[e]ducation as an academic subject has singularly failed to produce a due supply of professors from within the field'. Professors had been appointed in the related areas of psychology, history and philosophy, but, he admitted, 'I cannot think of one who has succeeded in developing his amateur interests in a related field into an established academic reputation in that field'. His solution to this had therefore been to look for people 'who have already established a reputation in the related field and are prepared to make such a reorientation of their interests in such a way as to bring their knowledge and experience to bear upon the problems of education'. This policy had, he felt, been successful in the cases of Arnaud Reid, recruited from philosophy, and Vernon from psychology, 'and I had hoped that we could do the same kind of thing with sociology' (Jeffery 1952).

Nevertheless, sociology posed a specific problem because of the still nascent state of the discipline itself, and Jeffery's advisers both inside and outside the IOE were divided about the best direction to take. One IOE professor, Margaret Read, argued in favour of finding a good sociologist in the tradition of Clarke's *Education and Social Change* and Karl Mannheim (Read 1952). Others pointed out that this might not be straightforward. Vernon suggested that 'sociology, while a subject that merits the greatest possible development, is as yet too indefinite and immature for it to be easy to find a suitable person'. He noted that there was a significant overlap with social psychology but recommended maintaining an emphasis on administration. On the basis that educational administration was a 'relatively well established subject' that 'attracts many students, who combine it with a variety of other subjects', he favoured looking for 'an administrator with sociological interests – in other words, someone rather similar to Lester Smith' (Vernon 1952). Lauwerys, by contrast, declared that sociological studies should be separated from educational administration, although he admitted that they were unlikely to receive a strong field of candidates (Lauwerys 1952).

This debate went beyond pragmatic issues about attracting strong candidates to a senior post into the identity of the sociology of education and the character of education as a field. Sociology as pioneered by Clarke and Mannheim was the high road, one with strong academic and intellectual potential, bringing the status of education alongside the social sciences and the IOE itself alongside the LSE. Educational administration was the low road, an applied, professional area of study with limited academic pretensions that suggested a future for the IOE as what Clarke had described as a 'glorified Training College'. Morris Ginsberg at the LSE and Barbara Wootton at Bedford College favoured combining the sociological and administrative features of the professorship, so that it assumed both an intellectual dimension and an element of 'practical experience' (Ginsberg 1952; Wootton 1952). It was Judges at KCL who perceived most clearly the academic opportunities represented by sociology as a discipline: 'Sociology has joined the company of scientific disciplines with its own elaborate theoretical structure – *un*disciplined though this still looks – and those in the educational world who speak of sociology as a mere matter of "social aspects" do not generally understand that there is a special language and equipment to be acquired with pain through academic application.' He noted that Mannheim had been 'a real professional', but on the other hand, 'that is not why he was a success' (Judges 1952a). The implication was plain: Mannheim was a success because he was recognised as a top flight sociologist and social scientist. By contrast, Ginsberg added, 'Personally I do not think that Administration stands on its own feet as an academic subject; it seems to be covered by the existing provision of posts' (Judges 1952b). T.H. Marshall at the LSE concurred that sociology should be separated from educational administration, although he agreed that there would be few candidates for such a post at the professorial level (Marshall 1952).

The situation was further complicated by the intervention of Lionel Elvin, then the director of UNESCO's Department of Education, who wrote to Jeffery to indicate his own interest in the post. He was concerned, as he affirmed, with the relationship between education and society, and continued: 'The immediate function of the holder of this Chair would be, it seems to me, to impregnate [sic] future teachers with a sense of their role in society, and especially English society: the function of the schoolmistress in the village, of the master or mistress in the slum or the suburb, and so on'. However, he freely admitted that he was not a 'trained sociologist' nor yet a 'school educationalist in the narrower sense of the word' (Elvin 1953). Carr-Saunders advised Jeffery that Elvin's works were 'well informed and exhibit a balanced outlook' but that he 'makes the impression of a practical reformer rather than an investigator' (Carr-Saunders 1953). Jeffery agreed to meet with Elvin informally to discuss the post further but was clear that the successful applicant would need to take the subject forward. As he pointed out:

> There is now an established body of knowledge under the title of sociology that is cognate with education. It would be an advantage to our work if we had someone of professorial standing whose business it would be to know current work in sociology, especially as it is being carried on in British universities and to pursue the consequences of this work in educational theory and practice.
>
> *(Jeffery 1953)*

Jeffery continued: 'We are looking for someone who would create a new subject for, while he might draw on the resources of academic sociology, he would be primarily concerned to tackle educational problems from a new angle.' If this indicated a compromise between sociology and administration, Jeffery was also at pains to emphasise that '[i]t is an important part of our conception that the professor would help to break down the isolation of education from the other social sciences which has been traditional in this country' (Jeffery 1953). Jeffery met Elvin over dinner but decided that Elvin was not the right person for such a role.

The outcome was a classic compromise. Jean Floud was appointed, with the advantage of being employed at the LSE and having active contacts with leading sociologists, but at the rank of senior lecturer rather than professor, with the professorship being held open to await further developments in the field. There is a significant gender dimension here that should not be overlooked as we glimpse the informal and indeed convivial dynamics of the mainly male professorial elite. Floud, like Susan Isaacs before her, never was recognised with a professorship. For the moment, while Floud supported the established position of the sociology of education and maintained its close association with mainstream sociology in the 1950s, the larger problem of how the sociology of education would be established both in its own right and as part of educational studies was held in abeyance.

Another decade was to pass before the sociology of education discovered its new champion. Basil Bernstein was appointed to succeed Jean Floud as a senior lecturer in the sociology of education in January 1963 and was instantly recognised as a future star because of his clear sociological prowess. Later the same year, Elvin supported Bernstein to be recognised as a qualified teacher of the university, although he had not yet taught for the requisite three years, and was rewarded with a generous tribute from the leading sociologist A.H. Halsey at the University of Oxford. Halsey gave his 'absolutely unequivocal support' to Bernstein on the basis of his contribution to the sociology of education: 'He is most prolific in ideas, and I know from first-hand that his excitement communicates itself to students very readily' (Halsey 1963). Bernstein was soon promoted to a readership in October 1965 and to a full professorship in 1967 – itself a landmark, as it was later regarded, in the institutionalisation of the sociology of education in Britain (Szreter 1980, p. 297). Ten years later, Bernstein's chair in the sociology of education received the further signal honour of becoming the first named chair at the IOE, named, very fittingly, after Karl Mannheim.

Educational administration and curriculum studies

In the 1960s and 1970s, the discipline-based approach of the IOE was at its most rigid and influential. This was the intellectual home and heartland of Richard Peters, the successor to Louis Arnaud Reid as the professor of the philosophy of education at the IOE. Peters used his inaugural lecture in 1963, as well as many other public platforms, to preach that education was not an autonomous discipline but 'a field, like politics, where the disciplines of history, philosophy, psychology and sociology have application' (Peters 1963/1980, p. 273). Intellectual depth in a particular disciplinary area was prized above breadth or range of studies. As the Institute grew rapidly in size, it was also most convenient to compartmentalise studies in different areas rather than attempt to embrace educational issues in general terms. From this point of view, a typical exchange took place in November 1965 between Peters and a comparative educationalist, Brian Holmes. The latter agreed with Peters that teacher training courses should be based mainly on specialist teaching by philosophers, psychologists, sociologists and comparative educationists rather than through seminars conducted by every member of staff. He emphasised that '[t]here are too many areas of special study to make it possible for teaching to be undertaken in every area by non-specialists' (Holmes 1965). Nonetheless, there were at least two notable attempts to challenge or mitigate this dominant regime. The first was designed to rehabilitate educational administration as an area of study in its own right with both an academic and a professional dimension. The second was to develop the emerging area of curriculum studies as an alternative to the disciplines, again combining theory with practice.

The rise of educational administration as a field of study in its own right was largely the achievement of George Baron, who was appointed to the IOE as a schools relations officer in 1946 and eventually made his way through promotions to become in 1971 the first professor of educational administration in the country (see also Glatter 2004 and McCulloch 2014b for more detailed discussions of Baron's career). Baron's career exemplifies the challenges that confronted staff with a broad range of experience as opposed to specialised expertise in one of the disciplines. He was regarded as experienced and knowledgeable in his area, but he was not recognised by the University of London Senate as a university teacher until 1956 (Baron 1956). Lionel Elvin, who had been appointed to a different professorship in 1957 and then succeeded Jeffery as director, observed that Baron was 'one of our best informed people about many sides of education in this country, especially perhaps on questions of the structure and administration of our education' (Elvin 1962). At the same time, in academic terms Elvin accorded Baron only faint praise. He noted that Baron had no qualifications in sociology and could apply himself to practical problems but did not have the theoretical depth of a sociologist (Elvin 1962, 1966). Baron tended to be regarded as a versatile generalist rather than as a specialist in a particular discipline, and this seemed to hold him back from being awarded the highest recognition.

The path to Baron's professorship became clear not through his practical experience or problem-solving abilities but as he led educational administration in the direction of being accepted as a separate integrated subject associated with the social sciences. In the early 1960s, national education policy came to the fore with the Newsom and Robbins reports (Ministry of Education 1963a, 1963b) and then with a Labour government that advocated the spread of comprehensive schools (see for example McCulloch 2015; 2016). Baron responded to this political context by arguing that the study of educational administration should be seen in relation to policy issues to comprise a field of study, as opposed to a discipline, which would be the concern of 'a number of people drawn in from sociology, philosophy, comparative education and history' (Baron n.d., 1963?). He proposed that a small group of those substantially concerned with sociology and the other disciplines should be brought together to work out a general plan, with individuals then being given responsibility for organising courses and for other elements in the work. These would include issues around policy functions, administrative agencies, the legal framework of education and the economics of education and educational finance (Baron n.d., 1963?). This led in 1964 to the establishment of a Department of Educational Administration under Baron's leadership.

Baron also co-edited with William Taylor, another education academic whose work straddled educational administration and sociology, a book entitled *Educational Administration and the Social Sciences* (Baron and Taylor 1969). This was organised into two sections, 'Analysis' and 'Applications', but the editors were anxious to emphasise the theoretical aspects of educational administration as a field of study, and the collection focused attention on 'some of the ways in which the thinking of social scientists may have relevance for both the study and the practice of educational administration' (Baron and Taylor 1969, p. v). Baron himself argued in one chapter in this collection that 'it should now be possible to conceive of the study of educational administration in England as stretching from political science on one side of the spectrum of social sciences to organisation theory and management studies on the other' (Baron 1969, p. 3). It was this, together with Baron's increasingly international profile and contributions to conferences, that earned Baron his deserved chair.

Another new initiative designed to lessen the IOE's dependence on a discipline-based approach was the creation in 1972 of the Department of Curriculum Studies (DCS). This reflected the prominence of curriculum change as a national issue in which teachers and LEAs had key roles and the significance of the Schools Council for the Curriculum and Examinations, introduced in 1964, as both an initiator of curriculum innovation and a provider of funding. 'Curriculum Studies' was intended to be a means of evaluating the success of these new initiatives and of understanding them in their broader context. A new journal, the *Journal of Curriculum Studies*, was concerned with issues such as, 'How does the curriculum change? What is the nature of curriculum evaluation? How is the curriculum related to teaching, and what kind of statements give an inner consistency to discussion about the curriculum?' (*Journal of Curriculum Studies* 1969, 1/1, p. 1). In 1970, the University of Leeds established a Centre for Studies in Science Education, located within its large School of Education, so that, as its founders recognised, 'institutional barriers between researchers in science education and in the basic disciplines of education were removed' (Layton and Lovell 1982, p. 216). The new Centre also introduced an annual publication, *Studies in Science Education*.

Within the IOE, this trend was led by Denis Lawton, appointed initially as a researcher in a sociological project in 1963 and later as a senior lecturer in curriculum studies from 1967 before being promoted to a professorship in 1974 (Aldrich 2002, pp. 150, 172). Richard Pring, a philosopher and lecturer in the department and later a professor at Exeter and then Oxford, has recalled that the IOE was 'a rather feudal society, ruled by the strong, "autonomous barons" of the "foundation disciplines" and chaired by a director with limited power over his baronial subjects' (Pring 2005, pp. 195–196). The DCS was intended to provide a means of bringing these disciplines together in the study of the school curriculum, as well as linking theory to practice. However, it largely failed to bring into existence a distinctively interdisciplinary approach to educational studies and research.

According to Lawton himself, the rationale for the DCS was that, as he put it, 'there is a need in the highly specialised Institute for one department which would (a) be concerned with the development of educational theory generally and curriculum theory in particular, and (b) be concerned with interdisciplinary courses and encourage other departments to contribute to the work' (Lawton 1974). He suggested that the DCS should be relatively small and avoid becoming a 'mini-Institute' and that it would be helpful to establish a formal structure to 'make decisions about proposals of an interdisciplinary kind' (Lawton 1974). It was committed from the beginning to bringing the different disciplines together to study the curriculum as a whole, an endeavour that was reflected in its staff members who had experience of one or more of the foundation disciplines (DSC 1981). In practice, it retained an emphasis on the separate disciplines working together more than a fully integrated approach.

This emphasis on the disciplines was reflected in Lawton's own publications. For example, Lawton's *Social Change, Educational Theory and Curriculum Planning*, published in 1973 (Lawton 1973), was organised first in terms of the principles of curriculum planning, including separate chapters on social factors and psychological theories, then a socio-historical study of the school curriculum in the UK, and finally an examination of how theory was implemented in practice to become what he called the 'common culture individualised curriculum'. By the time of his professorial inaugural lecture in 1978, Lawton recognised the increasingly active role of the State in the school curriculum by also stressing the importance of politics in shaping the curriculum, but he retained a fundamentally disciplinary model in his argument that 'curriculum, perhaps even more than other educational issues, needed to be studied simultaneously from the viewpoints of several educational disciplines' (Lawton 1978/1980, p. 306).

Nor was this approach unusual among curriculum theorists elsewhere. John Kerr, professor of education at Leicester and a specialist in the science curriculum, edited a volume entitled *Changing the Curriculum* (Kerr 1968a) with chapters based on a series of public lectures on the contributions of philosophy (by Paul Hirst), history (by Kenneth Charlton), psychology (by Philip Taylor) and sociology (by Frank Musgrove). Each of these contributions was anxious to stress its theoretical base in the relevant parent discipline, while at the same time asserting practical relevance to the curriculum. Kerr himself, in his inaugural lecture at Leicester, argued that philosophy, psychology, sociology and history, in cooperation with one another, could establish a more coherent theoretical framework for the curriculum. He also proposed that practising educationists should be able to consult specialists in the disciplines for advice about particular problems 'in the same way as the medical profession calls upon physiologists, biochemists, bacteriologists and so on' (Kerr 1968b, p. 36). This argument suggested the promotion of a closer affinity between 'practice' in the training and everyday work of teachers and the 'theory' embodied in the disciplines.

Such texts and the intellectual frameworks on which they were based served to structure courses in curriculum studies such as the IOE lecture programme in the DCS in 1978–79 (Figure 3.1), which began by outlining the philosophical, psychological and sociological issues at the heart of a 'multi-disciplinary' approach to the curriculum.

By the early 1980s, with Malcolm Skilbeck having succeeded Lawton as the head of the DCS, the disciplinary model of curriculum studies was under review but with little consensus as to what should replace it. According to Skilbeck's summation at a staff conference held in July 1982, 'There was general agreement that curriculum studies had developed beyond the discipline based model that the department originally embodied (according to DL [Denis Lawton] more for pragmatic than ideological reasons) but less clarity as to what it had developed into' (Skilbeck 1982). Skilbeck went on to propose three potential models for courses and research in curriculum studies that the department might adopt. On the first, curriculum studies would be treated as a picture of the field of curriculum studies itself – its history, literature, methodology and current position. On the second,

---

4.10.78 – Why curriculum studies?
11.10.78 – The nature of curriculum theory
18.10.78 – Philosophical issues
25.10.78 – Psychological issues
1.11.78 – Sociological issues
8.11.78 – Language and curriculum: some developments in the teaching of language
15.11.78 – A multi-disciplinary approach to curriculum
22.11.78 – Learning theories
29.11.78 – Motivation and education
6.12.78 – Theories of cognitive and moral development
13.12.78 – The theories of instruction: Bruner and Gagne
10.1.79 – Creativity and intelligence
17.1.79 – Tradition and change in the curriculum
24.1.79 – Problems of justification
31.1.79 – Curriculum content: problems of selection
7.2.79 – Curriculum content: sociology of knowledge
14.2.79 – Curriculum objectives
21.2.79 – Curriculum evaluation: with reference to some projects
28.2.79 – Curriculum evaluation: new approaches
7.3.79 – Methods of assessment
14.3.79 – The changing role of the teacher
21.3.79 – Teacher as researcher
25.3.79 – Accountability
2.5.79 – Control of the curriculum
9.5.79 – Authority and participation

FIGURE 3.1 IOE DCS Department of Curriculum Studies lecture programme, 1978–79 (readings and questions omitted) (DCS 1978)

it would focus on current issues or problems. On the third, it would become an orientation to action, and it was argued that courses should be framed more clearly around this overall approach rather than one of understanding and reflection. Staff discussion around the relationship between the core courses and the disciplines, according to Skilbeck, 'generated the most discussion and the least agreement!'. Indeed, the contribution of the disciplines remained unresolved (Skilbeck 1982).

Conclusions

Over the medium term, this chapter has shown how the new IOE represented a new model for educational studies in the UK from the 1930s onwards, under the leadership of first Nunn and then Clarke, as it shifted away from a model of the field as being based on psychology towards a multifaceted internationally oriented field in which sociology became the dominant sector. It retained vestiges of its applied, professional roots, which were seen as second-rate in a university context, but moved towards an increasingly disciplinary social science orientation in the post-war years. The IOE played a pivotal role in the institutionalisation of the sociology of education, albeit that this was contested and debated even within the institution. Disciplinary depth was the main route to academic prestige and success, although the IOE also helped to nurture two of the most significant alternative approaches to emerge in the post-war period in educational administration and curriculum studies. As Fred Clarke had hoped, the IOE as a specialist institution was *sui generis* but still became recognised as the leader of the field in the UK. All the gates of knowledge were indeed thrown wide open, but they remained on the whole fixed and separated from one another.

4

ORGANISING THE FIELD

From the Standing Conference to the British Educational Research Association

Before 1945, there was no national organisation to represent educational studies and research in Britain apart from SCRE in Scotland. In the thirty years after the Second World War, the founding first of NFER and then of SCSE and, by the end of the period, of BERA and SERA transformed this situation. From the 1940s until the 1970s, the State showed increasing indications of being willing to intervene actively in a number of educational domains, and by the 1960s educational research was an increasingly crowded arena. Nevertheless, although there were signs that political control would be exerted increasingly at a national level over the nature of educational research, there remained scope for those actively involved in educational studies and research to seek to define their own aims and approaches (see also Nisbet 2000). The spread of higher education over these three decades also affected the way in which this was achieved. In the 1940s higher education was still a narrowly elite institution, whereas by the 1970s it had acquired a broader mass basis. This in turn helped to shape the elite character of the SCSE, compared with the broader representation to which BERA and SERA aspired.

A national infrastructure offered new possibilities in terms of organising the knowledge base of the field as a whole. For example, it might permit greater efficiency in giving priority to particular approaches or issues or in encouraging new types of work. It might also be able to encourage more collegiality and teamwork, going across specialist interests to combine forces with common aims in view. Both SCSE and BERA, in their different ways, originated with interdisciplinary ideals to the fore. As they became established, nevertheless, it was their specialist and discipline-based forms of study that tended to emerge in the years that followed.

The growth of educational studies and research over this time was closely related to the expansion and nature of formal education and of higher education and also to wider social, political and economic issues. Generally this was a phase of sustained growth in terms of the economy as a whole, punctuated by short periods of retrenchment, with economic problems developing more strongly in the early

1970s (Timmins 1995, p. 177). Educational expenditure grew steeply over these years. In 1953–54, central government spent £46.9 million and local government £460.3 million, with educational expenditure as a whole at 3 percent of the gross national product. By 1963–64, these figures were £198 million, £1,129 million and 4.3 percent, and a decade later in 1973–74 they had increased again to £670 million, £3,566 million and 5.7 percent (Simon 1991, p. 599). Higher education also expanded markedly over this period. The Education Act of 1944 introduced secondary education for all pupils, up to the age of 15 from 1947 and finally up to 16 in 1972, and this helped to provide a platform with growing numbers of students staying on in school up to 18 for a growth in numbers in higher education (see Woodin et al. 2013). Numbers of university students in the United Kingdom as a whole grew from fewer than 50,000 in 1945 to nearly 300,000 by 1975, an expansion that was stimulated further through the Robbins Report on higher education in 1963 (Committee on Higher Education 1963).

Some key contextual factors also favoured the further development of educational research during this period. As Ben Morris of the NFER observed in 1955, there were intellectual, social and professional aspects to this. Intellectually, scientific modes of thought helped to promote the growth of educational psychology (Morris 1955, p. 79). The educational psychologist Robert Thoulness, for example, argued in the 1960s that the climate of opinion was changing so that it was being increasingly understood that 'education is too important to be allowed to develop without control by the expert knowledge that is to be obtained by scientific research' (Thoulness 1969, p. 287). Thoulness himself was optimistic that educational research would yield comparable results to that of another applied science, agricultural research, so that in relation to the teaching of reading, 'It may not yet have reached the level of that on potato-growing, but in a few years it should be adequate to provide a basis for guiding school practice' (Thoulness 1969, p. 286).

Socially, too, aspirations towards equality of opportunity, symbolised for instance in the Education Act of 1944, also encouraged research in education. Professionally, the implementation of the McNair Report of 1944 on the education and training of teachers, and then the Robbins Report of 1963 on higher education provided incentives for universities to review their responsibilities (Morris 1955, p. 79). Moreover, as William Taylor, then at the University of Bristol, pointed out in the early 1970s, a precondition of the growth of educational research was 'the existence of a climate of political, social and educational ideas sympathetic to research pursuits, and in which research is seen by policy makers, administrators, heads and classroom teachers as capable of making a real contribution to the rationality of decision making' (Taylor 1972, p. 7).

The Standing Conference on Studies in Education

In some other countries, the organisation of educational studies and research was well advanced in the early decades of the twentieth century. In the US, the National Society for the Study of Education (NSSE) was created in 1901, with its *Yearbook* beginning the following year, and the American Educational Research Association

(AERA) was founded in 1916. The Carnegie Corporation supported the foundation of national organisations in South Africa, Australia and New Zealand in the 1920s and 1930s. In Britain, despite a number of tentative initiatives, a national organisation was not founded until after the Second World War.

In 1930, for example, Percy Nunn of the IOE proposed that there should be 'some organisation for promoting inquiries in this country and abroad', somewhat on the lines of the Department of Special Inquiries and Reports towards the end of the nineteenth century and also of the International Institute of the Teachers College at Columbia University. He commended the efforts of the BPS's Committee of Educational Research, which involved a small executive body with a secretary based in London and a larger advisory body of which all professors of education and psychology in the British universities were *ex officio* members, 'together with other persons who were qualified to assist in educational research of the more narrowly scientific type' (Nunn 1930). Nunn noted:

> The business of the Committee was not itself to prosecute research but to execute a coordinating function, to keep a census of researchers in progress so as to prevent overlapping and to facilitate cooperation, to put young workers in connexion with more experienced guides, and to foster certain inquiries which involve detailed work by moderately qualified observers over a large area.
>
> *(Nunn 1930)*

He concluded that this enterprise was 'soundly conceived' but that it 'has not fulfilled its promise because it needed a definite home with office conveniences and a paid expert secretary' (Nunn 1930). These were the first hints of an initiative to organise and promote British educational studies that was to culminate two decades later in the Standing Conference.

As the director of the IOE in the late 1930s, Fred Clarke took the lead in helping to build a national infrastructure for the field, with the strong support of senior colleagues such as Philip Hartog. In 1939, Clarke was invited to chair a special committee of Section L of the BAAS to consider and report on the possibilities of organising and developing research in education in England and Wales. This committee discussed various ways of organising educational research and quickly agreed that 'some form of central council would be needed, co-ordinating the activities of many autonomous bodies, and in close touch with similar bodies in the Empire and in other countries' (BAAS 1939a). For the first time, it conducted a full audit of the research in education that was being conducted in different institutions around the country, comparing this with current work in Scotland, the United States, Geneva, South Africa, Australia, New Zealand and Canada. Clarke's verdict on the current state of the field in England was scathing:

> My own impressions, having written it all down, are:
>
> i) That it's mainly exploratory in nature, or else is 'committee work'. The amount of real research is tiny.

ii)   That most of it is *merely* empirical – try this, try that rule-of-thumb
      stuff.

iii) That it's very unco-ordinated, i.e. the bits are not related to each
      other; one authority will cheerfully repeat without improvement
      what has been done better by another . . .; that there are big gaps –
      some promising lines of research are simply not explored at all.

iv)   That it's all small-scale stuff. . . .

v)   That there's a great lack of means of spreading new knowledge, of
      coordinating what is known, of planning new research, of letting
      people know what is being done by others.

(Clarke 1939a)

Through this means, the committee decided that educational research in England
and Wales needed to be better coordinated. Such coordination might be achieved
through a Central Council to direct and support research, as with the Research
Councils overseas, but it was agreed that this might reduce the spontaneous activity that was already going on in many centres. Another alternative was to establish
a Department of Educational Research either at a centrally situated university or
else as an autonomous unity, but again this was ruled out, this time on the grounds
that the tradition of English education was against central control or a monopoly
of activity (Committee on Research in Education 1939).

It was therefore decided that a greater benefit would be gained if a central
committee were formed to stimulate research and to supply relevant information
to all who were interested. Such an organisation would coordinate research rather
than undertake it, to register and record it and thus prevent duplication of effort,
and to guide students, thus forming an administrative rather than an executive
national committee. This in turn would be controlled by a large number of supporting bodies and work in cooperation with these and would also maintain active
contact with the Board of Education and with Research Councils overseas (BAAS
1939b). It is worth noting, too, that as the committee reached this decision, Richard
Oliver of Manchester University commended the IOE for being so 'wide and non-
monopolistic' in its suggestions for a bureau of enquiry and research (Oliver 1939).

Clarke was hopeful, as he confided in Oliver, that '[w]ith reasonable luck we
might be within reach of something like a real national organisation within the
next three years or so' (Clarke 1939b). In the event, the outbreak of the Second
World War in September 1939 prevented immediate action to implement these
steps. Yet there remained further obstacles in the path to their realisation. The first
was the difficult question of how such a body would be financed, especially since
the Board of Education did not provide any money for educational research out of
the annual educational estimates of £45 million. The second was to achieve a more
secure position in the universities for education departments to develop the study
of education. The third was to establish a coherent vision or goal for this kind of
study. H.G. Stead, chief education officer for Derbyshire, showed a keen awareness
of these problems in a book that he produced in 1942. He observed that the staff of

training colleges had too little experience of research to be able to develop it successfully and that their work also lacked coordination by anybody that might record the results attained or bring to bear any comprehensive knowledge of the work being attempted (Stead 1942, p. 141). He suggested the establishment of research institutes in which selected teachers might be able to take part for a period and devoting much more money to educational research than was presently the case (Stead 1942, p. 143).

That these challenges came to be resolved over the following decade was primarily due to the cycle of educational reform and reconstruction during the Second World War culminating in the Education Act of 1944. This provided fresh legislative provision that favoured an expanded role for educational studies and research across the UK. It also provided an opportunity to articulate ambitions for the field that had rarely been entertained before. After R.A. Butler became president of the Board of Education, one of several advisory committees that he established was the McNair Committee on teachers and youth leaders, in 1942. This committee reported in 1944 with recommendations that university schools of education could be developed as an alternative scheme for teacher education (Board of Education 1944). Section 82 of the 1944 Act itself made explicit provision for LEAs to be able to contribute to educational research. More broadly and even more significantly, the Act was informed by a reforming vision that accorded it a place in the formation of the Welfare State after the war.

After the war, Clarke helped to create the NFER, which was founded in 1946 with financial support from the Carnegie Corporation of New York and other agencies, and he became its first president. The NFER was based on corporate membership through organisations that represented the LEAs, teachers, higher education institutions and the Ministry of Education. These organisations also provided a regular income through subscriptions and a Ministry grant (Morris 1952). It was intended to supplement the existing work of university education departments and to undertake independent research, which allowed it support research projects in specific areas, and it maintained a national presence through subsequent decades and into the next century.

In 1949, Clarke became the president of Section L of the BAAS, Educational Science. He was also a key figure in the founding of the SCSE, which was launched at an inaugural conference held in London on 19 December 1951. The conference was held 'to discuss the problems raised by the growth of educational research over the last few decades' (*BJES* 1952, p. 67). It agreed that 'British studies in the various fields of education – philosophical, historical, social, psychological and pedagogic – need to be better organised and better known' (*BJES* 1952, p. 67). It aimed to maintain close contact with the NFER and SCRE and with a group of advisers and consultants from overseas, with the ultimate purpose of providing 'greater continuity to the efforts of those responsible for research in the University Departments of Education and elsewhere, to exchange views on research and devise means for co-ordinating it' (*BJES* 1954, p. 170). Clarke chaired the conference but died a few weeks later (Judges 1952). Roy Niblett from the University of

Leeds became the SCSE's first chair and J.W.Tibble of University College Leicester its first secretary.

An example of the problems of educational research in particular was in the research degrees being produced as a basis for the further development of the field. The number of theses being produced as part of higher degrees in education in British universities was an indication of increasing research capacity, but they were produced mainly in relatively few universities and were largely of one particular type. In the three years between 1948 and 1951, 373 theses were produced in psychology and experimental education, 82 on history and comparative education, 58 on teaching methods and 32 on philosophy and principles, making 545 in all, or an average of 136.3 per year, double the number per year produced in previous decades. Over three-quarters of these theses were produced in six universities – London more than twice as many as at any other institution, and then Glasgow, Edinburgh, Leeds, Manchester and Birmingham (Wiseman, 1953, p. 62). Nearly all of these theses were for master's degrees rather than for doctorates, especially in the provincial universities, and although many were substantial pieces of work, they varied greatly in terms of quality (Wiseman, 1953, p. 64).

The SCSE itself was an elite body mainly consisting of professors and heads of departments of education, professors of adult education and other professors concerned with 'pedagogical studies' in the field of education in universities or university colleges (*BJES* 1955). In 1953, it had 74 members, of whom 46 were professors of education from across England, Wales, Scotland and Northern Ireland, with a few others from overseas, from schools, and representatives of other research associations (*BJES* 1953). It was indeed a 'select association' (*BJES* 1982, p. 5; see also Richardson 2002, pp. 11–12), reflecting an established hierarchy, besides being mainly male due to the lack of women professors of education and directors of institutes in Britain at this time. In certain ways it was a respectable body somewhat akin to the Royal Society, the British Association or indeed the Headmasters' Conference before it (see Stimson 1948; Percival 1973; MacLeod and Collins 1981; Morrell and Thackray 1984). If it was a parliament of education that was assembled here, it resembled a Senate rather than a House of Commons or House of Representatives.

The further growth of educational studies and research over the following two decades produced two competing sets of pressures. One was to coordinate and organise this research more effectively and to develop a coherent and cumulative body of research findings. This suggested a fundamentally interdisciplinary approach in which the distinctive contributions of different specialisms and disciplines would crystallise in a new configuration of knowledge that would itself represent an independent and separate discipline, on equal terms with other, more established disciplines. The other was to cultivate and reinforce the different specialisms and disciplines involved to promote a multidisciplinary approach in which the disciplines would combine rather than be subsumed in the cause of education. These different outlooks generated tensions that would last well beyond this period and encouraged the establishment of a large number of organisations to represent both generic and specialist concerns.

The SCSE, first conceived as a loose network that would represent educational studies in general, soon became a forum of debate between specialised and more generalised accounts of research in education. The annual meeting in 1953 for instance explored new projects to collect and disseminate information about research in education, the role of the history of education in teacher training courses and the nature of educational studies in Scotland (*BJES* 1954). In January 1955, it considered the activities of the International Conference of University Teachers of Education, which had recently met in Ghent, Belgium, and discussed the relationship between the study of education and the initial training of the graduate teacher (*BJES* 1955). In December 1955, it examined the place of the philosophy of education in one-year courses of training for graduates, together with the relationship of this study to psychology and sociology (*BJES* 1956). The following year, it developed further discussion of the relationship between educational psychology and philosophical studies in education and of a sociological approach to the study of education (*BJES* 1957). The record of this meeting notes that a prolonged discussion took place that 'produced support for all ten of the possible family relationships between philosophy, psychology and sociology, as well as exogamous connections, but displayed a drowsy unanimity in allowing all three of them to work on the family small-holding with no more formality than a change of name here or there' (*BJES* 1957, p. 166). Which approach should take precedence, if any, was less clear, but evidently all agreed that the reputation of their common calling should be their overall priority, since 'academic respectability' was 'the only armour against disdainful colleagues' (*BJES* 1957, p. 167).

These regular discussions among leading figures in the field, hosted by the SCSE and recorded faithfully in the *BJES*, reflected an awareness of the tensions that existed within and around educational studies and research, especially between the specialisation of the different core disciplines and their more generalised contributions to an understanding of education as a whole. Contributors were also conscious of the conflicting pressures between the need to encourage 'academic respectability' due to their precarious position in the academy and the importance of retaining a close and meaningful relationship with teacher education and the requirements of schools.

'Undifferentiated mush'?

By the early 1960s, with growing numbers of staff, students, funding and resources, at least in the main centres, specialisation on the basis of disciplinary study became increasingly widespread. In 1960 the college course was extended to three years in length, and the Robbins Report of 1963 proposed the creation of a new degree, the bachelor of education, for students in the colleges of education who were capable of work at degree level. The colleges, departments and institutes of education were also to be reorganised into university schools of education, with the colleges being considerably expanded in size (Committee on Higher Education 1963; Taylor 1969, pp. 74–75). In 1964, there were still only 31 professors of education in England and

Wales, but this figure almost doubled in the next three years (Taylor 1969, p. 224). By 1968–69, there were 166 colleges of education and 28 university departments of education in England and Wales (Taylor 1969, p. 78). In the three-year course, as William Taylor's study found, previous arrangements in which students undertook all their work with a single tutor gave way 'to a more systematic treatment of educational issues along philosophical, psychological, historical and sociological lines' (Taylor 1969, p. 117). This led to larger numbers of staff with specialist qualifications in particular disciplines. As Peter Chambers of the West Midlands College of Education in Walsall affirmed, 'The sociologists, psychologists, philosophers, historians and methodologists in the education department have come together as a team to replace the principal's lecture and the Master of Method's demonstration as the unifying element in the professional preparation of teachers' (Chambers 1971, pp. 78–79).

The total number of staff employed by university education departments and institutes of education, mainly for teacher training, was 500 at most; moreover, the Parliamentary and Scientific Committee (PSC) judged that 'few, if any, are engaged on full-time research and their total empirical research effort would not be equivalent to a hundred full-time workers' (PSC 1961, Appendix A). It observed that the Register of Current Research in Education, maintained by the NFER, recorded 233 empirical studies of education in the UK that were currently taking place, of which 121 were being carried out by individuals working for postgraduate degrees in education and mainly on a part-time basis. Seventy-one involved work by university departments, while three were undertaken by LEAs and two by teacher groups. Other educational research was conducted by professional organisations related to other disciplines, but the PSC considered that 'the all important "feed back" of information to educational institutions is not always available or may be unused' (PSC 1961). The PSC concluded that a rapid expansion of empirical research into educational problems was essential and overdue and recommended that an Educational Research Council should be established, comparable to the medical and agricultural research councils and reporting to Parliament. Moreover, it argued, 'Research in such a field must be independent, and should not be completely or directly under the control of any one of the main users of the researchers involved' (PSC 1961).

These figures reflected some growth in the amount of educational research conducted in university education departments, at least in the major centres. An ad hoc committee of the Association of Teachers in Colleges and Departments of Education (ATCDE) was established in 1965 to examine the prospects for research. It observed that '[t]he Colleges have for a century been in a position of inferiority in the context of higher education; the introduction of the three-year course and the B.Ed. provides an opportunity for building up the academic standing of the Colleges and enhancing the status and intellectual quality of the teaching profession' (ATCDE 1965). In order to achieve this end, the committee advised creating a 'climate of opinion in the colleges that was favourable to advanced study and research, with an expectation that a substantial proportion of any college staff should be engaged in this. At the same time, it added that this should not be allowed to operate to the detriment of teaching or of personal relations with students. The main problems that it identified were a lack of time, especially with increasing student numbers, a lack of interest on the part of college lecturers whose previous experience was of working in schools and a lack of competence in research that would need to be addressed through training in the context of higher degree work (ATCDE 1965).

Another new factor besides these radical developments in teacher education was a rapid growth in the amount of funding available to studies and research in education in the 1960s. The Crowther Report of 1959 observed, 'In view of the very large sums of money that are spent on education every year, the expenditure on educational research can only be regarded as pitiable. If there is to be a consistent programme of educational development, almost the first step should be to review the provision for statistics and research' (Ministry of Education 1959, para. 697). In 1961, the Parliamentary and Scientific Committee (PSC) calculated that while national expenditure on education in Britain had reached £800 million per year, empirical research into education and its achievement was only about £125,000 per year, or 0.014 percent of the total amount spent on education. This compared for example with £4.3 million per year spent on the Medical Research Council, £5.3 million on the Agricultural Research Council and £12.7 million on the Department of Scientific and Industrial Research. Industry also spent over £300 million on research, amounting to 4 percent of its £7,500 million contribution to the GNP (gross national product) (PSC 1961). It noted that most research conducted by teachers and LEAs was 'robbed of its principal value' because it did not receive skilled advice on matters such as experiment design, test construction and statistical analysis. The annual income of SCRE in 1959–60, which had just one full-time professional member, was only £8,338. The NFER, supported like SCRE by subscriptions from LEAs, teachers' organisations, universities and the education department, had a total grant in 1959–60 of £32,559 and employed eight full-time research staff.

The IOE in London began to accept research funding in the 1950s to support research from a range of agencies, including the Simplified Spelling Society, the Nuffield Foundation and other sources for reading research, as well as the Ford Foundation for research on the economics and administration of education (Aldrich 2002, p. 152). The low level of funding for educational research was widely debated at this time, including in the House of Commons a special debate initiated by the Labour MP James Bowden in April 1962. Bowden pointed out that the total amount spent on research into cast iron, welding and ceramics was in each category a quarter of a million pounds, or nearly twice the amount spent on educational research (House of Commons Debates [HOCD] 1962, col. 726). Moreover, he added, more was known about training capstan lathe operators than about the training of classroom teachers (HOCD 1962, col. 727). In his reply to the debate, the Minister of Education, Sir David Eccles, emphasised that the Ministry was beginning to establish new machinery for undertaking educational research and providing funds for charitable foundations, while also acknowledging the importance of independent sources of research: 'There naturally ought to be complete freedom for people outside to say, "The Minister is asleep. He does not realise that this wants looking into. We think it should be. May we have some help?"' (HOCD 1962, col. 751).

A wide range of agencies became directly involved in funding educational research during the 1960s. A separate Educational Research Council was not set up, but the new Social Science Research Council (SSRC) that was created in 1965 instituted an Educational Research Board that reported to it and enabled projects of fundamental research in education to be established. The NFER conducted research projects, produced and disseminated tests, provided information on research and offered technical advice and assistance on such matters as experimental design, the use of measuring instruments and statistical analysis (*BJES* 1969, pp. 209–210). The Ministry of Education, subsequently the Department of Education and Science (DES), began to commission research in 1962, and this provision grew rapidly so that in 1969 grants totalling £500,000 were made to support a total of 109 projects. The DES was advised within its planning branch by Dr A.H. Halsey until April 1968, when he was succeeded by Professor William Taylor (*BJES* 1969, p. 210). The Schools Council, established in 1964, was financed by the LEAs and the DES to promote curriculum innovation and by the end of the 1960s had a budget of about £1 million per year (*BJES* 1969, p. 211). Such curriculum development was also supported by the Nuffield Foundation, especially in science, mathematics and languages (*BJES* 1969, pp. 213–217).

Meanwhile, SCRE continued to conduct, sponsor, coordinate and advise on educational research in Scotland on an annual budget of about £38,000, of which £14,000 was used in 1967–68 for grants to other bodies and people, now clearly dwarfed by the infusion of funding from other quarters (*BJES* 1969, pp. 211–212). In Wales, the Schools Council Welsh Committee admitted in 1968 that comparatively little educational research had previously been conducted, although it suggested that this situation was changing rapidly: 'More work is being attempted; it reflects the needs of schools, and consequently it ranges over nearly the whole of the curriculum' (Schools Council Welsh Committee 1968, p. 1).

There were already fierce disputes between the DES on the one hand and the Treasury on the other about the level of funding for educational research and the causes for which it should be used. For example, J.F. Embling, on behalf of the education department, explained to J.P. Carswell of the Treasury in April 1963 that, although the 1963–64 estimates might look 'high', they reflected 'the importance which Ministers attach to research generally', together with 'the amount of public money we are putting into the educational system, and the extent of our ignorance'. In the light of these factors, Embling insisted, neither the expenditure of £30,000 per year on new projects nor a total expenditure of £250,000 per year was excessive, and indeed 'I am tempted to say that it is a minimum which could be effectively defended in the educational world' (Embling 1963). William Taylor estimated in 1971 that about £3.5 million was now spent annually on research and development activities in education. This remained a low figure by many standards; as Taylor observed, it still amounted to only 0.16 percent of the total budget for education (Taylor 1972, p. 4). Yet it was a large amount compared with the figure of only £125,000 ten years earlier or indeed with the sum total of zero twenty years before that.

The DES clearly had a stake in these new developments around teacher education and research funding, and it was itself contributing to organising the field when it convened and hosted a national conference on the course in education in the education of teachers, held at the University of Hull in March 1964. Such was the interest in this conference that the full text of the principal addresses was sent to all university departments and institutes of education and to all colleges of education in England and Wales (DES 1965). The first address, by the chief inspector at the Ministry, C.J. Gill, confronted the key issue: how far to integrate the study of education and the trend towards specialisation. He acknowledged that the recent introduction of a three-year course in training colleges, the expansion of student numbers and new demands on teachers in schools were serving to promote a more specialised approach. According to Gill, it was becoming increasingly difficult to keep pace with the growing amount of knowledge in psychology, sociology, philosophy, history and comparative education and with the expansion in departments; he commented, '[T]here is a growing tendency for specialist lecturers to take over the work in particular disciplines' (DES 1965, p. 3). It was in this context that he posed the fundamental question 'whether, to achieve recognition as an academic discipline, unification of the studies should be attempted or whether, to avoid too superficial a treatment of say, psychology or sociology, some degree of specialisation will be called for' (DES 1965, p. 3).

For the team of leading educational researchers who had been invited to address this conference, the answer to such a question was clear. These were all prominent and well respected in their own specialist areas: Richard Peters of the IOE London for philosophy, Stephen Wiseman from Manchester for psychology, Basil Bernstein of the IOE London for sociology and Joseph Lauwerys, again of the IOE London, for comparative education. It was Peters who set the tone with his conference paper. Peters had only recently presented his inaugural address as the professor of philosophy of education at the IOE London. In this inaugural address, he had described tendencies towards the integration of educational theory as 'undifferentiated mush' that had 'contributed so much to the low standing of the study of education in this country' (Peters 1963/1980, p. 273).

The Hull Conference gave Peters an opportunity to expound further on this thesis on a national stage, and he did so with a subtle argument about the proper relationship between integration and differentiation. He noted that logically all questions of educational policy were 'hybrid questions', that is, 'a crossing of value judgements with different forms of empirical inquiry'. Therefore, he argued, 'the first step towards answering such questions must be the breaking down of the questions into their logically distinct components'. This meant that the disciplines had a prior role in addressing educational issues. However, he continued, '[O]nce the various voices that speak about education, emanating from the different disciplines, have been separated out and trained, they need to join together in an orderly and coherent conversation about matters of common concern to teachers and practical administrators'. Thus, he concluded, '[W]e must make sure that the research and training carried out under the aegis of the different disciplines is brought together again in an integrated concentration on matters of common concern' (Peters 1965, p. 3). He insisted that there should be at least one specialist in the philosophy of education on the staff of every university education department and training college, although adding that they should also have experience in teaching if they were training future teachers (Peters 1965, pp. 8–9). While directly addressing the problems involved in the training of teachers, these strictures had clear relevance for the nature of educational studies and research.

The other keynote papers presented at the Hull Conference similarly insisted on the importance of particular disciplines as part of a broad but differentiated course. The psychologist Wiseman expounded on what he saw as 'the necessity for us to create an intellectual discipline as part of professional training, one that makes serious demands of our students – and particularly the best of them – and one which in quality of content and in rigour of methodology can bear comparison with any of the other sectors of our students' studies' (Wiseman 1965, p. 10). Bernstein, representing sociology, emphasised that the distinctive disciplines of psychology, philosophy, history and sociology should in his view 'retain their integrity as separate but related inquiries rather than for them to form some kind of educational stew' (Bernstein 1965, p. 2). He argued that the intellectual tensions between the disciplines should underlie the education course as a whole: 'At one level the student must feel the force of forms of thought which interpret how men have attempted to clarify and control the consciousness of being alive, and at another level the student must experience the direct bearing of these disciplines upon his specific consciousness as a teacher' (Bernstein 1965, p. 2). The comparativist Lauwerys also contributed a keynote paper on the place of the theory of education in schools of education, pointing out how 'the study of comparative education offers concrete examples of the way in which sociology and history of education can illuminate the analysis of educational problems' (Lauwerys 1965, p. 1). No historians of education contributed to the Hull Conference, but both Bernstein and Lauwerys, from their own particular perspectives, underlined the distinctive role of history as a discipline in education courses.

A further demonstration of the importance attached to the separate disciplines was the publication of a volume entitled *The Study of Education*, edited by J.W. Tibble of the University of Leicester (Tibble 1966a). This was to be the forerunner of a book series, the Students Library of Education, published by Routledge and Kegan Paul. The editorial board of this influential series, under the leadership of Tibble, consisted of the psychologist Ben Morris from Bristol, the philosopher Richard Peters from the IOE London, the historian Brian Simon from Leicester and the sociologist William Taylor from Bristol. This initial volume established the dominant discipline-based pattern with chapters on philosophy, history, psychology and sociology contributed by the members of the editorial board (see also Biesta 2011). Tibble, in his introduction to this first book, chose also to set out his aspirations for the series as a whole:

> Some will illustrate the contribution to the study of education made by the various forms of thought referred to in this introductory volume: the philosophy, psychology, history and sociology of education. It is also our intention to include some books which deal with a major educational topic in an interdisciplinary way, showing the contributions which different forms of thought can make to it.
>
> *(Tibble 1966a, p. vii)*

In practice, there were relatively few contributions that highlighted an 'interdisciplinary' approach.

Simon had emerged in the early 1960s as the leader of the 'new' history of education, his approach taking its cue from Fred Clarke's ideas about a social history of education but interpreting this on Marxist lines (see e.g. McCulloch 2010, 2011, chapter 4). His discipline-based contribution to Tibble's collection emphasised the importance of the history of education in terms of understanding education as a social function, or 'a vital contribution to social history' (Simon 1966, p. 95). He thus rejected what he characterised as its traditional production of 'a somewhat indigestible mass of dates and facts, orders and Acts' (Simon 1966, p. 91) and elsewhere as 'a flat record of acts and ordinances, punctuated by accounts of the theories of great educators who entertained ideas "in advance of their time"' (Simon 1966, p. 95). It was much more important, according to Simon, to consider the social origins of such ideas, which would in turn illuminate 'the elements in society ready for change at different times . . ., why changes of a particular kind were needed, what assisted or prevented their realisation, what compromises were made, break-throughs achieved, and with what effect' (Simon 1966, pp. 95–96). This was an approach to the history of education that resonated with contemporary political tensions over the direction of educational policies, for example on comprehensive schools designed for all abilities and aptitudes, and especially with controversies over social class and education.

Simon's inaugural lecture as the professor of education at Leicester University, also in 1966, reiterated these ideas but also attempted to explain his perspective on education in general and emphasised the interdependence of the disciplines. He aspired towards a 'fruitful cooperation' between the disciplines in education, 'in which no one lays down all the laws but everyone rubs off corners' (Simon 1966/1980, p. 91). Indeed, he insisted, 'There cannot be a permanent leasing out of concessions in the field of education to other disciplines which then operate exactly as they would at home' (Simon 1966/1980, p. 91). Simon therefore argued in favour of a conscious cultivation of interrelations. As befitted a historian, he chose an arresting historical analogy to make this point, proposing that what might be hoped for was 'something like that settlement whereby an Anglo-Saxon country, invaded in turn by Danes and Normans, triumphantly emerged from the process as English'

(Simon 1966/1980, p. 91). This notion of 'interdisciplinary cross-fertilisation' (Simon 1966/1980, p. 92) is interesting as it marks Simon out as a leader and champion of his own discipline who also promoted interdisciplinary ideals.

Simon's own department at Leicester University was one of the leading education departments in the country at this time. Its head of department was J.W. 'Billy' Tibble, the editor of *The Study of Education* (Tibble 1966a), who also supported the disciplinary approach at Leicester. Tibble had graduated in English at the University of Leeds in 1922 before going on to teach and then being appointed as a lecturer in education at the University College of the South West (later Exeter University) in 1929, where he stayed for thirteen years. In 1946 he was appointed to a professorship of education at what was then Leicester University College and built the department up over the next twenty years. In the 1960s, the disciplines of education were offered in the context of a general education course outside a subject-method course component, with Simon teaching the history of education, Geoffrey Bantock taking educational philosophy in the form of a historical study of educational theorists, Tibble himself teaching sociology and Mary Swainson and Mildred Collins taking psychology (Jones 2001). Simon himself had joined the Leicester department as a lecturer in 1950, and when Tibble retired in 1966, he, Bantock and the science educator J.F. Kerr were all given professorships. While generally sympathetic to the 'four disciplines' approach, which he later argued had 'promoted a higher level of educational studies generally than had existed before' and gave many of its students 'a wider, more informed, view of the nature of education as a social process', Simon was nevertheless critical of some of its more adverse effects. For example, as he recalled, students were asked to follow courses on any two of the disciplines according to their choice, and a split developed between the 'method' tutor on the one hand and the 'basic course' tutor on the other that betokened a tension between theory and practice (Simon n.d.).

In his role as head of the Leicester department in the 1970s, Simon continued to support a fundamentally disciplinary approach. In a formal note to the university's vice chancellor in February 1974 to recommend future developments in the School of Education, he requested that strength should be built up in the relevant specialisms in order to support the further development of work for higher degrees and diplomas. The original four disciplines approach now required modification, and cooperation with the education service and schools now required greater expertise in research design and statistics. In terms of the disciplines, he argued that the School was best known for its work in his own area, the history of education, which had also developed links with other areas of the university such as urban history and the history of science, although he pleaded that it needed more cover in pre-nineteenth century history of education. He explained that his own wife, Joan, who was well known as an author of academic studies in Tudor history of education (Simon 1965) was only 'called in unofficially' (Simon 1974). Simon noted that staffing in the philosophy of education appeared adequate, while the sociology of education was tending to publish in sociology journals rather than supporting interdisciplinary work in educational studies. There was meanwhile, he proposed, a 'crying need for a good educational psychologist with experience in teaching in ways relevant to the intending teacher, who could also participate in research' (Simon 1974).

Arising from this emphasis on disciplinary specialisation in university departments of education, a number of new societies were formed to promote research in specific areas and to organise conferences and journals in which their members and associates could take part. The Philosophy of Education Society of Great Britain (PESGB) for example was established in 1964 under the chairmanship of Louis Arnaud Reid, with an annual conference starting from 1965 and a journal, the *Journal of Philosophy of Education*, launched in 1967. The History of Education Society was created in 1967, also with an annual conference, and a journal followed five years later in 1972 under the title of *History of Education* (*HoE*). Although such a society was not established to represent the sociology of education, there were new developments designed to promote this specialist area too. Sociologists of education generally attended the British Sociological Association's (BSA) annual conference, and it was here that in 1970 in Durham. a self-styled 'new sociology of education' was promulgated with the resulting publication of a seminal text edited by Michael Young of the IOE, *Knowledge and Control: New Directions for the Sociology of Education* (see Young 1971; Szreter 1980; Banks 1982).

Other societies, formed at around the same time, also recognised the opportunities for coordinating research on specific areas within education. The Society for Research into Higher Education (SRHE) began in 1964 with a conference held in London at the end of the year. Although it drew from no single discipline, it expanded rapidly so that by 1971 it had well over 500 members of whom 358 were members of academic staff, 10 were students, and 179 were corporate members, and it also established a channel of communications through the publication of books and journals. It was awarded a grant of £2,500 from the DES, but most of its income came from its members until its support for publications developed. Regional bodies were also established in London and the south-east, the Midlands, the north-west, Scotland and Wales (Greenaway 1973).

The British Educational Research Association

At the same time, contrary pressures were building towards a more inclusive, interdisciplinary organisation to promote educational research in general. Impetus towards a new association that would be broader in its membership than the SCSE gathered momentum during the 1960s, stimulated by interest in cultivating new and radical configurations of knowledge that would challenge the traditional disciplines.

By the end of the 1960s, a number of new initiatives based in different university departments of education began to reflect growing interest in finding a means of promoting interdisciplinary research in education. In Manchester, for example, the faculty of education established in 1969 a new journal entitled *Research in Education*. The first issue of this journal remarked in its editorial notes that '[f]ields of research are becoming narrower and more specialised, and within the whole area of educational research, sociologists, psychologists, researchers in higher education and so on are having greater difficulty in understanding each other's discoveries' (*Research in Education* 1969). The aim of this journal was therefore 'to improve communication by producing an inter-disciplinary research journal designed to be as widely intelligible as possible without gross over-simplification' (*Research in Education* 1969). In 1970, the University of East Anglia established a Centre for Applied Research in Education (CARE) under the leadership of Lawrence Stenhouse, Jean Rudduck, Barry MacDonald and Rob Walker (Norris 2012, pp. 31–34).

According to one of our interviewees (pseudonym Hugh, a philosopher of education), Stenhouse's basic vision was that 'educational studies should be focused on the problems of education as they were experienced in schools and by teachers'. Thus, Hugh continues, '[H]e had a view of educational studies being disciplined by the problems of practice . . . and actually being concerned with the design of strategies for tackling and resolving some of their persistent questions'. On the other hand, Hugh adds, '[I]t wasn't that he was against the disciplines at all, but he had more of a renaissance view [that] the role of the disciplines was to provide resources for thinking about those problems' (Hugh, interview). Stenhouse's view of the Schools Council's Humanities Curriculum Project, which he directed, is a useful illustration of this approach. Although he was sceptical of the idea of academic disciplines 'informing and giving grace to living', he endorsed their relevance in relation to a curriculum broadly conceived in terms of its humanities: 'To cross subject boundaries successfully one must grasp – or at least see the need for – standards of quality in each of the subject fields involved' (Stenhouse 1968, p. 217; see also Elliott and Norris 2012).

Such aspirations and initiatives provided a climate of opinion that helped to encourage the formation of the British Educational Research Association (BERA) in 1974. Edgar Stones, at the University of Liverpool, found that classroom studies brought work in different fields to a common focus, leading to agreement that there was a need for an 'interdisciplinary forum' in the form of BERA (Stones 1985a, p. 17; see also Stones 1985b). A meeting to discuss classroom studies had been held at Lancaster University in 1970, initiated by John Garner. According to Stones, 'From the start the group was interdisciplinary which, together with the focus on a relatively unexplored field, engaged and enthused participants.' Sara Delamont from Cardiff took over as the organiser of the seminars when Garner left to go to Australia, and the numbers involved increased to about 80, with funding also being received from the SSRC. Stones recalled:

> The interesting thing about these gatherings was that people with similar interests from different disciplinary backgrounds were coming together for the first time. Indeed, many well known to each other by publications had never actually met. It was this coming together of people from varied disciplinary backgrounds in informal stimulating discussion that provided the context and the impetus for the birth of BERA.
>
> *(Stones 1985a, p. 18)*

Brian Start of NFER noted in private correspondence with other key figures in the formation of the new association – Brian Dockrell of SCRE, John Nisbet at Aberdeen, Noel Entwistle at Lancaster and Gordon Miller at the Institute of Education London – that '[t]he lack of a central association and forum in which the interdisciplinary study of education can be promulgated has exercised the minds of most of us in the last few years' (Start 1973). At present, Start reflected, individuals with interests in education tended to have diverse professional links with the education sections of organisations such as the BPS and BSA. According to Start, 'The idea of a British Educational Research Association to which can be brought all those with interests in education as an area and with skills involved in other disciplines has obvious attractions' (Start 1973). Entwistle acknowledged the need for further discussions to 'help to emphasise the multidisciplinary nature of Educational Research' (Entwistle 1973).

A meeting was held in Birmingham in October 1973 to discuss the formation of an association, attended by about 24 individuals from around Britain. Dr R.C. Whitfield of Aston University, who took part in the meeting, reported general enthusiasm for the idea of a national association (Whitfield 1973). Nevertheless, there were several issues to be resolved. One was the question of whether the system of membership should be open, in which anyone with an interest in educational research could join, or restricted, as the SCSE had favoured. For example, Neville Postlethwaite of the International Institute for Educational Planning (IIEP) recommended to Stones that membership should be based on 'quality' and thus selective in nature:

> In general, I believe that the more people can interact with each other, the better it is, but there is the problem of hangers-on and if you do get the hangers-on in education, all you get is a very large convention once a year where people meet their friends. This, I presume, they could do at the British Psychological Association [sic] anyway. Therefore, I would again plead for some quality-type membership.
>
> *(Postlethwaite 1973b)*

A second question was defining 'interdisciplinary commitment', in order that 'whatever disciplines relevant to educational research in the widest sense shall be included' (Whitfield 1973). A third was privileging 'research' over 'development'. It was agreed that overall there should be an academic orientation, although it was noted that 'in due course there may be a political spin-off in terms of promoting educational research'. An initial discussion took place on establishing a related publication, but it was agreed to confine this initially to a regular newsletter, leading in due course to 'the sponsoring of a journal of a rigorous kind, either new or growing out of an existing one' (Whitfield 1973).

The potential implications of these new developments for established organisations and interests were not lost on those involved. Professor Alec Ross, who had recently established the only specialist university-based Department of Educational

Research in the UK at the newly founded Lancaster University, pointed out to Stones that a new national association might damage SCSE and also SRHE. He was hopeful that he and others, including Alan Blyth at Liverpool, might be able to develop the membership base of SCSE, with the aim of 'reviving, broadening and developing to make it something more significant than the prof's club!' (Ross 1974a). Ross was also at that time the chair of SCRE, which he observed had good membership figures, a regional organisation and a healthy publishing programme, with an office and staff maintained in London. He proposed that a central office might be established to support several educational bodies or else find some way to bring these bodies into a relationship with one another rather than compete. His own preference was for a national society such as the National Society for the Study of Education (NSSE) in the US, with sections in psychology, sociology, history, philosophy, curriculum, economics, educational studies, research 1 (empirical), research 2, teaching, higher education, preschool education, fundamental education, further education, adult education and others, but, as he acknowledged, 'what kind of jamboree would that be!' (Ross 1974a).

Stones responded sympathetically to the points raised by Ross but was clearly already committed to the new organisation. The problems facing both SCSE and SRHE, he commented, were 'something that BERA will have to grapple with (and which it is in fact currently thinking about)'. He suggested that BERA might develop along the lines of American Educational Research Association (AERA), with special interest groups being formed, but added cautiously: 'Whether we should permit the indiscriminate spawning that you itemise for NSSE is another question' (Stones 1974). Both Ross and Stones understood that the field might fragment into different organisational groups and potentially also splinter into a larger number of interest groups as a consequence of these new developments at a national level. This possibility differed considerably from the broad ideals of interdisciplinary cooperation that had initiated the discussions around a new national organisation and also from the relatively small number of foundation disciplines that had provided a base for the field in the 1960s. Ross responded to Stones by agreeing that 'indiscriminate spawning' was not desirable but added that 'I listed them to indicate what could happen'. He remained of the view that the 'identifiable groups' were psychology, sociology, philosophy, history and curriculum, together with SRHE and 'possibly special education', while warning at the same time that the relationship of the new organisation with SCSE, the longest established society in UK educational studies, was 'the most difficult' (Ross 1974b).

Another issue was the relationship between the new national organisation and the State. The DES had begun to fund educational research both directly and indirectly during the 1960s, and in 1973 the leaders of the new initiative approached it for financial support. This proved unsuccessful, with the DES declining to provide a grant for a meeting (Forrester 1973), and, as Stones noted, 'We got a dusty answer from the DES when we asked for a "pump-priming" grant' (Stones 1974). This failure to establish practical support from the State meant that the new national infrastructure would need to develop independently, based mainly on the resources of institutions of higher education and their members. If BERA was to be organised as an open membership society, its members would need to pay what might become a substantial individual fee to maintain the organisation and also to attend regular conferences.

The prospect of a new European association was also mooted at this time, in the context of regular conferences now being held on a cross-national and European basis and the likelihood of Britain joining the European Economic Community (EEC), confirmed by national referendum in 1975. Postlethwaite took the lead in proposing the establishment of a European Educational Research Association (EERA), which he suggested might be modelled on AERA (Postlethwaite 1973a, but in the event EERA did not come into being for another two decades, in 1994.

Meanwhile, in Scotland, the Scottish Educational Research Association (SERA) was also established in 1974, led by Bryan Dockrell at SCRE, with an open membership that grew to 156 the following year and to 289 the year after that (SERA 1994). Discussions had originally been initiated by the Scottish Universities Council for Studies in Education (SUCSE) in 1965, with the journal *Scottish Educational Studies* being established from 1967 (Nisbet 2003). In May 1973, a meeting convened by Bryan Dockrell, the director of SCRE, had discussed the forming of a new Scottish association (Nisbet 1984). SERA was formed at a meeting held at Moray House College of Education in September, led by Stanley Nisbet, as chair of its planning committee, followed by its first annual general meeting held at Stirling University on 31 January 1975 (SERA 1975). A formal relationship between SERA and *Scottish Educational Studies* was agreed on the following year (Wilkinson and Morrison 1976).

BERA's inaugural meeting took place at the University of Birmingham on 4–5 April 1974, chaired by Edgar Stones. It agreed to establish informal relationships with kindred organisations 'to avoid conflict and reduce duplication of activities'. It was hoped that this would both strengthen the achievements of BERA itself and promote the representation of other bodies (BERA 1974, minute 4). It was agreed also to avoid a duplication of dates with those of other conferences. The first annual conference of BERA would be held in September 1975, with the aim also of maintaining a principle of interdisciplinary approaches to educational research (BERA 1974, minute 5). The first president of BERA was John Nisbet (the brother of Stanley Nisbet) from the University of Aberdeen, then the chair of the Educational Research Board of the SSRC. Nisbet chose to present his inaugural address to the Association at this first meeting on the state of the art of educational research. He emphasised the growth of the field over the previous thirty years, which he suggested had carried with it the danger that the study of education might 'split up into less and less meaningful sub-divisions' (Nisbet, J. 1974, p. 2). His own department at Aberdeen, although still relatively small, held special meetings to ensure that there was some link between the various aspects of educational research, and every member of staff was required to carry out some tutorial work across all the boundaries. Nisbet's research, conducted with Noel Entwistle at Edinburgh, included theoretical issues, a historical section, a chapter on comparative studies, an empirical study and a small piece of action research. Overall, Nisbet took the opportunity that his presidential address at BERA afforded him to 'argue strongly against the fissiparous trend in current educational research' (Nisbet 1974, p. 2).

Other early presidents of the fledgling Association, from different specialisms and disciplinary backgrounds, concurred with Nisbet's generalist outlook on educational research. Jack Wrigley from the University of Reading, then the chair of the Educational Research Board of the SSRC, noted in his presidential address in 1975 the 'intended interdisciplinary nature' of BERA despite his own empirical and statistical preferences (Wrigley 1975, p. 1). Wrigley chose this occasion to suggest that educational research was akin to engineering as 'a problem solving subject drawing on the disciplines of anthropology, philosophy, psychology and sociology for its insights and techniques' (Wrigley 1975, p. 7). Moreover, he added, 'BERA ought to be an excellent organisation to promote the kind of interdisciplinary study necessary for good research. The bringing together of workers from the various disciplines should help to expose the pitfalls due to blinkered thinking' (Wrigley 1975, p. 7).

Two years later, the historian Brian Simon argued in his presidential address that BERA represented 'a coming together from various disciplines' (Simon 1978, p. 2), which would in his view encourage 'submerging the undesirable aspects of contributory disciplines while extracting the most from them from the educational point of view' (Simon 1978, p. 4). Simon, indeed, was emphatic in his belief that '[t]he study of education has manifestly suffered from subordination to disparate modes of approach and methodologies deriving from fields quite other than education which have simply been transferred to the educational sphere, and which, once there, have tended to maintain their own distinctive languages and approaches, to pursue their own ends' (Simon 1978, p. 4). He also warned against a growing tendency to 'let a hundred flowers bloom', which might encourage a tendency to 'pull in different directions' rather than focusing on the conceptual and practical problems of education as a whole (Simon 1978, p. 4).

Other leading educational researchers, such as Alan Blyth from the University of Liverpool, regarded the advent of BERA as an opportunity to consolidate education as the subject of an independent and integrated study, constituting, as Blyth argued, 'an academic unity which could draw upon – and contribute to – other disciplines without being subordinated to any of them' (Blyth 1982, p. 13). Blyth himself was insistent that, as he expressed the matter, 'the nature of educational research is such that it requires collaborative effort, not a partitioning of the educational field among experts, as though it were the academic equivalent of eighteenth-century Poland' (Blyth 1977, p. 109). On this view, educational research, based on an integrated study of education, should be regarded as a collaborative activity. Blyth saw BERA itself as having a broad membership representative of different kinds of research activity that would enable it to sustain the 'essentially integrative quality' of educational research (Blyth 1977, p. 122).

Conclusions

Thus, by 1974, debates within and around educational research had shifted from a focus on the distinctive and complementary role of the disciplines to an emphasis on interdisciplinary study, with the founding of BERA the apparent harbinger of a more integrated approach. Disciplinary and specialist societies, conferences and journals continued to exist alongside the new body, as did the SCSE and NFER, but it seemed possible that these might become less popular as BERA established itself and brought them together as an umbrella organisation.

These were formative years for educational research in Britain, during which it grew in resources and staffing and established the institutions that would provide the framework and organisation for research in education in subsequent decades. These developments took place at a time when the economy at a national level was expanding over the medium term after the Second World War and education was regarded as central to the development of a more equal and prosperous society. Educational research was widely supported as a means to improve education on a scientific and rational basis. These were promising indications for further development.

Yet 1974 also saw signs of change that would challenge the position of educational research in fundamental ways. The economic situation deteriorated, and political consensus around educational changes became increasingly fractured as successive governments sought to intervene more actively. William Taylor had already intimated, in 1972, that 'the future prospects of educational research are dependent upon adequate resources, both of money and of manpower, upon the existence of appropriate structures for initiation, execution, and dissemination, and a climate of opinion in which both the promises and the limitations of educational research evoke a positive and understanding response' (Taylor 1972, p. 8). In 1974, these relatively benign conditions were coming to an end, and more hostile ones were about to take their place.

5

A JOURNAL FOR THE FIELD?

The *British Journal of Educational Studies*

With James Thomas

The post-war years witnessed new growth in journals in educational studies and research, and this became especially strong in the 1960s. Journals provided a further means of scholarly communication and were potentially a key part of raising the academic status of educational studies as a field. The national flagship journal for educational studies was the *British Journal of Educational Studies* (*BJES*), which has continued over a sustained period of rapid educational, social and political change. This chapter reviews the role of the *BJES* in supporting disciplinary, multidisciplinary and interdisciplinary approaches in different ways over this time, as well as the relationship between this journal and other journals in the field. It draws on citation network and text-mining analyses of the outputs of the *BJES* and other key journals, the details of which are described in an addendum to this chapter.

An apparatus of scholarship

The *BJES* was established in 1952 under the auspices of the SCSE, with the aim of representing the field as a whole in Britain, as opposed to taking a partial approach based on a particular discipline or aspect. The sole exception to this intended breadth was to be educational psychology, on the grounds that it already had a well established journal. According to an editorial note in the first issue of the new journal, it would give prominence to articles embodying research, but at the same time would not be 'narrowly specialist'. Indeed, it continued, it was 'intended to serve the needs and interests of everyone concerned with education whom the implications of specialized research affect' (*BJES* 1952, p. 67). The founders of the journal took the opportunity to vow that it would never lose sight of its broad objects, which were 'to explain the significance of new thought, to provide philosophical discussion at a high level, and to deepen existing interest in the purposes and problems of current educational policy' (*BJES* 1952, p. 67).

This new initiative had been widely canvassed over the preceding decade. As early as 1943, before the end of the Second World War, Fred Clarke had argued strongly in favour of a new publication. As he noted, 'There is nothing that is really comparable to the specialist journals that serve students of the physical and natural sciences' (Clarke 1943, p. 22). Educational news was well catered for through publications such as the weekly *Times Educational Supplement*, the regular periodical *Education*, produced monthly by the Association of Education Committees, another periodical, the *Journal of Education* (published since 1879), and also the daily newspaper, the *Manchester Guardian*, for which the radical educational reformer R.H. Tawney regularly provided well informed campaigning editorial columns (McCulloch 1996). On the other hand, Clarke observed, '[T]here is great need for a periodical Review to take more weighty discussion and lengthier articles which need not all be the work of professional educationists' (Clarke 1943, p. 22).

Richard Oliver, Sarah Fielden Professor of Education at the University of Manchester since 1938 and a leading educational psychologist, also argued that the new conditions after the war would require a rapid improvement in what he described as the 'apparatus of scholarship' in education. This would include developing courses of study and research with high quality and also academic journals that would gain national and international currency. Oliver explained that he was not thinking of the many periodicals that already existed for the benefit of teachers and other educationists but envisaged a new journal along the lines of 'the more learned journals which report the results of research and discussion at the highest level of scholarship'. Oliver conceded that education already had a journal in the area of educational psychology, his own subdiscipline, but insisted nonetheless that there was a need for one or two more journals with international standing in the area of education. These, he affirmed, would have a similar role in other branches of the study of education to that of the *BJEP* and should also provide bibliographies, annual reviews of various fields and other aids to scholarship. This was, he concluded, 'a field in which university departments of education could play a leading part' (Oliver 1951–52, pp. 52–53).

The established journal in the field, the *BJEP*, had already 'come of age' with 21 years of publication under this title by the time the *BJES* made its first appearance. C. W. Valentine, who was still the journal's editor as he had been at its inception, could now reflect on a much enlarged size of journal with the improved supply of paper after the war and over 2,000 subscribers from the BPS and ATCDE (Valentine 1951). Since 1948, the journal had been published by Methuen, a well regarded publishing company. There was also fresh activity on the part of the new Institutes of Education that had been created in some universities following the McNair Report of 1944. At the University of Birmingham for example, the *Educational Review* was established in 1948. No less a figure than the vice chancellor of the university, R.E. Priestley, wrote a foreword for the first issue of the new journal to highlight its potential role in supporting partnerships between university departments of education, training colleges and LEAs (Priestley 1948). Another university, Durham, established a *Research Review* to be published by its Institute of Education from 1950.

There was indeed a growing audience for such journals, as well as an increasing number of individuals who were capable of contributing to them. On the other hand, Richard Oliver at Manchester felt obliged to warn of likely problems in a frank two-part article carried by the prestigious *Universities Quarterly* (Oliver 1950–51, 1951–52). He detected a number of weaknesses and dangers in the new arrangements for training teachers and studying education. According to Oliver, there were disparate standards not only between universities and training colleges but also between institutes of education. The training colleges had lower entry qualifications and, he argued, intellectual standards of students that were now 'less exacting than they had been before the war', with the result that 'the training college is tending to live down to its name' (Oliver 1950–51, p. 365). He was also anxious lest the institutes of education became tempted to finance too many publications. He acknowledged that they were encouraging interest in research but counselled against overinflation: 'Too often, however, research in education means sending out an elaborate questionnaire to a good many people and summarizing their answers. Hundreds of opinions are made to look like a scientific fact, and a pooling of ignorance is accepted as a substitute for knowledge' (Oliver 1951–52, p. 50). He insisted that there were only a limited number of people who were capable of independent and original work in education. Most teachers had received two years of higher education since leaving secondary school, with only part of it devoted to an elementary study of education, while graduate teachers had one year's study of education. Oliver concluded scathingly: 'In no other academic field would students be thought capable of research with so little foundation' (Oliver 1951–52, p. 51).

Topic modelling and citation network analysis

The emergence of the *BJES* in 1952, with the imprimatur of that elite body of professors, the SCSE, was designed to elevate the academic status of educational studies while also offering a means of scholarly communication across a broad range of topics and approaches. The extent to which it provided such depth and breadth together tended to vary in practice and was affected over the medium term by changes in the size and nature of the field and also a rapidly changing wider social and political context.

The availability of journal repositories, such as JSTOR and Web of Knowledge, has changed the way in which it is possible to examine academic outputs. While there is no substitute for reading articles, machine-assisted tools now enable researchers to analyse more content than would be possible using manual methods and to make connections between papers and across time and publications that would be impractical to undertake without machine assistance. This chapter has made use of two novel analytical tools in order to analyse the outputs of the *BJES* and other educational journals. The first technique has analysed the content of all of the research articles from *BJES* over its history, and the second has examined the journal's disciplinary 'reach' in terms of where its outputs are cited. Each technique is described here, and a technical appendix is provided at the end of the chapter.

In order to analyse every article published by *BJES* in its history, a technique called 'topic modelling' was used. Topic modelling analyses every word in every article and clusters together those groups of papers that use similar combinations of words. The technique employed here has many applications beyond the analysis of topics from journal articles but is particularly appropriate for this type of analysis as it aims to identify the topics that underlie the documents being analysed (rather than only examining how frequently words appear, as simpler methods do) (Blei et al. 2003). As the technical appendix outlines, after downloading data on all articles from JSTOR, the topic modelling analysis was conducted, and fifty topics were identified, which are summarized in Appendix 2. Each topic contains many articles, with some being more strongly associated with a given topic than others. It is extremely difficult to give topics comprehensible labels (an area of current research in computer science), so current practice is to 'label' each topic with a list of the most important terms used by the documents in a given topic, leaving the reader to interpret the topic's meaning for themselves. For example, the most important words used by the articles in Topic 17 are:

> curriculum national policy paper development des england emphasis debate subject key science hmi role wales

('des' is the Department for Education and Skills, and 'hmi' is Her Majesty's Inspectors). The table in Appendix 2 also contains a small graphic that shows when the important papers in that topic were published. In the case of Topic 17, it is clear that almost no papers were published until after the 1988 Reform Act, when issues concerning the National Curriculum in England became a hotly debated issue. This paper discusses the content of topics that show a strong temporal character (that is, they show when particular issues became important or when authors lost interest in publishing papers about them) and where the papers in the topic reveal information about disciplinarity or interdisciplinarity. (A comprehensive examination of all topics is beyond the scope of this chapter.)

The second analytical tool used is citation network analysis (White 2014). Using Web of Science, all papers in the following journals were identified, and then all the papers – from any journal – that cite papers in the specified journals were identified.

- *British Journal of Educational Studies (BJES)*
- *British Educational Research Journal (BERJ)*
- *Oxford Review of Education (ORE)*
- *Journal of Education Policy (JEP)*
- *British Journal of Educational Psychology (BJEP)*
- *British Journal of Sociology of Education (BJSE)*
- *History of Education (HoE)*
- *Journal of Philosophy of Education (JPE)*

As described in the technical addendum, networks of citations were then created, linking journals and showing which journals were most closely associated with one another. These networks of links between journals can then be analysed, and those journals that show similar patterns of citations can be identified and grouped into clusters. An important aspect of network analysis is visualization, and this chapter uses several visualizations of journal networks in order to examine their relationships. Each journal is represented as a circle on the visualization, and the size of the circle represents how frequently that journal appears in the analysis. (For example, in Figure 5.4, the *Journal of Education Policy* has quite a large circle, indicating that its papers cite the outputs of many of the other journals in the analysis.) The positioning of the circles on the visualisations is also important: those journals that are most related to one another, in that the papers they contain frequently cite one another, are positioned closely together; and those with few – or no – connections are positioned further away. An iterative mathematical algorithm simultaneously 'attracts' and 'repels' the positioning of journals in relation to one another, until a satisfactory graphical representation of their relationships is reached. Finally, lines connect those journals with the strongest connections to one another, and the clusters of closely related journals are indicated using different shadings (or colours).

The outputs of the *BJES*

In the first two decades of its publication, the *BJES* remained unchallenged as the national generic journal of educational studies. At the same time, its editor throughout this period was Professor Arthur Beales, a leading historian of education at King's College London. With no specialist journals in the history of education until the 1970s, the *BJES* tended to become the journal of choice for historians of education, thus providing the history of education with a broad educational audience but limiting the journal's success in representing the field of education as a whole. It had a disciplinary emphasis, especially associated with history and tended to be multidisciplinary rather than interdisciplinary in its approach. This section reviews the outputs of the *BJES* from its initial focus on history, through changes in its focus over time, which were often caused by external factors. Particular focus is given to the journal's outputs in terms of their disciplinarity, multidisciplinarity and interdisciplinarity, as well as the extent to which it is able to claim to be the 'journal for the field'.

An emphasis on historical papers until the 1970s is apparent when the focus of its outputs is examined over time, with a range of topics discussed. A number of papers investigate school history (Topics 19 and 46), with an interest in this subject strong during the 1960s and 1970s. The issues covered ranged widely, sometimes being focused fairly specifically, such as 'A Charity School in the Nineteenth Century: Old Swinford Hospital School, 1815–1914' (Hopkins 1969), or the history of significant approaches to education, including 'The Grammar School and the Education of the Poor, 1786–1840' (Sanderson 1962). The historian-friendly journal showed a particular fondness for the more specialist issue of historical sources and records. A short series of general introductory papers covering 'Educational Records' in the early 1950s was followed by pieces covering sources in the history of technical education; grammar schools; French, Spanish and German educational history and other general historical sources (Armytage 1956, 1957a; 1957b; Barnard 1954, 1958; Beales 1954, 1955; Bowyer-Bower 1955; Gordon 1966; Henderson

1960; Kerr 1959; Mallinson 1955; Peters 1964, 1965; Pritchard 1963; Pugh 1952; Reid–Smith 1965; Tate 1953a, b, 1954; Tempest 1960; Tropp 1958).

Some interdisciplinary dialogue was attempted in 1969 by C.M. Turner in a paper entitled 'Sociological Approaches to the History of Education' (Turner 1969). Turner argued that it was difficult to use theoretical frameworks when studying the history of education and that the 'models and concepts' of sociology and social psychology might be a solution. This suggestion did not lead to a longer debate on the applicability of sociological constructs in the journal, however; no other papers in the *BJES* refer to this paper (it has been cited seven times in total, according to Google Scholar), and the automated topic modelling places the paper firmly amongst papers from a sociological rather than historical perspective. Another foray into interdisciplinarity can be found in the paper 'Towards a Socio-Psychological View of School Achievement' by D.S. Finlayson in 1973 (Finlayson 1973). Here, Finlayson argued that, while the impact of social class on educational outcomes was becoming widely understood, it was necessary to recognise the limitations of an exclusively sociological perspective. It was proposed that these limitations might be overcome through the use of psychological perspectives and approaches. Again, though, this is an isolated paper, which does not appear to have prompted a wider debate within the *BJES* (or beyond).

The disciplines naturally converge in some areas of educational research, and one such area identified by the topic modelling is assessment, concerns about which run throughout the journal's history. Early papers include 'The Examination at Eleven Plus' (Burt 1959) and 'The Marking of G.C.E. Scripts' (Black 1962), with later papers expressing concerns from a sociological perspective: 'GCSE: Does It Support Equality?' (Radnor 1988) and 'Using Assessment to Drive the Reform of Schooling: Time to Stop Pursuing the Chimera?' (Torrance 2011). Philosophy also contributes to this examination of assessment with 'Michael Young's the Rise of the Meritocracy: A Philosophical Critique' (Allen 2011). While assessment can be seen as an area where the different disciplines contribute, there is little overt cross-disciplinary dialogue, and the interaction among disciplines in the journal's outputs in this area is far more 'multi-' than 'inter'-disciplinary.

The discipline of psychology is not entirely absent from the *BJES*'s output, but psychological issues certainly do not form the bulk of the journal's output. Ironically, the topic in which the term 'psychology' appears strongest is the topic containing papers that discuss the field of educational studies from an analytical perspective (that is, what the field might, could, or should be) (Hofstetter 2012; McCulloch 2002; Pirrie and Gillies 2012; Thomas 2012). Only one other topic contains papers that clearly discuss psychological issues, and this is a somewhat 'confused' or disparate topic, containing papers from numerous perspectives.

In the 1960s, as university departments of education and the new colleges of education expanded, new courses developed and access to funding increased, a large number of new journals in education were introduced. These were usually not generic but specialist in nature, brought into being by societies and associations that were responsible for one particular sub-discipline, educational sector or topic. They thus provided an alternative outlet for specialist articles based on a specific discipline. For example, the *Journal of Philosophy of Education* (*JPE*) was established in 1965, while the *Journal of Educational Administration and History* was founded at the University of Leeds in 1968 and *History of Education* (*HOE*) by the fledgling History of Education Society in 1972.

The impact of the advent of specialist historical journals is pronounced in the story of the *BJES*'s output, with papers with a historical focus abruptly drying up after the initial burst of enthusiasm in the 1950s and 1960s. One of the topics focused on historical sources (including Arundale 1968; Bowyer-Bower 1954, 1955; Tropp 1958) is depicted in Figure 5.1, showing how papers that focused on these topics declined rapidly after the 1960s.

In the following decade, the *BJES*'s position as the premier generic education journal in Britain was effectively challenged, first by the introduction of the *British Educational Research Journal* (*BERJ*) under the auspices of SCSE's new neighbour, BERA, in 1975, and then by the founding of the *Oxford Review of Education* (*ORE*) by the University of Oxford Education Department in 1976. Specialist journals continued to proliferate so that, by the end of the 1970s, educational studies and research comprised a crowded field so far as journals were concerned. The *British Journal of Sociology of Education* (*BJSE*) for example was introduced in 1980. The citation network analysis detailed in the next section shows the relationship between the *BJES* and these newer journals.

On the thirtieth anniversary of the *BJES*, in 1982, the journal published a special issue reviewing the progress of the field over the period since 1952. It did so squarely in terms of the separate disciplines and their contributions to educational studies. Olive Banks examined the development of the sociology of education (Banks 1982), Brian Simon that of the history of education (Simon 1982), R.F. Dearden the career of the philosophy of education (Dearden 1982) and Ann Clarke, in a rare concession by the journal, the role of psychology in relation to education (Clarke 1982). It also included articles on educational administration (Bone 1982), the economics of education, in what its author claimed to be only the second paper in the journal ever published on this topic (Williams 1982), and comparative education (McDade 1982). While it focused on this familiar disciplinary framework, however, it did exhibit a relatively novel awareness of the differences among the constituent parts of Britain. This was not quite the case for Wales, which was as usual yoked together with England in an overview by Peter Gosden of the educational system since 1952 (Gosden 1982). James Scotland discussed the recent development of

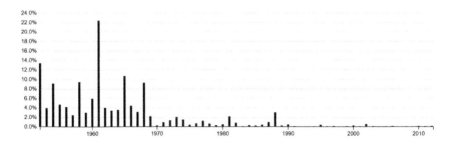

FIGURE 5.1 Topic 34: *BJES* papers detailing historical sources

Scottish education (Scotland 1982), while the editor, Margaret Sutherland, explored
the progress and problems of education in Northern Ireland (Sutherland 1982).

At the same time, this special issue reflected anxieties about the disciplinary nature
of the journal in an educational and political context that was showing ominous signs
of change. Sutherland's editorial emphasised the different areas of study, arguing force-
fully in favour of the various disciplines, and defended specialisation, although it also
expressed unease that 'uncoordinated digging at the chalkface' might achieve little
and that too few specialists were able or willing to generalise (*BJES* 1982, p. 6). At the
same time, it commented that 'the major problem we confront today is that of inte-
grating the practices of all these fields of endeavour' (*BJES* 1982, p. 6). In fact, it asked:

> Is there indeed one discipline of Education or are there simply a number of
> disciplines of education? Specialisms have grown: for professional advance-
> ment in Education it seems necessary today to be a specialist. Yet what is the
> outcome of uncoordinated digging at the chalkface? Surely specialists must
> achieve and retain awareness of the work of colleagues in other disciplines?
> Surely there must be some over-riding principles which determine the value
> judgements and policy dimensions of the educative process?
>
> *(BJES 1982, p. 6)*

These were troubling issues, to which Sutherland added that advancing beyond the
'precision' of the disciplines towards an ability to generalize was attempted by only a few
and might be too demanding for most. Yet it acknowledged that 'it is a function of this
Journal to provide such encouragement and to facilitate this task by offering knowledge
of what is being thought and done in different aspects of education' (*BJES* 1982, p. 6).

This message was reinforced by a reflective essay by Alan Blyth of the University of Liverpool. Five years previously, Blyth, also one of the leaders of the nascent
BERA, had contributed a combative paper to *BJES* championing 'integrated study'
in educational research (Blyth 1977). In that paper, he had argued that 'the nature of
educational research is such that it requires collaborative effort, not a partitioning of
the educational field among experts, as though it were the educational equivalent
of eighteenth-century Poland' (Blyth 1977, p. 109). The 'foundation disciplines' had
emerged and developed to acquire 'independent importance' in their own right, with
conceptual and methodological differences between them, so that, as he complained,
from being a two-faced study between the arts and social sciences, '[e]ducation has
become something of a Babel, in which an increasing number of disciplines claim a
share' (Blyth 1977, p. 114). Moreover, he observed, 'Adult education, physical education, special education, science education, and so forth became separate worlds with
their own professional identities and journals and conferences' (Blyth 1977, p. 114).
According to Blyth, this situation led to a profusion of committees and conferences,
with mutual misunderstandings that would be viewed with impatience by policy
makers and teachers (Blyth 1977, p. 116). He had concluded that:

> despite the welcome infusion of funds and interest in recent years, educa-
> tional research stands at present in a curiously vulnerable position, one in

which the producers and consumers of research misunderstand each other and in which, while the consumers are divided between administrators and teachers, the producers themselves are split up into camps with different characteristics.

(Blyth 1977, p. 116)

Blyth's contribution to the 1982 special issue offered by its own description a 'personal account' and retreated somewhat from his earlier warnings to present on the face of it a more optimistic vision of the future: 'The edifice of scholarship in education is much stronger now, and Education as itself an autonomous but inter-related field of study is much more widely accepted, not least by teachers as a whole who have come to participate more widely and purposefully in it' (Blyth 1982, p. 16). Nevertheless, he counselled, to respond to new demands and issues would require 'studies involving interaction with other disciplines as well as . . . response based on autonomy' (Blyth 1982, p. 17). According to Blyth, indeed, 'Through the general strengthening of the bases of scholarship, the study of aesthetic judgment or seventeenth-century French education alongside more obviously "relevant" issues does, in fact, facilitate sophisticated response and enable immediate problems to be considered with greater professional authority' (Blyth 1982, p. 17).

A further edited collection, published the following year, also expressed continuity rather than change in the cultivation of the disciplines (Hirst 1983a). Edited by Paul Hirst, the format of this volume was reminiscent of Tibble's earlier collections (e.g. Tibble 1966a). Hirst introduced the collection with an essay on educational theory that did signal some retreat from the confidence that he had shown on behalf of the disciplines in the 1960s. He now pointed out that although educational theory drew upon the disciplines in order to develop rational principles for educational practice, the disciplines did not in themselves embody principles for practice (Hirst 1983b, p. 6). The remaining contributions of the volume constituted reviews of how different disciplines had developed in their curricula and methods over the previous two decades. Each of these surveyed a struggle to adapt to changing and threatening conditions, but all were able at the same time to detect promising signs for their survival. For example, Richard Peters, examining the philosophy of education, noted the onset of what he called 'a period of consolidation – some would say a struggle for survival' (Peters 1983, p. 35). Nonetheless, Peters was also able to observe that the Philosophy of Education Society of Great Britain now had over 500 members, while the *JPE* sold over 1,000 copies per issue (Peters 1983).

The 1980s witnessed growing turbulence in higher education with growing economic difficulties and a challenge to its activities on the part of the State. This encouraged increasing attention being given to education policy, and a new journal, the *Journal of Education Policy* (*JEP*), was created to represent this in 1986. Educational theory and the disciplines of education were deemed by the Conservative Government to be either dangerously unsound for the training of the next generation of teachers or irrelevant to the practical needs of schools. This left a generic educational journal such as *BJES* dangerously exposed to the vagaries of national policy changes. Finally, by the turn of the century, internationalisation came to bear on the field, as networks that had once been local and national in nature became increasingly international and even global. Authors in different parts of the world began to offer their work to *BJES* for publication, and, as will be highlighted later in the chapter, broad international themes made their presence felt in the pages of the journal.

The sudden changes in the wider political environment are revealed starkly in the chronology of journal outputs. To begin with, the 1988 Education Reform Act established a National Curriculum for England and Wales, and debate about this is reflected in Topic 17, depicted graphically in Figure 5.2. Here, we can see that the bulk of papers about this issue appeared after the legislation had been passed, suggesting that academic debate has followed rather than led practice. Interestingly, the rise in interest in this issue in the UK led to a flurry of papers offering an international perspective (Bartlett 1992; Kennedy 1989; Morris and Chan 1997).

The same pattern is shown in a series of papers on the benefits – or, more frequently, the undesirability – of increasing marketization in education (Topic 5), for example 'Free Marketeers or Good Citizens? Educational Policy and Lay Participation in the Administration of Schools' (Deem 1994). Accompanying this are wider debates about power (Ball 1993) and control (Cutler and Waine 2000). The peak of paper writing about national curricula and marketization appears to have been reached by the turn of the century.

Detailing contemporary issues, where interest has not yet peaked, are several clusters of documents containing sociological critiques and debates about the nature and uses of knowledge. Figure 5.3 shows the rapid increase in the publications

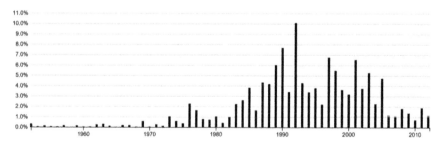

FIGURE 5.2 *BJES* publication of papers about national curricula

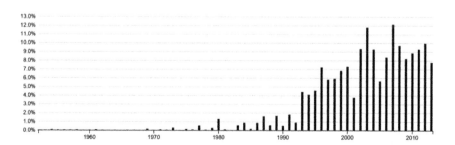

FIGURE 5.3 Sociological perspectives

clustered in Topic 47, concerning sociological perspectives on the wider benefits of education. Examples of these papers include 'Learning throughout Working Life: A Relational Interdependence between Personal and Social Agency' (Billett 2008), 'Emotional Capital and Education: Theoretical Insights from Bourdieu' (Zembylas 2007) and 'A Theory of Collective Competence: Challenging the Neo-Liberal Individualisation of Performance at Work' (Boreham 2004). Like the other topics mentioned, these papers can be seen as a reaction against increasing neoliberalism in education and the value of education being understood in narrow economic terms.

Another area of debate that has received increasing interest has been the nature and potential uses of educational knowledge. Two topics intersect in this area (43 and 15), discussing evidence-based policy and practice (Davies 1999; Hamilton 2002; Pirrie 2001) and methods and approaches for education research (Andrews 2005; Avis 2003; Connolly 2006; Gorard 1999, 2002, 2005; Hammersley 2001). Many of the papers debating evidence-based education make the point that this is an initiative that stems from similar moves in medicine, where evidence-based medicine has been a hugely influential force since the early 1990s. Elements of disciplinary thinking can be discerned in some of these critiques with, for example, sociological perspectives of the nature and possibilities of knowledge being deployed to critique the instrumental use of education research for decision making (Pirrie 2001).

Debates about what knowledge is and how legitimate (and illegitimate) knowledge claims are made are a perennial concern of educationists and philosophers alike, and papers dealing with epistemological issues are spread fairly evenly throughout the history of *BJES*. Topics 10 (epistemology) and 13 (philosophy and ethics) show this even temporal distribution, with Topic 10 including papers such as 'Epistemology and Justifying the Curriculum of Educational Studies' (Walker and Evers 1982), 'Education without Theory' (Carr 2006) and 'Educational Theory, Practical Philosophy and Action Research' (Elliott 1987). This topic (10) contains a number of papers marking skirmishes in the qualitative/quantitative paradigm wars that loomed large towards the end of the twentieth century. Few of these papers appear to promote what might be considered radical positions at either ends of the spectrum, though there is a clear thread of argument in favour of 'Reclaiming Metaphysical Truth for Educational Research' (Willmott 2002) and 'Overcoming Veriphobia – Learning to Love Truth Again' (Bailey 2001). Philosophy is also an important perspective in Topic 13, which is dominated by papers on ethics and values. Here, papers range from Dearden's 'Education and the Ethics of Belief' (Dearden 1974), published in 1974, and Dixon's 'On Teaching Moral Procedures' (Dixon 1968), through to later papers concerning 'Is Education a Good Thing' (Wilson 2002) and 'Education and Values' (Carr 1991). This topic is tightly focused and represents several streams of debate in which authors reply to one another (for example, Peters 1967; Wilson 1967; Dixon 1968; Hare 1968).

In summary, the output of *BJES* can be broadly characterized as having a historical focus for the first twenty years of its life, and it has now moved, along with the other journals in its domain, away from disciplinary-led publications towards policy analysis and critique.

The position of the *BJES* in the organization of scholarly journals

We now move to the picture provided by the citation network analysis of journal outputs. The citation network enables us to examine the 'destination' of the knowledge published in any given paper. We might expect to see the outputs of journals with strong particular disciplinary affiliations to be heavily used by papers in other journals in the same discipline and for papers published in inter- and multidisciplinary journals to be cited across the disciplinary landscape. This is the pattern we might expect to see from *BJES*, given its avowedly cross-disciplinary target audience.

Figure 5.4 shows the big picture: the entire network of citations across all the journals included in the analysis. It is a striking image, showing the organization of the field at a high level. At this level, we see the field organized into three main overarching areas. At the top of the graphic is a cluster of journals that focus on educational policy, sociology and social research. On the left of the diagram we see a cluster of journals with a more applied focus and at the bottom a large cluster of journals on educational psychology. (One additional cluster is on the right, containing international journals.)

The psychology cluster, as might be expected, contains the *British Journal of Educational Psychology*, the *Journal of Educational Psychology*, *Learning and Individual Differences* and *Contemporary Educational Psychology*. The sociology cluster contains the *British Journal of Sociology of Education*, *Journal of Education Policy*, *British Journal of Educational Studies*, *Oxford Review of Education*, *British Educational Research Journal*, *Journal of Philosophy of Education* and *History of Education*. The more applied cluster – containing journals such as *Teaching and Teacher Education*, *Studies in Higher Education*, *Instructional Science* and the *Journal of Research in Science Teaching* – is located between the two aforementioned major clusters. This visualization indicates that both the sociology and psychology clusters are closer to the applied cluster than they are to one another, emphasising the lack of connection between the sociology and psychology clusters. This indeed is the defining feature of this visualization: the disconnection between psychology and the other disciplines showing that papers in the psychology and sociology clusters have very little use for the content of papers in their opposing cluster.

The other issue emerging from this high-level picture that warrants further investigation is the apparently close relationship between ostensibly quite different journals in the sociology cluster. Figure 5.5 looks more closely at this cluster, showing the organization of this part of the field. *BERJ* is closest to the psychology cluster, being located at the bottom of the picture, and the *JEP* further way, further even than the *BJSE*. The other general journals, the *BJES* and the *ORE*, are located in between. While the *JPE* and *HoE* are present, the circles representing these journals are very small, illustrating that the other journals depicted here use their outputs much less frequently than most of the other journals shown in the visualization.

The high-level image represents the sociology cluster as a homogeneous entity, where possibly important distinctions between journals are blurred. If we run the

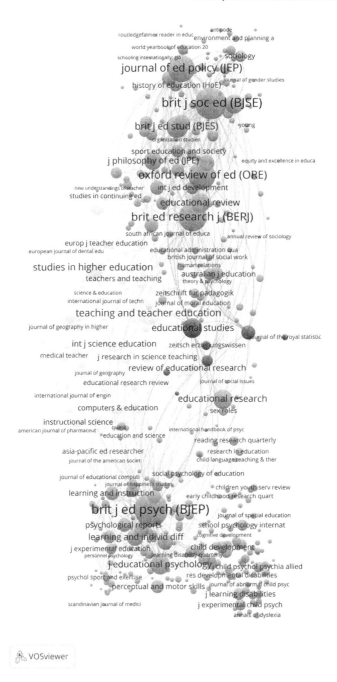

FIGURE 5.4 The entire network

analysis again, this time omitting those papers that are in the network due to the fact that they cite *BJEP* (and not the other main journals previously listed), we obtain the structure presented in Figure 5.6, which gives much more nuance to this cluster's organization – and breaks the cluster down into several sub-clusters. We can now see that the journals in our analysis have more distinctive character- istics than had previously been apparent. *BJSE* is clearly identified with a range of other sociology journals, far more so than the other journals in this analysis. Both *ORE* and *BJES* are located in the same cluster, which also contains the *JPE* and *HoE*. Both journals (*ORE* and *BJES*) are located between sociology and the policy-orientated cluster dominated by the *JEP*. Interestingly, the other general education journal (*BERJ*) has not been placed in the same cluster as the *BJES* and *ORE*. Instead, its more applied focus is reflected in its inclusion in the cluster of journals, including *Teaching and Teacher Education, Studies in Higher Education* and the *BJEP* (which is present in the visualization but is almost invisible due to the almost complete lack of interest in psychology displayed by the papers that cite papers in *BJES, BJSE, BERJ, HoE, ORE* and *JEP*).

Appendix 3 contains network diagrams depicting the connections for each jour- nal individually. They provide further nuance about the individual characteristics of each journal and facilitate some comparisons to be drawn. As might be expected, given the range of outputs just described, the network of journals associated with the *BJES* reflects its generalist position, with its papers being cited most frequently in the *ORE, BERJ, BJSE* and *JEP*. After sociology, its closest disciplinary affiliation appears to be philosophy, with history being a more distant satellite towards the

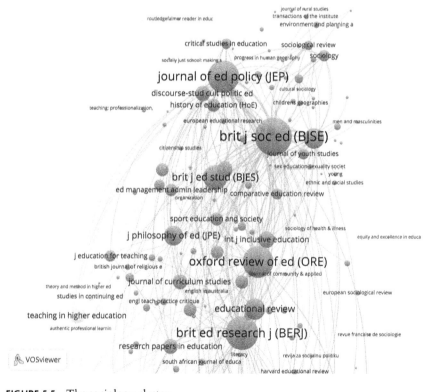

FIGURE 5.5 The sociology cluster

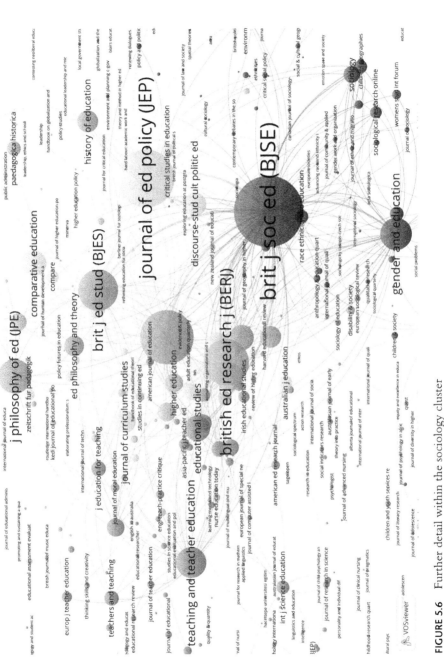

FIGURE 5.6 Further detail within the sociology cluster

bottom right of the image. No papers in the *BJEP* cite any papers in the *BJES*. *The ORE* and *BERJ* have similar characteristics to the *BJES*, with *BERJ* papers being cited more frequently in the cluster of journals concerned with teaching and assessment than in those concerned with sociology, and the *ORE* being rather closer to sociology. Papers in the *JEP* are frequently utilized in the generalist journals, in particular in sociology and critical studies.

The journals with explicit disciplinary affiliations show more striking differences than the generalist journals. The papers published in the *BJSE* are cited in mainstream sociology journals a little more than those of the generalist journals, but, in the main, papers from *BJSE* have a similar appeal to papers published in the generalist journals. This is in stark contrast to papers published in the *BJEP*, which are mainly taken up in a huge range of other psychology journals. Psychology papers are not limited to pure psychology journals, however, with a large number being utilized in journals concerned with higher education, medical education and information science. Papers published in *HoE*, in contrast, are rarely cited beyond other papers published in the same journal or in *Paedagogica Historica*. Somewhat surprisingly, a larger number of clusters of journals are associated with *HoE* than with other journals in this analysis, which probably reflects the lack of a clear 'outlet' for papers in this journal. Papers published in the *JPE* are utilized in a range of different areas. Unsurprisingly, they are picked up in *Educational Philosophy and Theory* and *Studies in Philosophy and Education* but also in more applied journals – such as *Studies in Higher Education* and *Teaching and Teacher Education*. They are also included in international journals and frequently used in the *ORE, BJES* and *Journal of Curriculum Studies*.

An interdisciplinary or multidisciplinary journal?

Finally, we turn to the question of whether the *BJES* achieved its original aim of being an interdisciplinary journal – or whether it might better be thought of as multidisciplinary. One of the *BJES*'s main weaknesses in its aim to represent the field of educational studies must surely be its exclusion of papers with a psychology focus. While the historical reasons for this are understandable, in that psychology already had a major journal when *BJES* was founded, it resulted in a publication that did not foster interdisciplinary thinking between psychology and the other disciplines. It accepted that psychologists had (and have) their own disciplinary-specific outlets and did not seek to draw them into a more interdisciplinary dialogue.

The involvement of the discipline of history in the story of the *BJES* is more complex than that of psychology. With the positive promotion of the journal in its inception as a location for historical work, many historical papers were published in the 1950s and 1960s. However, once alternative destinations for historical research became available from the 1970s, the *BJES* has, to all intents and purposes, not been a journal containing historical papers. Philosophy has not received priority treatment in the *BJES* – of the kind that history enjoyed – and another 'interdisciplinary' journal – the *ORE* – might claim to contain more philosophy than the *BJES*, but many papers with a philosophical perspective have been published in the *BJES*, and, unlike many historical papers, they have addressed contemporary issues with interest well beyond the their main disciplinary affiliation. Indeed philosophy, with its ability to speak with authority about perennial epistemic concerns, has regularly reached out beyond its disciplinary boundaries in order to provide a counterpoint to the epistemological claims made by sociologists.

The story of sociology, as seen through the *BJES*'s outputs, mirrors what has been seen elsewhere: an increasing focus on policy analysis has led to a blurring of the lines between what might be described as 'sociology' as opposed to 'social research'. While some have raised concerns about this move, it would also be fair to observe that contemporary sociological analyses of policy have the potential to foster dialogue and understanding beyond the discipline of sociology – and into discourses outside the academy.

In conclusion, the fact that it has been so difficult to identify papers that take an explicitly interdisciplinary perspective suggests that the *BJES* itself does not appear to have succeeded in its aim to be an explicitly and distinctive interdisciplinary journal covering the whole of the field of educational studies. This aim was limited from the outset, with the exclusion of the major discipline of psychology, and the advent of new specialist journals for historians and philosophers of education and the evolution of sociology into policy analysis and social research have made many of the outputs of the *BJES* very similar (and, at times, indistinguishable) in character from those published in other journals.

The question of whether or not interdisciplinarity is desirable and should – and can – be advanced by a journal is beyond the scope of this chapter but is an important issue for this book as a whole. While this analysis might conclude that there is little evidence of interdisciplinary work in education, another conclusion might be to question whether the idea of interdisciplinarity, as originally conceived by the founders of the journal, might need to be updated. Rather than thinking of this in terms of the four foundational disciplines, perhaps it is more useful to look at the citation network that shows how outputs from psychology, policy analysis, sociology and philosophy are used in the journals with an applied focus – even though this picture is not apparent within any specific 'interdisciplinary' journal. Indeed, perhaps the idea of interdisciplinarity without a supra-disciplinary focus is problematic, in that extra-disciplinary problems may be required to prompt the type of interdisciplinary investigation that the founders of the *BJES* were looking to support. If so, the idea of a generic interdisciplinary journal – which is able to foster dialogue among all disciplines equally – might be problematic because practical problems are required to 'force' disciplines into dialogue with one another. Thought of in this sense, the aims of the founders of the *BJES* to deepen interest in the "purposes and problems of current educational policy" might be more achievable than expecting disciplines to interact in a generic sense without a focus for their interaction. Here, the *BJES* might be considered to be achieving its aims, as its contemporary focus on policy analysis speaks clearly to current concerns in educational policy, with its outputs being utilised in journals with a focus for interdisciplinary dialogue.

APPENDIX 5.1

Technical details

This chapter has drawn on emerging information technologies and associated methods in order to generate the data and visualisations used in its analysis and discussion. Two quite distinct technologies were used: topic modelling, which is concerned with identifying the substantive issues discussed in the journal papers analysed, and citation networks, which facilitate an examination of the 'reach' of papers (that is, where papers in each journal are being cited).

Topic modelling

Topic modelling is a statistical method that analyses the combinations of terms used in a corpus (that is, a set of documents). The method used in this chapter was latent dirichlet allocation (LDA) as operationalized in the R package dfrtopics (which utilizes the mallet LDA engine). The theory on which LDA is based is that papers (and groups of papers) are based on an underlying distribution of topics, and the LDA algorithm seeks to identify these by analysing the combinations of terms used in each document (Blei et al. 2003). The data used in this case were the full text papers from all the outputs of the journals analysed that were available in JSTOR. After LDA topics were modelled, data were then transformed for use in the HTML (Hypertext Markup Language) model-browser interface, which was written by Andrew Goldstone. This browser interface is particularly useful for the type of analysis conducted, as it allows the user to examine the way in which topic foci change over time. The source code for the model browser is available on GitHub (http://agoldst.github.io/dfr-browser/). The steps taken to produce the visualisations were as follows:

1. Searches were carried out for all the research papers in each journal (individually) on the JSTOR data for research platform (http://dfr.jstor.org). Word

frequencies were downloaded for every paper. (At the time of writing, this involves 'queuing' a request for data. JSTOR sends an email when the data are ready for downloading.)

2. The LDA topic modelling R package was run against the data downloaded for each journal. Some iteration was necessary at this point in order to remove a lengthy list of 'stopwords' from the analysis (i.e. words that did not have informational value, such as the journal publisher's name and address, which appeared on every page of some journal outputs). The R code used is in the following box.

3. The topic models were then visualized in a standard Web browser. Topic models do not speak for themselves, and a lot of judgement and interpretation is then needed to determine which topics are meaningful in terms of understanding the unfolding narrative of a journal's output over time.

BOX: R CODE TO VISUALIZE TOPIC MODELS FROM JSTOR DATA

```
options(java.parameters="-Xmx2048m")
library(rJava)
library(mallet)
library(dfrtopics)

m<-model_dfr_documents(citations_files="C:\\...citations.
tsv", wordcounts_dirs = "C:\\...wordcounts", stoplist_file =
"C:\\ . . . stopwords.txt", n_topics=50)

export_browser_data(m, out_dir="c:\\browser", internalize=T,
overwrite=TRUE, supporting_files=TRUE)

* N.B.: you will need to have installed the following packages:
rJava, Mallet and devtools.
```

Citation networks

The citation networks used in this chapter were based on data downloaded from the Web of Science Core Collection. Searches were carried out for each of the journals in the analysis (individually). A 'citation report' was then produced, and then the 'citing articles' for each journal were downloaded (in plain text → other formats → full record and cited references), 500 records at a time. These files were then imported into the VosViewer software, and a citation network was created based on 'bibliographic coupling'. When there are many thousands of citations in a network, it is possible to run out of memory. This limitation can be overcome by running 64- rather than 32-bit Java and starting VosViewer from the Windows command prompt using, e.g.:

```
java - Xmx4000m -jar VOSviewer.exe
```

This will start VosViewer with about 4 gigabytes of memory, which was sufficient to run the analyses presented here.

APPENDIX 5.2

Summary of topics, the top words they contain and their temporal distribution

Topic	1952–2013	Top words	Proportion of corpus
Topic 1		art creativity creative aesthetic physical arts music sport sense imagination expression movement activity artistic body	0.8%
Topic 2		academic freedom disciplines university studies speech history educational disciplinary journals discipline knowledge study universities free	0.8%
Topic 3		women boys girls men love sex london female white physical novels male class sexual boy fiction	0.7%
Topic 4		schools school pupils secondary system london number comprehensive england primary pupil schooling high likely staff	3.0%
Topic 5		new policy government quality market public management local state control labour performance policies paper private	3.5%
Topic 6		child experience human life mind thinking nature world man natural intellectual individual understanding process development	2.4%
Topic 7		educational new years labour government system change reform political party policy act age major war	2.7%
Topic 8		religious religion christian catholic god faith ireland jewish theology church northern secular beliefs religions belief	1.4%

(*Continued*)

Topic	1952–2013	Top words	Proportion of corpus
Topic 9		learning society adult life new lifelong economy learners economic change human open people myth global	1.2%
Topic 10		knowledge educational philosophy theory truth philosophical hirst university forms practice theories understanding newman practical world	2.3%
Topic 11		history citizenship london identity ethnic values british cultural people culture historical singapore pupils global group	1.2%
Topic 12		training economic vocational technical skills industry london employment british work qualifications development technology industrial studies	1.8%
Topic 13		moral values human good value particular different life sense question peters general view concept person	5.0%
Topic 14		schools board elementary report system school committee instruction london government commission society local classes boards	2.4%
Topic 15		data table analysis social effect gorard effects level achievement cent attainment boys educational differences girls	1.5%
Topic 16		university training college colleges universities scotland scottish teachers years courses new institutions deaf teaching teacher	2.1%
Topic 17		curriculum national policy paper development des england emphasis debate subject key science hmi role wales	2.3%
Topic 18		change public crisis basil black media discourse pressure ie case group news sphere don ve	0.7%
Topic 19		school schools years children grammar public boys early age year century three private old number	2.8%
Topic 20		teachers teaching teacher children primary london pupils classroom english subject class years pedagogy pupil report	1.9%
Topic 21		children parents educational child choice social schooling equality class parental justice parent rights provision opportunity	1.4%
Topic 22		european la europe france educational paris international countries national french des states order compliance unesco	0.8%

(Continued)

Topic	1952–2013	Top words	Proportion of corpus
Topic 23		teachers professional teacher teaching practice training development practical knowledge profession professionalism theory model educational role	1.6%
Topic 24		history school london john schools william grammar signed vol master st thomas old rev college george	1.0%
Topic 25		rousseau mathematics numeracy man emile action practices world nns strategy life practice discussion ideas capability epistemic	0.5%
Topic 26		work need course people given good less little far point great whole fact thought place	12.0%
Topic 27		different study problems particular studies general view approach terms problem possible case question analysis form	6.6%
Topic 28		social educational new society life adult modern movement development world working system class interest century	2.4%
Topic 29		knowledge learning skills new assessment competence understanding information learn process experience outcomes performance thinking students	1.5%
Topic 30		german comparative germany dewey childhood history american der historical new york grundtvig see und university	0.7%
Topic 31		social people young educational capital class exclusion children family school studies families community justice behaviour	1.4%
Topic 32		citizenship students civic community higher engagement service learning participation university political public student democracy active	1.1%
Topic 33		assessment examination tests standards examinations ability test testing intelligence admissions results achievement performance marking level	0.9%
Topic 34		london history educational university books england royal sir book library john sources national see society	1.5%
Topic 35		needs special uk provision http available www cent skills support early inclusion dfes years london	1.1%
Topic 36		children health care medical child play group voice bias early difficulties adhd pastoral mental years	0.7%

(Continued)

Topic	1952–2013	Top words	Proportion of corpus
Topic 37		argument paper needs hope action justice white dilemma contrary case freedom consequences principle liberty positive	1.4%
Topic 38		students higher university academic student system courses universities study institutions degree level course vocational graduates	1.9%
Topic 39		english life literature arnold study man william later england farrar book books latin learning classical	2.3%
Topic 40		educational london sociology leadership new power social school critical knowledge theory management studies schooling field	2.2%
Topic 41		bill church national act voluntary lord question support liberal july parliament balfour commons times birmingham	1.7%
Topic 42		school improvement inspection ofsted effectiveness leadership innovation learning performance headteacher change staff authors external inspectors	0.9%
Topic 43		research educational studies researchers practice evidence policy development british evaluation review uk project capacity systematic	2.1%
Topic 44		committee council report teachers local act authorities secondary authority secretary members general ministry board reports	2.1%
Topic 45		science scientific subjects sciences arts mathematics college natural teaching physics century chemistry general professor subject	1.2%
Topic 46		schools leach grammar english history england church records chantry st little monastic later reformation foundation medieval	0.9%
Topic 47		social practice practices development individual work university cultural culture context particular process processes different individuals	3.8%
Topic 48		american infant states state south national australia united africa australian canadian hong kong african america music	0.8%
Topic 49		literacy language writing reading text children word texts communication words oral grammar skills alienation languages	0.7%
Topic 50		society political public state right community liberal social individual politics common power tradition culture autonomy	2.7%

APPENDIX 5.3

Network diagrams of individual journals

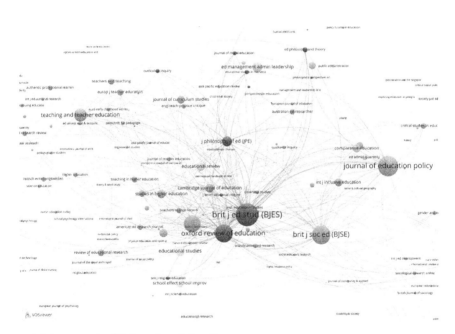

British Journal of Educational Studies

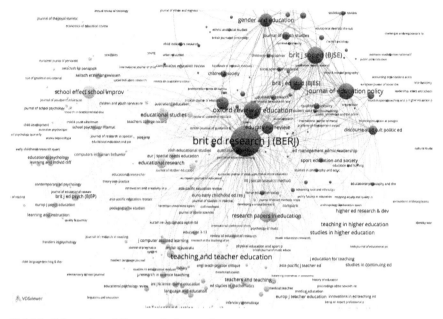

British Educational Research Journal

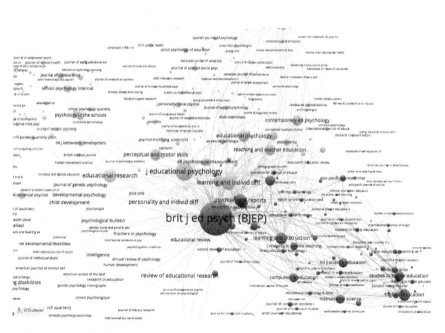

British Journal of Educational Psychology

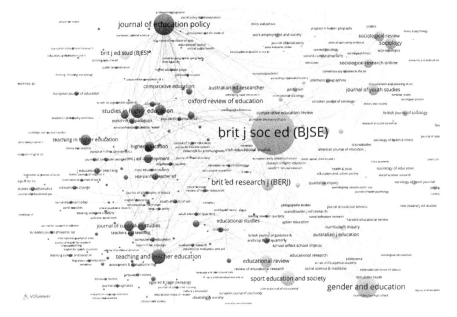

British Journal of Sociology of Education

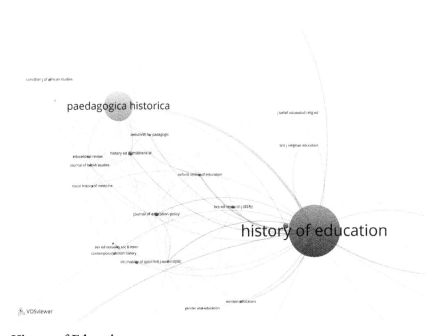

History of Education

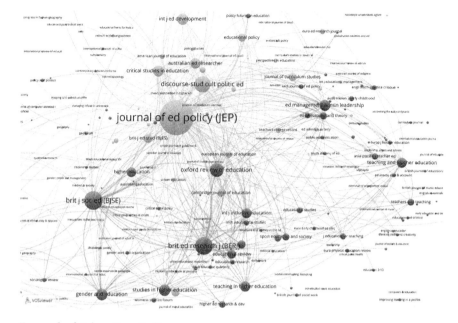

Journal of Education Policy

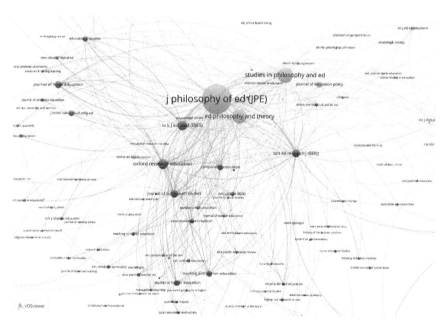

Journal of Philosophy of Education

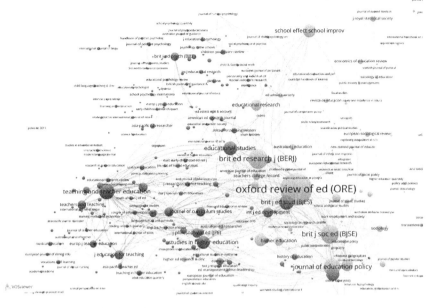

Oxford Review of Education

6

PUBLISHED REGISTERS AND TEXTS OF EDUCATION

Introduction

Textbooks provided a further means of defining or codifying the field. As John Nisbet noted, a 'textbook', in this sense, is 'a book which reviews and summarises research procedures, surveys and experiments, rather than reporting new work or introducing new concepts' (Nisbet 2003, p. 37). Moreover, according to Nisbet, 'It is written for students and their teachers, as an introduction to a defined field of study, and thus implies the existence of this field of study and its acceptance by the academic community' (Nisbet 2003, p. 37). Nisbet concluded that this highlighted 'the role of textbooks in the creation of a new discipline, in marking its boundaries and shaping its content, and also in legitimating new extensions as the study develops over time' (Nisbet 2003, p. 44). The existence of textbooks requires authors to be in a position to survey the field in a particular way, a student base or market of some kind to receive the work, and publishers to be active and receptive in its production.

In educational studies and research, there were relatively few textbooks of this kind produced before the Second World War. In the nineteenth century, the Rev. R.H. Quick's *Essays on Educational Reformers* (Quick 1868) is regarded as the earliest British textbook in the subject (Gordon 1980c, p. ix). In the early twentieth century, most textbooks were in psychology, such as R.R. Rusk's *Introduction to Experimental Education* (Rusk 1913). The interwar years witnessed the production of a few key general texts, the clear leader in the field being Percy Nunn's *Education: Its Data and First Principles* (Nunn 1920). Collections of articles arranged and edited to cover the field also began in this period with *The Yearbook of Education* from its foundation in 1932, published by Evans Brothers Ltd, initially edited by the ubiquitous Fred Clarke and from 1937 sponsored by the IOE London. From the 1940s, both authored and then increasingly edited texts began to proliferate as the field itself expanded and diversified. At the same time, it became progressively more difficult for such works to map the field as a whole, so that they typically mapped only a particular area of it, from the perspective of one of the disciplines or by focusing on a specific theme or topic. For many years, such texts had a mainly postgraduate student market, for student teachers and other courses in education or for research students, but in the early twenty-first century, a new set of texts began to cater for an undergraduate market with the spread of courses in educational studies.

The particular focus for the present chapter is how academic studies and texts reflected and represented changes in the field during the post-war period, focusing in particular upon those publications that aimed to map education studies, as well as those that sought to delineate a particular sub-field or discipline within the broader field of education studies. They were themselves maps of the field and represented a significant aspect of the relationship between disciplinary, multidisciplinary and interdisciplinary images of educational studies and research. Often, they continued to be prominent in the field for many years after their publication, with many running into several editions. In some cases, this served to codify the field in a way that ignored new insights in a rapidly changing educational, social and political context.

Attempts to represent the field of educational research from the 1940s through to the present day assume a variety of forms including single-authored summary reviews and descriptions of the constituent elements of the field (Thoulness 1969), surveys of the types of research being undertaken (Cohen et al. 1982), registers of research in education being undertaken with ancillary referencing information (NFER 1976), multi-authored summations of sectors within the field (Butcher 1968; Butcher and Pont 1970, 1973), attempts to delineate a sub-field as part of an academic programmatic project (Halsey et al. 1961) and critical studies assessing the present state of play within educational research (Yates1971;Young 1965). Another stream of publications casts eyes into the future to lay out where education research might be heading (Brownell 1963; Culbertson and Hencley 1963). Edited collections containing specialist short studies were the dominant form rather than the broad synthesising works that typified the previous generation (Nunn 1920; Adams 1922). A notable example of comprehensive edited collections aiming to survey an entire field was the series of compendium studies under the title *Scottish Education* (Bryce and Humes 1999, 2003, 2008; Bryce, Humes and Gillies 2013). These are a response to research developments within the research community, as well as being a response to significant changes brought about by political events.

One reason for a hesitation to produce synthesising 'maps' of the field is the seeming enormity of the task, especially during a period of expansion and reconstruction. Nonetheless, as the field was growing in volume and importance, it was recognised that it deserved detailed recording, dissemination and analysis. Edited collections were a means of encompassing the field as a whole but consisted of linked chapters by specialist authors focusing on their own particular areas. When they were framed on a disciplinary basis, they therefore tended to be multidisciplinary rather than interdisciplinary in their design. It is also notable that the field was not nationally insular but made extensive reference to companion literature flowing from the US and to a lesser extent from elsewhere (Culbertson and Hencley 1963; Yates 1971). Another key feature of the post-war literature is the extent to which mapping education studies and research involved quasi independent bodies, especially the NFER and the Schools Council, as opposed to university education faculties. The British educational research scene was therefore not wholly led or indeed centred within university institutes and departments of education, which may explain in part its applied and practical, professional orientation rather than having a theoretical character. There was, however, a close interrelationship with research foundations and the leading professors of education within universities.

The range of published studies emanating from within the field of education studies began to reflect growing state priorities and interests. Research undertaken from within the university became increasingly linked to major policy concerns and priorities, and this led to greater accountability to the State. Szreter (1980, p. 294) went so far as to propose the publication in 1954 of the report *Early Leaving* by the Central Advisory Council for Education as an early landmark in the institutionalisation of the sociology of education in Britain (Ministry of Education 1954). An example of a stream of policy-led research publications is that which examined the gap in productivity and educational attainment of a hypothesized British industrial worker when compared with their equally hypothesized German counterpart (Green 1993; Martin 1977; Thompson 1949). Another example is the rise within university sociology departments of studies seeking to address the perceived crisis in youth attitudes and behaviours (Dawson 1968; Friedmann 1971; Ramsey 1967; Willis 1977). The former can lay claim to primarily economic concerns, while the latter situates itself within the terrain of social policy, thus illustrating one of the core characteristics of education as a field – its interrelatedness to concerns and fields lying beyond itself.

Registers and surveys

The first attempt to map the field after the war came on the initiative of Fred Clarke for the NFER's first publication, although it did not chart the contemporary field in relation to published works but instead collated all of the unpublished research produced in the form of theses over the past generation, from 1918 to 1948 (Blackwell 1950). The bulk of the list comes from MA and PhD research projects, with over half of the theses presented in this period falling into the category of psychology and experimental research (Wiseman 1953, p. 62).

This emphasis continued in the immediate post-war period, as for example four of the six books published by the NFER by 1950 were related to the topic of testing undertaken by researchers working within the discipline of psychology using their statistical knowledge and skills. Yet educational publishing was already burgeoning to stimulate the expanding field. In the library catalogue of the library of UCL Institute of Education, which records acquisitions of books, there are 722 separate titles for 1956, 794 separate publications dated 1958 and 1,050 dated 1960, most of which are British with a small peppering of US volumes. These figures reveal the expansion of education-related publications during that period and the range of reading available to students of education. It was indeed a continuing trend of growth, and the same IOE library accessed 3,975 publications in 1980, 4,217 in 1982 and 4,619 separate titles for 1984. This alone suggests why producing a coherent synthesis of the field proved challenging, as it was expanding exponentially. Taking the book reviews within the *Times Educational Supplement*, which has been a weekly publication since 1912, provides another source to survey the range of books falling within education studies (Tuckett 2014).

Blackwell's (1958) revised NFER list demonstrated the degree to which the field had recovered from the sparse base that was presented in 1950. Blackwell's list was revised for 1952, 1954, 1956, 1958 and finally in 1961, by which time the process became too complex for a small team to undertake. This series of lists, issued biennially, provide us with a comprehensive mapping of the field of education studies in the immediate post-war period, revealing not only the growth but the diversification that were taking place. We can trace subtle shifts in organisation within sub-fields through a search for key concepts within the titles of individual research projects.

Additionally, we begin to discern the shifting of the substrata of the field as the sub-disciplines of philosophy and sociology begin to grow at the expense of educational administration, history and psychology. Library cataloguing and shelving are often premised upon identifying a work by its perceived disciplinary affiliation, leading to some confusion when it crosses boundaries or eschews such narrow placement (Banks 1968; Brim 1958; Ottaway 1953). Many studies set out to establish a multidisciplinary profile, arguing that their focus is best seen from differing perspectives (Butler 1983; Ferguson 1981; Floud 1956).

The most sustained project to map the field came from the NFER Registers produced over four large volumes between 1973 and 1980. These were A4-sized volumes reaching 469 pages for the third edition. The project was designed to create a comprehensive and standardized register of all educational research across the UK and was convened by the NFER in 1972 and chaired by Professor John Nisbet. The project was broadly representative, containing government, professional, academic and other interested groups. Funding was secured from the SSRC. The project gathered existing specialized registers from 33 other organisations and was the first to work within the computerized European Documentation and Information Systems in Education database initiative. Adjusted questionnaires were sent out to all organizations undertaking educational research, and the data could then be fed into the computing system. Thus the first volume of the NFER register is significant as it represents an early form of computer-generated text for printing using a system operated by the British Library. By 1976, over 2,000 separate entries were submitted for processing, revealing another indication of a massive growth in the field since the initial work by Blackwell in 1950. The NFER felt that they had finally succeeded in making feasible the collection of comprehensive information that was a 'centrally stored, national register of current educational research' (NFER 1976, p. 9).

Addresses of all organisations where education-related research was being conducted were supplied. This ran to 276 locations (NFER 1976, pp. 15–26). Some 2,094 separate research entries were recorded across 224 pages. These were then identified by a subject index beginning with '*A Level*' and concluding with '*Zoology*', thus providing a comprehensive account across 96 pages of the diversity of topics and themes currently being researched, with each page containing approximately 80 separate theme/subject entries. Within each subject heading, references led to an appropriate research project. There then followed a list, with reference locations of authors or named research leaders running across 24 pages, thus presenting for the first time a full picture of the cohort across the UK who were directly involved in educational research. Each page contained approximately 220 names, although there were instances of double entry as individuals were involved in more than one project, showing approximately 2,600 active researchers within the field. Aberdeen University recorded 25 research projects and Stirling University 11, illustrating the strides that had been made since John Nisbet had estimated a maximum of five across the whole of the country.

Educational research had become a substantial endeavour while still remaining relatively limited in terms of internal professional organisation. As a result of this comprehensive mapping of the field of education, it became possible to identify features such as the research profiles and activity of institutions, the emergence of sub-fields with disciplines and themes, the ebbing away of others, the national or cultural background of researchers based upon name entries and the number of university research bases. Most importantly for funding agencies, the register became an instrument that was intended to help prevent allocating resources to preexisting projects.

The NFER survey, led by Robert Thoulness (1969), reveals how discourses that had become challenged in the early twentieth century, remained in place through the continued academic and professional role of exponents several decades later. In 1969, Robert Thoulness held an emeritus positon as Reader in Educational Psychology at the University of Cambridge. He was part of the generation who pioneered psychology in universities (Manchester and Glasgow) during the early part of the twentieth century. An area of special concern for Thoulness had been the field of parapsychology investigating the occult, chance and the irrational in thought and perception. Stephen Wiseman's introduction stressed the need for the dissemination of findings and results of research. He opined that 'scientific knowledge' was doubling every ten to fifteen years. The review was to survey selectively the field of empirical and experimental research in education and excluded historical and comparative studies in education on the basis that there was no room to include them (Thoulness 1969, p. ix). The volume was delayed for three years, with Wiseman adding a final chapter to bring the survey up to date. Thoulness and the NFER maintained areas of enquiry such as 'Intelligence Testing', 'Educational Backwardness', 'Maladjusted Children' and 'Moral Development' in a key position within experimental educational knowledge, at a time when such categories were coming under critical examination.

Textualising the field

Some general texts that covered the field as a whole come from what can be described as 'transdisciplinary' sensibilities where the intention is to sidestep altogether the disciplinary traditions that come from the organisational arrangements within universities and instead aim to connect across social spheres linking for example academic, parental and professional readerships around common educational concerns. Brian Simon's early book on intelligence testing is one such transdisciplinary study, which seeks to bring teachers, parents and political reformers together around a key issue that he saw as being central to the reproduction of social class divisions (Simon 1953). Edward Blishen's BBC (British Broadcasting Corporation) publication, *Education Today: The Existing Opportunities*, ostensibly sets out to present 'facts' as part of the BBC's remit to provide information (Blishen1963). However, the book was part of a growing library emanating from the BBC's Schools Broadcasting Department and was aiming to link into The Campaign for Education, launched in 1963 by the Archbishop of Canterbury Michael Ramsey saying:

> 1963 must be the Year of education. The campaign calls upon the government to commit itself to a progressive plan for advance in education, the basis of which must be the implementation of the 1944 Act and a massive expansion of higher Education which will make this a practical possibility.

Such was the social and political context within which educational research found itself in the 1960s, a far cry from the barren terrain described by Clarke only a few years previously. The growth in educational research that began during that decade rode on the back of changing public sentiment in favour of 'a progressive advance in education' as expressed by Archbishop Ramsey. As research funding for education expanded, those with vested interests began to see opportunities for open competition. According to the 1963–64 Annual Report of the NFER:

> . . . educational research has become something of a bandwagon [on which] individuals and bodies with scanty experience and minimal competence are now turning their attention to matters which they think may provide rapid (and sometime sensational) returns. Some of these are commercial interests who skilfully conceal their origins or convince a reputable educational organisation that they will finance research without strings. Others are self-appointed pressure-groups often with innocent and high sounding titles . . . Questionnaires are a favourite instrument of such groups since they appear simple to construct and interesting to fill.
>
> *(Quoted in Griffith 2003, p. 46)*

One of the most ambitious schemes of publication, the Students Library of Education series, evolved as an inter-university initiative involving IOE director Lionel Elvin (Elvin 1987) and J.W. Tibble, professor of education at Leicester. Elvin's particular academic background was from the interdisciplinary field of English studies. Tibble had special interests in the life and work of the poet John Clare and co-authored a biography of Helen Keller. In Tibble's introductory chapter to the keystone book of the series, *The Study of Education* (Tibble 1966b), he outlines a series of major contributory figures (all male) within the history of education studies in English universities. He presents a view shaped by the established disciplines of psychology and history and then highlights early progenitors of what was to become the philosophy of education, citing for example the cross-disciplinary profiles of previous IOE directors Percy Nunn and John Adams. The purpose of the series, published by Routledge and Kegan Paul, was to provide a range of individual titles to address the need for disciplinary specific studies to be used within teacher training and B.Ed. courses. Tibble described these as 'basic books'. His critical approach reflected adherence to the established study of great educators from the past, an amalgam of philosophy and biography with some elements of comparative studies. Tibble identifies a key turning point in the history of education studies at universities with the appointment in 1947 at the IOE of Louis Arnaud Reid as professor of the philosophy of education – a post bearing an unequivocally academic and disciplinary profile, rather than being a post designating both seniority and the range of senior administrative duties undertaken by a chair of education. The contributors to Tibble's volume and also members of the editorial board of the Students Library of Education were Ben Morris (psychology of education), Richard Peters (philosophy), Brian Simon (history) and William Taylor (sociology) (Tibble 1966a).

Tibble established the Students Library series on the basis of a disciplinary division that framed the curriculum of existing teacher training and courses of study leading to the innovation of the B.Ed. degree. The foundation areas were to be history, philosophy, psychology and sociology. Two books in particular in the series that were to exert considerable influence were *The Logic of Education* by Paul Hirst and Richard Peters (Hirst and Peters 1966), then both based at the IOE, and Robert Dearden's *The Philosophy of Primary Education*, which became widely used as a key reference in training colleges (Dearden 1968). Dearden was yet another senior figure who was teaching at the IOE London and later became professor of philosophy of education in the University of Birmingham from 1978 to 1989. Tibble emphasised that the disciplines in relation to education were distinct from pure subjects studied for their intrinsic worth in that they made sense through their application to method. Education studies was to be viewed as a practical field of study.

As the series progressed, monographs on historical topics and titles appearing under the subheading of "Method etc." came to predominate. The majority of works of the series fell within what was broadly history but also contained elements that placed them into comparative education studies, especially the titles written by Harry Armytage of the University of Sheffield (Armytage 1967, 1968, 1969a, 1969b). Many under the broad heading of 'Method etc.' focussed upon special areas of the curriculum such as *Change in Art Education* by Dick Field (1970) and *Environmental Studies* by D.G. Watts (1969). As the various volumes appeared, the lines defining a particular ideological orientation within the field became progressively blurred, and the series became a display of the heterodox nature of the field itself. Thus, far from delineating an emerging and coherent field of study defined by self-contained disciplines, the Students Library series came to reproduce the complexity and cross-currents that had been captured by other attempts at mapping the field.

The development of specialised sub-literatures

Richard Oliver's *Research in Education*, published in 1946 (Oliver 1946), was an early pioneer text addressed specifically to intending postgraduate researchers. In the same year Charlotte Fleming published *Research and the Basic Curriculum* (Fleming1946), which John Nisbet cited as one of the only available British written research texts offering guides beyond that of psychometric approaches (Nisbet 1974). Apart from the extensive statistical and psychometric literature that supported quantitative research within the field of psychology, there was little on research methodology linked to other fields. US texts were available to support students with some technical research basics. Works such as those of John W. Best (Best 1959) and Deobald Van Dalen (Van Dalen 1962) offer a glimpse into what US university–based academics identified as the foci that constituted the research field. Van Dalen for example offers three pages on documentary analysis (211–214), while offering 44 pages on inferential statistics (written by William C. Meyer, pp. 369–413). The prevalence of statistical analysis derived from psychology continued to predominate, reflecting the weighting within education courses during the early careers of academics trained during the 1930s who matured professionally in the post-war decades. W.A. Brownell for example, who was born in 1895, reached retirement in 1962 and during the following year wrote *Education Research in the Decades Ahead*. His academic research had primarily been in psychological studies of teaching and learning of mathematics including the comparative study of the English and Scottish approaches (Ohles 1978, pp. 189–190). Thus in some respects, much of what was being published by senior figures within the field in the mid-twentieth century reflected thinking and practices that had been developed in the interwar period.

Such methodological aides acted to fill a gap in British publication. Where a sub-field was similarly undeveloped, US texts such as Gale Jensen's *Educational Sociology* (Jensen 1965) were available. Moser (1958) from the LSE produced a pioneer text on *Survey Methods in Social Investigation* in 1958 working from within the social demographic movement in the survey traditions of Charles Booth and continued into the twentieth century by the Mass Observation (Jeffrey 1978) and Gallup survey work (Elam 1995). Michael Young's *Innovation and Research in Education*, published by the Institute of Community Studies in 1965, focused upon the nature of research within departments and institutes of education and included a joint study on the subject with William Taylor (Young 1965, pp. 137–144). Through publications such as this, we can identify insights into educational research at this time. One sceptical and unnamed respondent wrote:

> Over the past 17 years I have observed EDUCATION develop as a professional study, atomised and careerised; meanwhile the background philosophy

and thinking have steadily become more uncertain. In the 1920s I left a Day training college with a satisfying philosophy of mathematics and of education: today I find we are in danger of having neither. Meanwhile the research theses in the basement multiply: what does it all add up to?

(Young 1965, pp. 138–139)

The survey of colleges and departments by Young and Taylor found that 20 percent of research fell within the teaching of a particular subject, 12 percent within historical topics and 10 percent in teaching methods, with other sub-fields falling into less than 10 percent. Of the professors surveyed, 83 percent said they were active in research, but this fell to 56 percent among lecturers. Young and Taylor pointed out the "paucity of research posts" across the system (p. 140). They found that the single greatest inhibiting factor was pressure from other types of work among academic staff. Their survey compared the average percentages who taught 12 or more hours per week compared with other academic departments and found 47 percent in education departments against 18 percent elsewhere. There was a corresponding inversion in relation to the numbers of research hours spent weekly. Within the HE Education Studies survey of 410 individuals, there was a concern to invest more in research into teaching methods, the curriculum, school structures and organisation, addressing problems of staffing particular subjects and of teacher supply generally and the effects upon child development (Young 1965, p. 143).

Another approach was to analyse prospects for the future of the field. One example of this was a keynote collection edited by A.V. Judges, professor of history of education at King's College, London (Judges 1955). His volume, *Looking Forward in Education*, was a conscious attempt to widen the remit of educational studies to include social policy areas relating to rural areas, professional training, voluntary schools, financial costs of expansion and transfer from schools to university. Here the aim of educational research is to highlight forgotten aspects, to widen enquiry and to emphasise links between policy and practice. The text is an example of a professional historian using disciplinary concepts in order to intervene in contemporary debates. Judges invited the reader to 'reflect on subsequent happening' (Judges 1955, p. 9). He asked whether progress was actually taking place when measured against the wartime aspirations of social reconstruction.

There were, however, concerted attempts to bolster a more orthodox perspective towards education studies as a field of study. The reaffirmation of the once dominant positivist, psychological paradigm was to appear in Butcher's volume *Educational Research in Britain*, under the imprint of the University of London Press (Butcher 1968). Of the eighteen papers in this collection, over half come from academics practising within the field of psychology. The paper on 'Social Class and Educational Adaptation' by Donald Swift, described as 'a tutor in sociology at Oxford', sought to argue that:

> The use of the concept of social class . . . is a categorizing device which will have some value at a particular stage in the analysis of cognitive development,

but which may be replaced as our ability to define the stimulus content of social class experience improves.

(Swift 1968, p. 288)

Swift was to be the editor of the Students Library series publication *Basic Readings in the Sociology of Education* (1970) and advocated a functionalist, psychodynamic approach to the study of social class and education. In the Butcher volume there are no contributions from the fields of philosophy, history or more contemporary strands of sociology. The editor is brief and to the point when it comes to defining 'educational research':

It is interpreted here as empirical research, based upon experiment, on social survey and on the clinical study of individuals.

(Butcher 1968, p. 13)

Five of the 18 contributors had direct experience of working within the leadership of the NFER. Almost all of the other papers sustain a focus upon psychologically derived studies such as the discussion by D. Graham, who is described as a senior lecturer in psychology at the University of Durham, on children's moral development.

For over a decade, Butcher's work was a key reference point in mapping the boundaries both of the field and of research approaches within the field. The first volume was followed by two more published in 1970 and 1973. As with the first volume, the second volume begins with a paper on the development of the work of the NFER. Jack Wrigley, professor of curriculum studies at the University of Reading, presented a paper on the Schools Council of which he was then the director. In this revised 1970 mapping of the field, sub-disciplines begin to appear such as 'medical education' and 'education for business and management'. Maureen Woodhall, a colleague of Mark Blaug at the IOE in the emerging area of economics of education, allocated half a page to E.G. West and his ideas about parental choice and school vouchers. Woodhall's research subsequently placed her work at the heart of debates about student fees and the business management of schools, as well as cost-benefit analysis in educational planning (Woodhall 1970). Butcher's three volumes are presented as summations of trends within the wider field and are intended to act as points of reference for students studying in colleges and universities. In volume 3, published in 1973, ten of the seventeen contributors came from academic psychology of education. However, the status of contributors was altered with the inclusion of Denis Lawton (head of the Department of Curriculum Studies, IOE), William Taylor (director, IOE), John and Elizabeth Newsom (Nottingham Child Development Research Unit) and Lawrence Stenhouse (director of Applied Research UEA).

Representative voices from within educational psychology were able to maintain their dominant position within educational studies through the diversification within their own disciplinary field. As Thomas (2012, p. 54) points out, four out of eleven members of the board of the SSRC represented psychology – Jack Tizard, Ben Morris, William Wall and James Drever. This was a group more notable for the distinctiveness of their interests within their field than for their similarities. Another luminary within educational psychology was Philip Vernon who more than most others established a critical discourse from within mainstream educational psychology challenging many of the previous and currently prevailing assumptions of Cyril Burt relating to intelligence and testing. Thomas's survey evokes a picture of a discipline that was itself internally contested and evolving, in particular in the way that many academics were seeking ways of making connections across disciplines. Liam Hudson's *Contrary Imaginations* (Hudson 1966) and *Frames of Mind* (Hudson 1968) sought in part to focus the study of schools upon social psychological phenomena. He represented a new spirit of questioning previous orthodoxies within the discipline, having himself trained in philosophy, history and psychology.

However, as new B.Ed. courses sprang up during the 1960s and expanded further into the 1970s, it was works originally written in the 1950s that persisted and acted as the principal references for study of educational psychology. *Psychology and Its Bearing on Education* by Charles Valentine was one of the most widely used study and reference texts, published initially in 1950 by Methuen and republished in a second edition in 1960 (Valentine 1950). This text had its genesis in Valentine's 1916 book *An Introduction to Experimental Psychology in Relation to Education* (Valentine 1916). Valentine is an example of an academic whose work in the field began in the second decade of the twentieth century and whose influence persisted through to the 1970s. He held the chair in education at Birmingham from 1919 to 1946 and was editor of the *British Journal of Educational Psychology* (*BJEP*) between 1931 and 1955. Fred Schonell and then Edwin Peel, who succeeded Valentine at Birmingham in the post-war period, also made significant contributions to educational psychology. Peel's texts, in particular *The Psychological Basis of Education* (Peel 1956), *The Pupil's Thinking* (Peel 1960) and *The Nature of Adolescent Judgement* (Peel 1971), differed from Valentine in their emphasis on individual development and increasingly on Piagetian approaches and were also prominent well into the 1970s (Platt 1979; Wall 1979). Another key text was that of Kenneth Lovell, of the University of Leeds, whose book *Educational Psychology and Children* appeared in a tenth edition in 1969, having first appeared in 1958 (Lovell 1958). This was also to help displace Valentine's publication in the 1970s as the staple reference for university courses in developmental psychology (see also Lovell 1979). Lovell had been one of Philip Vernon's students at the IOE (Orton 1998) and, despite his prominence within educational psychology, established his main reputation in the field of mathematics education and teacher training.

At the same time, published texts also represented shifting emphases within the discipline of sociology of education. Ottoway's *Education and Society* first appeared in 1953 and was not revised until 1962. This text continued to be reprinted throughout the 1960s in its second edition (Ottaway 1953). Olive Banks' *The Sociology of Education* was published in 1968, superseding Ottaway's text, and remained in publication through to the 1980s (Banks 1968). During that time, Banks remained the sole female professor at Leicester University. The field became identified through landmark single studies such as Banks' own *Parity and Prestige in English Secondary Education: A Study in Educational Sociology*, published in 1955 (Banks 1955). So a distinctive and extensive tradition of research-based educational publications was developing, some designed to service the growing numbers of active postgraduates, salaried and funded professionals operating within the field. Lauder, Brown and Halsey argue that the high point for sociology within educational studies was in the 1970s (Lauder et al. 2009, p. 569). While readership grew among training teachers seeking answers to how their roles within schools could serve as agencies for social change, new theoretical perspectives suggested that these roles were ambiguous. A key turning point came with the collection of papers edited by M.F.D. Young entitled *Knowledge and Control: New Directions for the Sociology of Education* (Young 1971), which argued that teachers were implicated in sustaining and reproducing social relations of power through their work. This prominent work offered teachers a view of themselves as insider agents complicit in helping to exercise social control, while distancing the discipline from the perceived needs of policy makers, especially those working in central and local tiers of government.

Another significant shift of disciplinary focus, a different mapping of the field, came with the publication in 1961 of *Education, Economy and Society* edited by Halsey, Floud and Anderson, identifying six broad areas for the study of the interconnection of education with economics (Halsey et al. 1961). Halsey and Floud were based at the LSE and had already made an impact with their 1956 book *Social Class and Educational Opportunity* (Floud and Halsey 1956). Anderson was professor of comparative education at the University of Chicago. The first part of this second-generation or revisionist mapping asserts the centrality of economic concerns, thus challenging the uncritically accepted quadrant of history, psychology, philosophy and sociology. It constitutes an attempt at questioning the existing disciplinary arrangements while proposing a wider multidisciplinary configuration. Chapter 3 consists of an uncut section from the Crowther Report (pp. 22–30), which forms chapter 5 of the actual report published by the Central Advisory Council for Education (England). This is a bold move implying that sources other than those of academic origin are deserving of recognition within the field. Another contributor was T.W. Schultz, who examined the net investment in education across the US and raised questions concerning the social, political and economic motives behind such investment. At the time of publication, Schultz held the Chair of economics at the University of Chicago from which he had influenced thinking about economic development and post-war recovery (Schultz 1963). His later development of human capital theory was to lead to a Nobel Prize. Thus within this mapping exercise of a redefined educational field, Halsey et al. were interpolating mainstream thinking from contemporary American economics, some of which was to exert radical influence upon succeeding waves of critical thinking concerned with human and cultural capital and development education theory. Another prominent American sociologist from Chicago to contribute to the Halsey et al. collection was Howard Becker, who at the time of publication in 1960 was president of the

American Sociological Association, at the age of 32. He was one of the sociologists whose work on deviance, labelling theory and use of life history methodology, was not only to transform sociology but to change the status of qualitative research within the field (Burgess 1995).

Thus the book breaks the framing of the field in national boundary terms and invites readers to study writing from elsewhere (the US). While the framing of the field is limited to the UK and US, there is however, a single exception, that of Dietrich Goldschmidt looking at teachers in institutions of higher learning in Germany. Instead of presenting education as a field unto itself, the studies are related to an overarching historical economic theme of changes taking place in the transition from earlier forms of industrial manufacturing towards advanced, technological industrialism. The broad argument of the book is that, unlike previous periods, education becomes essential, to an unprecedented degree, to economic transformations and consequently expands and changes its priority. Within this map of the field of the socio-economics of education, the editors highlight six broad themes designed to take readers into an interdisciplinary exploration weaving cultural, economic, pedagogic, historical and sociological strands into accounts of educational transformations. Education is depicted as a process that can only be understood in its relation to social structural dimensions.

The successor volume to this collection was *Power and Ideology in Education* (Karabel and Halsey 1977a). It was again co-edited by A.H. Halsey, by this time a widely celebrated leader of the field, on this occasion with another American sociologist, Jerome Karabel of the University of California at Berkeley. This new collection responded to the recent radical revisionist work that had been published in the US in the sociology, political economy and history of education by figures such as Samuel Bowles, Herbert Gintis, Martin Carnoy and David Tyack. The editorial introduction was an extensive critical overview of recent educational research that tried to make good its fundamental claim that '[o]ver the last generation educational research has come from the humblest margins of the social sciences to occupy a central position in sociology, as well as to receive considerable attention from economists, historians, and anthropologists' (Karabel and Halsey 1977b, p. 1).

The subsequent inheritor volume, *Education: Culture, Economy and Society*, once again involved Halsey but illustrated how the map of education studies had shifted in the 35 years since his first co-edited collection (Halsey et al. 1997). The previous presumption of nation states acting as the unit of reference for educational research, it was now argued, was being displaced by globalised economic interests and cross-national organisations setting agendas for change in education. The contributing authors proposed that education no longer served the needs of industrialised states but those of post-industrial multinational conglomerates. State bureaucracies, it was argued, were giving way to the management and control norms established by private interests. Educational research had shifted attention to the impact of private interests within and upon the educational system. Whereas Schultz's paper opened the first volume, the 1997 volume began with a paper by Pierre Bourdieu on *The Forms of Capital* (Bourdieu 1986/1997). A new focus upon gender issues reflected the shifts in female employment as the economy moved towards service sector employment and servicing employees for the communications industries. These transformations, the authors claim, have created education 'as a site of struggle' (p. 12). The postmodernist critique led to attention to the idea of the cultural politics of 'difference' within education. Developments in postcolonial societies had become central ones within education studies as the field internationalised it focus. However, the collection of 52 chapters reinforced the idea that earlier inequalities persist. The promotion of meritocracy and the rise of social exclusion provides a central node around which one strand of education studies can organise. The authors placed issues of the knowledge economy, changing curricula and cultural politics as another developing node within the wider field. The central new element was the emergence of the politics of the market within school management and its attendant politics of school effectiveness. Another focus was that of transformations in the role, training and status of teachers and teaching. With these we have moved a long way from the interest in subject disciplines as being the central organising agencies of knowledge and research.

Meanwhile, one of the most authoritative surveys or representations of the field of education as it exists within the UK comes from the publication *Scottish Education*, first published in 1998–99 under the imprimatur of Edinburgh University Press and edited by two of the pre-eminent figures in modern Scottish educational research, Walter Humes, who held chairs at three Scottish universities, and Tom Bryce, who had been vice dean of research at the University of Strathclyde. The fourth edition, published in 2013, acted not only to outline areas of currently active research interest but also as a register of people and institutions where research was being undertaken. The publication included 111 papers by 104 contributors, most of which presented a summation of the current state of the sub-field. Almost all contributors worked within universities, but there were some others such as George Kerevan, previously an academic economist transformed into a journalist, Janys Scott, a practising barrister and expert of Scottish education law, Ian Hulse, a mathematics teacher from Dundee, and Liz Niven, a poet. The collection was arranged not by academic disciplines but thematically in relation to a number of current and active areas of concern. Not surprisingly, much attention has been paid in recent years to policy making in the Scottish context in view of devolution for education and the rise of the Scottish National Party seeking to move towards national independence. This has led to a strengthening of discourses concerning 'Scottish' in distinction to 'British' education. Following from the transfer of the Scottish Office to the Scottish Executive and then Parliament, a new set of institutions was established requiring new relationships with local authorities and educational institutions, leading to the academic field of educational administration and control becoming prominent once again (Redford 2013, pp. 153–163). There are ten papers exploring aspects of educational change and culture, with Robert Anderson and Donald Gillies providing historical overviews leading to the present day and establishing an ethos that is both Scottish yet impregnated with values of diversity.

Twenty-first-century texts

The heyday of the B.Ed. degree and its associated texts had long since passed by the turn of the century. Nevertheless, in the early decades of the twenty-first century, there was a revival of the undergraduate text, this time linked with the spread of BA programmes in educational studies, designed not for intending teachers but for undergraduate students in the humanities and social sciences. Burton and Bartlett (2006) see this development as being based on the onset of a new type of under-graduate degree for a broader clientele in a mass system of higher education. These were modular courses in which education was often viewed as combining well with cognate subjects, whether primarily academic or professional in nature, or as the basis for an honours degree in itself (Burton and Bartlett 2006, p. 389), and they have led to burgeoning numbers of textbooks to cater for this fresh development. These works have also constituted maps of a changing field of study.

One example of these twenty-first-century texts was produced in 2004 by members of the Faculty of Education at Bath Spa University. Of the nineteen con-tributors to the volume, *Education Studies: A Student's Guide* (Ward 2004), all had previously been professionals working within some tier of the education system. In an attempt to provide coherence across such a broad field for their undergradu-ate students, the editors state that they strive for 'a deeper understanding of what education is about' (Ward 2004, p. 1). The editor acknowledged that '[e]ducation studies can be subject of pure academic interest without any particular vocational outcome' that can be 'intellectually challenging and interesting' (Ward 2004, p. 1). It was noted that courses such as that which they offered at Bath Spa University had been separated from teacher training pathways because of the external con-trol over teacher training programmes exercised by the Teacher Training Agency under the terms of the 2002 standard for Qualified Teacher Status. This marked a historic shift for education studies whose origins in Britain lay with teacher trade unions and with university departments who were involved with teacher training and then with applied education psychology. There is no attempt at synthesis of the field, but instead the aim is to 'introduce . . . a broad range of topics that will stimulate your ideas and your reading' (p. 2). The work presents three broad uni-fying themes: International and Global Perspectives, Teaching, Education Setting and Policy and Knowledge Learning and the Curriculum. Thus the social science disciplines have faded as forms for organising knowledge and research although Heather Williamson's chapter, 'Human Rights and Education' is subtitled 'A Philo-sophical Approach' (Williamson 2004, p. 57). Here, in 2004, in a text designed for BA graduates following education studies courses, the idea of disciplinarity has all but gone. As the post-war consensus evaporated, there emerged a strain of explicit commentary focused upon the politics and policy of education, so within Ward (2004) there is a concern about the shift from a framework of local authority sup-port for education towards a situation whereby, as Ward argues, 'the government perceived its duty to micro-manage schools with almost daily guidance, direction and exhortation about their day-to-day business' (Ward 2004, p. 88). The section on 'Knowledge, Learning and the Curriculum' is a survey of recent developments within broad areas of the national curriculum rather than a discussion of core ideas or traditions about knowledge and learning. Ward's collection was an effective contribution to the new courses and by 2013 was into its third edition.

Another collection, *Education Studies: Issues and critical Perspectives* (Kassem et al. 2006) was published by the Open University Press. Michael Totterdell, director of the Institute of Education, Manchester Metropolitan University, opened the book by declaring that 'Education studies has long been considered as the disciplinary arm of education understood as a "subject" or field of enquiry' (Kassem et al. 2006, Foreword). For Totterdell, the distinction is that education studies offer scope for 'serious thought about issues' that extend beyond the immediate concern of policy and practice. One of his concerns is the tendency for such 'serious' thinking to be parodied as mere 'theory', a tendency that can lead to de-intellectualising the study of education. His concern is not to lose sight of 'underlying principles, fundamental concepts, contextual factors and global dimensions' (Kassem et al. 2006, Foreword). His plea implies that such a tendency exists. However, the collection of sectorally arranged essays is not formed by a unifying introduction, and papers are arranged in categories that sometimes have only tenuous connections to what is included. The field is organised into the following sections: 'Inside the School'; 'Policy Politics and Education'; 'Education at the Margins' and 'Global Education, Global Issues'. One of the main justifications offered for education studies within this text is that it can provide an evidential basis for the evaluation of policies and practices, and the editors argue that most contemporary discourse is lacking in this respect. Dave Hill (Hill 2006) calls for a critical investigation into the aims, contexts and impact of educational policies in order to broaden awareness of the meaning such a policy has. Hill argues that education studies should interpret developments within three broad ideological frameworks that shape the educational system and its practices in England – those of social democracy, neo-liberalism and neo-conservatism. Hill exemplifies the trend towards emphasising the importance of policy focused research within the field, a merging of what previously would have been considered the purview of politics, history or administration studies within education. It is fair to say that publications such as Kassem et al. (2006) and Ward (2004), which have wide student readerships, are written from viewpoints that are critical of neo-liberal stances, so advocates of the values of neo-liberalism tend to be absent even though they have considerable purchase within the field. Both Kassem and Ward seek to reposition research into education within a unifying, globalising movement tracing tendencies towards the homogenizing of education across political boundaries. This shifts attention to the transnational influence of the OECD and its PISA assessment programme, arguing that we have moved away from framing education studies in purely national contexts.

One of the most widely used and recent representations of the field has been that produced by Steve Bartlett and Diana Burton, both from the University of Wolverhampton. Their publication *Introduction to Education Studies* (Sage) has, since 2006, been through a number of reprints and through four editions (2006, 2008,

2012, 2016). The aim is to consider education studies as a field in its own right that is essentially interdisciplinary in character. While focusing upon the school sector, in the main Bartlett and Burton emphasise the significance of five other broad areas within the field: further and higher education, lifelong learning, early childhood education, citizenship and social justice, and education and globalisation. Bartlett and Burton echo the view of Ward et al. (2004) that the turning point for contemporary education studies came from the removal of theoretical and academic elements from initial teacher training programmes (Bartlett and Burton 2006/2016, p. 5), which prompted the emergence of undergraduate courses distinct from the B.Ed. courses.

On the other hand, a further new text of this type, edited by Vivienne Walkup (Walkup 2011), resurrects a substantially discipline-based map of the field. It is divided into four parts: the history and philosophies of education, the psychology of education, contemporary policies and debates in education, and new perspectives in education. Within this general framework, a range of authors explore a number of themes, albeit with a lack of sociological theory in most cases. According to the editor, 'The study of education encompasses a range of disciplines, including but not limited to psychology, sociology, history and philosophy' (Walkup 2011, p. 1). She seeks from this stance to 'encourage critical engagement with education, and to equip readers with a basis from which to evaluate key issues' (Walkup 2011, p. 1).

Thus, students pursuing education studies in British universities now engage with a field characterized by authors as being 'young' and developing, taking a critical, analytical and 'resistant' approach to the study of education, grappling with fundamental, contested concepts, exploring a range of perspectives, not just those of teachers and schools and dealing with multiple rather than singular explanations or phenomena (Bartlett and Burton 2006/2016, p. 7). Whilst the idea that the field is young and developing might come as a surprise to those familiar with its history over the past century, much that is being said here is consistent with the social and educational ideas characteristic of educational studies in the early post-war years.

7

AN INTERDISCIPLINARY PROJECT?

The case of the Centre for Contemporary Cultural Studies

Centres are a particular kind of institutional development within the modern university that have tried to draw together expertise and knowledge in a particular area, often across departments and thus against the established social organisation of the university itself, challenging the authority of the disciplines. The Centre for Contemporary Cultural Studies (CCCS) at the University of Birmingham, launched in 1964, highlights contested issues of knowledge production in relation to the disciplines in modern universities. It constitutes a fascinating example of the social formation of configurations of knowledge that can be subjected to historical analysis. It enacted an explicit ideal of interdisciplinarity in its approach to research, teaching and social practices, but it also drew on the established disciplines to develop its radical agenda. It offers an instructive comparison in a cognate area of study with the more orthodox style of educational studies and research in the same period. It established an education subgroup in 1975–76, and its distinctive approach generated significant works related to education such as *Unpopular Education* (1981) and a collegial style of teaching and research. Its oppositionist and dissenting character also led to its isolation, political vulnerability and eventual closure in 2002.

Introduction

CCCS was founded in 1964 as a research grouping in the English Department of the University of Birmingham. Its founding director was Richard Hoggart, author of *The Uses of Literacy* (Hoggart 1957), and Hoggart's inaugural lecture in 1963, 'Schools of English and Contemporary Society' (Hoggart 1963), established its academic mission. Later directors were Stuart Hall and Richard Johnson, and it became a department in its own right, but it was closed in 2002.

CCCS does not make an appearance in Eric Ives' history of the University of Birmingham, published in 2000 (Ives 2000). The University of Birmingham was itself a civic university established in the late nineteenth century. As Ives notes, the study of universities is 'a late comer to the discipline of history' (Ives 2000, p. xiii), and analyses of departmental structures and even more so of the configurations of knowledge within and across them remain in their infancy. On the other hand, Richard E. Lee's *Life and Times of Cultural Studies: The Politics and Transformation of the Structures of Knowledge* (Lee 2003) provides a detailed study of CCCS. It argues that although it found intellectual ancestors in English, Hoggart's project did not respect disciplinary lines. Hoggart divided the new field into three parts, drawing on both the humanities and social sciences: historical/philosophical, sociological and literary critical. Hall also saw CCCS as a conjunctural practice developed from a different matrix of interdisciplinary studies and disciplines, emerging from a crisis in the humanities (Lee 2003, pp. 106–107).

It is possible to combine the institutional approach of Ives with the theoretical emphasis of Lee in order to reach a fuller appraisal of the work of CCCS in its social, political and historical context. A range of archival documentary sources sheds further light on CCCS, in particular the archive of Richard Johnson at the Cadbury Research Library, University of Birmingham. Interviews conducted as part of the preparation for this book are also revealing, including an interview with Johnson himself, as well as a number of other, anonymised witnesses of CCCS's development. CCCS is interesting in its own right as a significant episode in the international history of cultural studies (see for example Gibson 2007; Hartley 2007; Schulman 1993). It also reflects tellingly on the nature and development of educational studies as a field of knowledge over the same period. It constituted an interdisciplinary initiative in an area related to education and reaching across the humanities and social sciences, an example of an interdisciplinary 'space' developed through a university centre that also promoted courses, seminars, conferences, research projects and publications. CCCS was a forum that developed an intellectual project and social practice around interdisciplinarity and embodied the opportunities and challenges related to this. Ultimately, nevertheless, it became a victim of the educational, social and political changes of the past thirty years and, unlike educational studies, failed to survive these changes. CCCS can thus be interpreted as a project that exemplifies interdisciplinarity in action, contrasting vividly with the ideas and practices that usually characterised educational studies over the same period. Nevertheless, it also exhibits some features of disciplinarity underlying the interdisciplinarity that it chose to emphasise and cultivate.

The case of CCCS

From the outset, the annual reports of CCCS discussed the development of the Centre providing significant insights on the nature of interdisciplinarity in CCCS as an intellectual project and social practice, as they explicitly pondered the opportunities and threats around such an approach in the context of an English institution of higher education. The first report of the Centre, in September 1964, highlighted the establishment of a wide range of loose groupings working on particular projects, including one on the 1930s that was 'loosely-knit' and brought together 'people of differing ages, with widely different interests, and different academic experience' (CCCS 1964, p. 5). This group included two English specialists, one of whom was also a social anthropologist, together with several literary critics, a political historian and a biographer. It was observed that there was a wide age range, with the two youngest being in their early twenties, graduates in English from Keele and Oxford. The eldest was a senior lecturer at the training college, also in English (CCCS 1964).

CCCS's initial report also suggested wider ambitions for the Centre that might be described as transdisciplinary as well as interdisciplinary, especially in seeking to develop connections with teachers and lecturers. Responding to the demographic changes then taking place with an influx of students from a wider range of social backgrounds than hitherto into higher education, it argued that there was 'a growing body of people in education who see the direct connection between our work and their educational careers' (CCCS 1964, pp. 11–12). Closer liaison with this group would be established initially through arranging occasional conferences, but, it continued, 'Over the years, we should like to see the Centre increasingly as a rallying point, both for research work on cultural change and also for those who are engaged in the same field, but express it in the practice of education and teaching at all levels' (CCCS 1964, p. 12). It suggested that there was a great deal of such work that might be done, alongside bodies such as the British Film Institute and Use of English groups and also overseas institutions (CCCS 1964, p. 12). This was followed up the following year. In June 1964, CCCS organised a meeting with 'a number of interested people in further education, adult education and teacher training' (CCCS 1965, p. 11), and collaborations were developed with the departments of music, geography, education and the German department (CCCS 1965).

From the beginning, CCCS represented resistance to the established disciplinary structures and conventions of higher education and also an aspiration to construct an alternative set of discourses that had broader social and political connotations. As Richard Johnson later recalled, its members were to be prominent in student protests at the University of Birmingham in 1968, reinforcing its reputation for dissent but also potentially creating opposition to its further growth over the longer term (Johnson interview 2013). CCCS also attempted from this early stage to define its contribution to what it explicitly described as an 'interdisciplinary' approach. For example, it argued, CCCS required 'a clear definition of the contribution which the various disciplines can make to "cultural studies" (which is, properly, an interdisciplinary and evaluative field of studies)' (CCCS 1965, pp. 3–4). For this reason, as it noted:

> We have agreed to organise a small, occasional, national seminar between critics, historians and social scientists, on the problems of method and analysis in cultural studies. This seminar should enable those closely engaged in this work from the standpoint of their different disciplines to contribute to the growth of an inter-disciplinary approach to cultural studies.
>
> *(CCCS 1965, p. 13)*

There was a clear awareness of both opportunities and threats from an early stage, and the additional requirements implied by interdisciplinary work quickly became apparent. As early as 1966, CCCS's annual report explained, 'As the interdisciplinary character of our work becomes more obvious to us, so the need grows for the "other disciplines" to be on the spot, a felt presence in the intellectual "ensemble" of the Centre. The frontiers between disciplines in cultural studies cannot be crossed from one side of the boundary only. It must be a mutual effort' (CCCS 1966, p. 33). Indeed, it added, 'With the recent large growth in social science teaching and research, there are only a few good people who are willing to take time out to spend in this intellectual "twilight zone" between disciplines – but there are some. Their presence would enormously enrich the intellectual work of the Centre' (CCCS 1966, p. 33).

There was in these early comments, as well as a consciousness of the additional time and effort demanded by interdisciplinarity, at least some optimism about the prospects for growth and expansion. However, by the early 1970s there was an increasing note of pessimism as the radical hopes expressed in the 1960s began to fade, and the Centre became more aware of the constraints involved and the resistance to its work. Its sixth report, in December 1971, had a noticeably more pessimistic tone than its predecessors. It observed that the problem of crossing boundaries between fields that it had set for itself was 'an extremely delicate undertaking, both politically and intellectually' (CCCS 1971a, p. 3). In the human sciences, it commented, disciplines were not only specialised and fragmented into 'intellectual empires', but 'they were often mutually untranslatable into one another's terms' (CCCS 1971a, p. 3). It lamented that this situation meant very difficult work, both theoretically and in terms of the methods involved. On the one hand, the traditional academic doctoral model of 'the lonely graduate student, with his text and his file cards, immured in the Library, with occasional visits to a supervisor who keeps his work on the scholarly straight-and-narrow path' was increasingly anachronistic (CCCS 1971a, p. 6). At the same time, alternative forms of practice had many obstacles in their way:

> Interdisciplinary work, especially, is poorly placed and supported: paid ritual obeisance, in terms of its contribution to 'advancing the frontiers of knowledge', in practice it runs up against the boundaries between disciplines, the division of labour in intellectual work, the awkward problem of relevance and action which flow from truly critical knowledge, the protocols of good academic manners, and the defence of institutional boundaries. . . . To live in a sort of no-man's land between fields places strains of an incalculable kind on students, staff, on the project as a whole.
>
> *(CCCS 1971a, p. 6)*

These difficulties, it acknowledged, could only be resolved through producing work of 'outstanding and distinctive quality', taking a set of problems to transform them, 'making it impossible for others to think and act those problems again in the same old way' (CCCS1971a, p. 6). This was indeed 'the last – perhaps the only – sort of intellectual work which . . . is worth doing in an iron age' (CCCS 1971a, p. 6). Nevertheless, it concluded, the further development of CCCS 'will be affected by the overall pattern of expansion in the University, and the place and position of interdisciplinary research at graduate level' (CCCS 1971a, p. 23), in other words by wider factors beyond its control.

Changing patterns of teaching, curriculum and research in higher education were appraised and further grounds for development established. By the mid-1970s, the Centre could argue that '[t]he question of proper, rigorous, inter-disciplinary work is, once again, on the agenda' (CCCS 1974, p. 4). Taught courses in the new polytechnics, established as a more technologically and vocationally oriented form of higher education in England in the 1960s, were beginning to be revised in the direction of 'communications' and 'cultural studies' (see also for example Robinson 1968), and similar steps were being taken even in some universities (CCCS 1974). In this changing context, CCCS was reviewed formally and established as an independent postgraduate and research unit, confirming its avowedly interdisciplinary character (CCCS 1976a), and in 1975–76 a Master of Arts programme in cultural studies was offered for the first time.

CCCS's publications provided a means of working out the Centre's philosophy of interdisciplinarity, in particular through the ideas of Stuart Hall and Richard Johnson. For example, Stuart Hall's introduction to *Working Papers in Cultural Studies* (CCCS 1971b) critically analysed the nature of cultural studies and the role of CCCS within it, observing that cultural studies as a field was still diverse and ill defined, 'working within too many divergent traditions for any single group, tendency or publication properly to command the field' (Hall 1971, p. 2). These *Working Papers* would therefore develop comments, discussions, work in progress rather than finished pieces of work, with a number of projects serving 'to clarify, by empirical and theoretical work, a field of inquiry with its own distinctive terrain and problematic, and to develop a critical practice in the study of culture' (Hall 1971, p. 2).

The aim of CCCS, according to Hall:

> was not to establish one more compartment in the already fragmented "map of knowledge", but rather to attempt to view the whole complex process of change from the vantage point of "culture"; and thus to make intelligible the real movement of culture as it registered in social life, in group and class relationships, in politics and institutions, in values and ideas.
>
> *(Hall 1971, p. 2)*

This required the Centre 'to trespass across boundaries traditionally well defined and well patrolled in normal academic life' and indeed 'to confront, as part and parcel of the enterprise, the costs for critical social knowledge, of the state of fragmentation in the domain of the human sciences', with the potential thus to 'reinvigorate the human sciences as a potential source of knowledge-for-use in the understanding and transformation of society' (Hall 1971, p. 2). To this end, too, graduate students engaged in their own projects but as part of a 'common intellectual enterprise' with a collaborative style of work (Hall 1971, p. 2).

A collection of *Working Papers in Cultural Studies*, 1972–79, was republished by CCCS in 1980 as *Culture, Media, Language* (CCCS 1980). This provides further evidence of CCCS's academic and social development. The preface of the collection noted that CCCS now had three staff members, two research fellows working on specific funded projects and over forty postgraduate research students. It had now left its original home in the English Department and had an independent programme. It was hoped that the present volume might help ongoing clarification of an emergent field of study, but rather than being recognised as a specific 'discipline', cultural studies would remain 'an area where different disciplines intersect in the study of the cultural aspects of society'. Moreover, as the Centre affirmed, 'The particular complex of disciplines involved, and the types of approach adopted, naturally differ from place to place' (CCCS 1980, p. 7). It was seeking an open approach, and orthodoxy was regarded as the enemy of a truly 'open' science. There were four main sections in the volume, dealing with ethnographic work, the media, language and English studies, each of which stressed the open and provisional nature of work in such a novel and emergent area, together with the diversity of the approaches that were involved (CCCS 1980, pp. 9–10).

Stuart Hall's contribution to this publication provides further evidence of intellectual development and reflections on this process (Hall 1980). Hall noted that CCCS worked with the intellectual raw materials to hand: 'It approached the problems of interdisciplinary research from those more established disciplines already present in the complement of staff and students working in Birmingham at that time' (Hall 1980, p. 15). The originating texts of the field were Hoggart's *The Uses of Literacy* (Hoggart 1958), Williams' *Culture and Society* (Williams 1958) and *The Long Revolution* (Williams 1961), and Thompson's *Making of the English Working Class* (Thompson 1964). These addressed long-term shifts taking place in British society and culture and provided an assessment of historical processes, which were being widely debated. There were tensions between political and intellectual concerns. It was not simply another academic sub-discipline, which Hall argued both 'prevented its easy absorption and naturalisation into the social division of knowledge' and also 'made the enterprise problematic from the outset in the eyes of the powers that be' (Hall 1980, p. 18). In the face of this resistance, it began to chart a more independent, ambitious, properly integrated territorial voice of its own, engaging with alternative traditions and emphasising qualitative methodology and ethnographic approaches. It also made use of translations of Western Marxist texts such as those by György Lukacs, Walter Benjamin, Jean Paul Sartre and Antonio Gramsci (Hall 1980, p. 38).

The emergence of feminism within the Centre's work challenged male-oriented models and assumptions and masculine subject-matter and topics. It sent certainties and orthodoxies back to the drawing board and redrew the map of cultural studies. The overall aim was to generate a new kind of intellectual practice and to give it an organisational form. Hall observed, 'Especially, it has experimented with ways of involving all its members, staff and students, in the shaping of that practice and in the decisions and responsibilities for setting that practice to work in a specific organisational setting' (Hall 1980, p. 43). It challenged the 'lonely, isolated, individualised and competitive-possessive form' of much humanities and social science research (Hall 1980, p. 43). To Hall, that was 'largely an obsolete and archaic kind of "knowledge production" (knowledge in the handicraft or artisan mode)' (Hall 1980, p. 44). CCCS preferred to practise the difficult exercise of genuinely sharing knowledge, exposing ideas at an early stage, trying to research and write as a collective group. A 'general theory' seminar was initiated, later becoming a compulsory requirement in CCCS's MA programme in introducing students to the interdisciplinary field. At the same time, work was divided between different research groups, each organised around a particular theme or field. This led to a more sustained engagement with existing fields and regions of research. An annual review took place in which each research group presented to the Centre as a whole some aspect of its work during the year, identifying cross-cutting themes (Hall 1980, pp. 44–45).

CCCS's journal, *Working Papers in Cultural Studies*, was essentially a collective venture, the product of staff and students working together. With the Stencilled Occasional Papers series, it gave the Centre and cultural studies 'a necessary public presence' (Hall 1980, p. 16). The first issue had been designed and overseen by Trevor Millum, one of CCCS's first successful PhD students. Through these individual and collective practices, in Hall's view, CCCS had developed cultural studies as a field, and despite difficulties and constraints, it had made some advances. As Hall pointed out, though, 'It is really exceedingly difficult both to do serious intellectual work in an advanced, interdisciplinary area and to write and produce in an immediately accessible way' (Hall 1980, pp. 45–46). CCCS was often criticised for use of obscure language, and Hall attributed this to 'the fragmentation of knowledge, its ruthless division into watertight compartments', which effectively defended and enforced orthodoxy. By contrast, CCCS was seeking to produce organic intellectuals and to actively forge a unity of knowledge and practice (see also CCCS 1977, Clarke et al. 1979).

Richard Johnson, Hall's successor as CCCS director, was also highly conscious of the social organisation of CCCS and of cultural studies as a whole, observing that, in Britain at least, cultural studies was now a 'movement' or a 'network', exercising 'a larger influence on academic disciplines, especially on English studies, sociology, media and communication studies, linguistics and history' (Johnson 1983, p. 1). Johnson saw the Italian Marxist Antonio Gramsci as providing a model for this kind of approach. It appropriated methods from literary criticism and history, with philosophy, especially Louis Althusser and Gramsci, also being important. There were continuing engagements with sociology, critiques from the women's movement and struggles against racism (Johnson 1983, p. 7). This meant that it became necessary to find a means 'of viewing a vigorous but fragmented field of study, if not as a *unity* at least as a *whole*' (Johnson 1983, p. 7). He argued that '[t]his is not a question of aggregating existing approaches (a bit of sociology here, a spot of linguistics there) but of reforming the elements of different approaches in their relations to each other' (Johnson 1983, p. 7). Cultural studies could be defined as an intellectual and political tradition, in its relations to the academic disciplines, in terms of theoretical paradigms, or by its characteristic objects of study (Johnson 1983, p. 8). In retrospect, Johnson had reservations about whether CCCS conceived of interdisciplinarity in theoretical terms and indeed whether it found an appropriate pedagogy for its teaching but pointed out that 'cultural studies' required a method for viewing the whole way of life (Johnson 2013; see also Johnson 2001). He also stressed the importance of students in the Centre being actively involved in its organisation and planning, to the extent of taking part in recruitment policies at an institutional level (Johnson interview 2013).

Both Hall and Johnson, therefore, were strongly interdisciplinary in their approach. Nevertheless, it should not be forgotten that both were also thoroughly grounded in their own disciplines, respectively sociology and history. Hall, born in Jamaica in 1932, did have exposure from an early age in a range of areas. He went to Jamaica College in Kingston, winning a Rhodes scholarship to study English at Merton College Oxford, and then became a lecturer in film and media at Chelsea College, London University, in 1961. He was appointed as the first research fellow in CCCS in 1962 and became its director in 1972. Alongside these strong interdisciplinary credentials, Hall also won widespread acknowledgement for his sociological expertise, and indeed he left CCCS in 1979 to become a professor of sociology at the Open University.

Johnson had a clearer disciplinary training but then went on to question this. He came from a prosperous family with a fruit import business in Hull, was educated at home by a governess and then went to a public school, Oundle. By his own account, although he was successful, he was 'never happy, really' and had 'quite negative feelings about schooling' (Johnson interview 2013). He read Hoggart's *The Uses of Literacy* and encountered working-class culture in Hunslet, Leeds. Although his main areas of study at school were history and English, he enjoyed art and drama in the sixth form and was accepted by Goldsmith's College London, but he accepted his father's wishes for him to study history at Clare College Cambridge. There, he recalls, 'I hated, hated Cambridge', and, 'For a year I was very miserable' (Johnson interview 2013). However, this was the college of the Elizabethan historian Geoffrey Elton, to whom he became attached. He was awarded an Upper Second in history and decided to study for a doctorate under the nineteenth-century constitutional historian George Kitson Clark, emerging eventually with a thesis on the growth of educational government in nineteenth-century England. Yet this was in the mid-1960s, when there was a growth of interest in the 'new' social history, including E.P. Thompson's book *The Making of the English Working Class* (Thompson 1964), which attracted widespread attention. Johnson was attracted to Thompson's approach to social history, adopted it in his own work, and never returned to publish work from his thesis (Johnson interview 2013). He was appointed to the Economic History Department at the University of Birmingham to teach social history and was then recruited by CCCS. Johnson thus again exemplifies the mutual synergies between disciplinarity and interdisciplinarity. He rebelled against the orthodoxies of his home discipline, history, to cultivate a more interdisciplinary outlook but was still informed by established historical methods. His work on radical education and working-class culture in the early nineteenth century and on the long-term historical roots of Thatcherism in English education exemplify Johnson's approach (Johnson 1979, 1989).

Johnson's conversion to the new social history of the 1960s exemplified the tensions within the discipline of history as a whole. The new social history was a radical movement both intellectually and politically. It rebelled against what was seen as the positivism or 'empiricism' of traditional history in which facts were gathered together from the archives to form a dominant image of the past (see e.g. Stedman Jones 1972). Politically, it belonged above all to the 'New Left', the anti-nuclear protest movement strongly influenced by Marxism that coalesced in the early 1960s. Its leaders were historians such as Eric Hobsbawm, who had left the British Communist Party after the Soviet Union's invasion of Hungary in 1956, with the aim of developing an independent intellectual and political force (Hobsbawm 1997). In the US, Graff also recognises these tensions within the discipline of history, highlighting the trend to draw on sociological concepts and to construct 'a 'historical social science' (Graff 2015, p. 163). According to Graff, 'The new histories' interdisciplinary conceptualisation lay in seeking to explore new questions by bringing the theories, sources, and methods of the social sciences to bear on the subjects and problems of the humanities' (Graff 2015, p. 163).

In the UK, the history of education as a sub-discipline was at its most popular in the early 1970s. The UK History of Education Society (HES) was formed in 1967, and it established a new journal, *History of Education*, in 1972. The leading historian of education, Brian Simon, was 'old left' in his political sympathies, still a member of the British Communist Party even after the Soviet Union's invasion of Czechoslovakia in 1968, although beginning to lose his enthusiasm for the Party at this time (Simon 1997; McCulloch 2010). Its other leading practitioners, such as Harold Silver and Kenneth Charlton, tended to follow the orthodox, more respectable social history line of mainstream social historians such as Asa Briggs (see e.g. Briggs 1972), rather than the more subversive, sociologically oriented approach of the new social historians.

The education group and *Unpopular Education*

During the 1970s, CCCS sharpened its interests in education, and especially under Johnson it aimed to make distinctive and substantial contributions in this area. This was in the context of a growth in controversies around education during the Labour government of 1974 until 1979. Under the Labour government, economic problems intensified, and plans for education became increasingly attuned to industrial and vocational needs while also seeking to alleviate renewed anxieties about declining educational standards. In October 1976, the new prime minister, James Callaghan, made an unprecedented direct intervention in a speech at Ruskin

College Oxford that was widely heralded as the start of a national 'Great Debate' in education. By 1979, the debates about education that had developed since the early 1960s had raised important questions about the nature of educational provision and its role in preparing pupils for a changing society and for the world of work. The Conservative government elected in 1979 with Margaret Thatcher as prime minister was presented with an opportunity to make radical changes in education in response to these demands.

In 1975–76, it was proposed to begin a new CCCS subgroup in education, with a programme that would be open to formulation by new people in the Centre (CCCS 1975). Its first task was to read through the basic theories of education. It was expected to host a number of academics from other centres who were visit irregularly, for example Simon Firth and Paul Corrigan at the University of Warwick, Michael Young at the IOE London and Steve Butters at Leicester. Second, it would convene sessions on educational problems directly linked to Centre members' interventions in further and higher education (CCCS 1975). Michael Green, a key member of the group, suggested several areas of theory for further development, in particular social democratic ideology, the ideas of Ivan Illich on 'deschooling' (Illich 1971), the 'new' sociology of education being taken forward by Michael Young and the work of the French social theorist Pierre Bourdieu (Green 1975). Green noted that there had been no proposal made for a section on educational history as such but that 'presumably when and where we can take in an historical dimension we will' (Green 1975). According to Johnson, who was active within this group, a historical approach was fundamental to the work of this group, informed by theory (Johnson 1976b). Thus, a disciplinary perspective remained strong within the general interdisciplinary project. A theoretical aspect was fundamental to this project; as meetings of the group held in May 1976 insisted, 'A proper history is *dependent on* and *part of* the formulation of an adequate theory' (CCCS Education group 1976b). It was suggested that the key historical phases for examination might be the period up to the Second World War, the 1950s–60s and the crisis of the 1970s but that also '[w]e need to decide where the main historical effort will go here – necessarily, organisationally, on the post-war period but an adequate theory must also be developed in friction with quite a long view of educational development within the capitalist mode' (CCCS Education group 1976b). The Bowles-Gintis work *Schooling in Capitalist America* (Bowles and Gintis 1976), published in the United States and widely influential at this time, provided a potential model, but Johnson argued that CCCS could improve on this because it was in a position to do its own research (Johnson 1976).

Progress in this work was slow, and Johnson conceded that the group had still not reached the stage of producing a first draft or a journal article and had only a weak grasp of the supposed 'crisis' or of the concept of ideology (Johnson 1976a). By July 1976, it was proposed that the education group would work on three distinct levels, first on a Marxist theory of education, second on the history of the current educational crisis and third on micro studies of schooling. Its theoretical studies were to start with a rereading of the work of the French intellectual Louis Althusser on 'Ideological State Apparatuses', which was then fashionable, developing the problematic of reproduction, including issues beyond schooling such as family, the reproduction of the sexual division of labour and patriarchal ideology, as well as class. The work was to connect with other groups, for example those on the State and on women's schooling. A 'proper history' was to be developed from these different strands of work (CCCS 1976b, item 5). The following year, the education group was ready to present a short working paper with part of the general argument of the planned book. It anticipated being able to begin the work with a rehearsal of different versions of reproduction, then to focus on education and accumulation of privilege and finally to develop the study of the crisis in education. It was still envisaged that the American work of Bowles and Gintis would provide the starting point for the book, although the group was by now critical of the notion of reproduction in *Schooling in Capitalist America* and found its use of the term 'both confusing and misleading' (CCCS Education sub-group 1977).

The education group was conscious of the need to maintain close contacts with key intellectuals on the one hand and with teachers on the other. It identified a number of significant institutions for maintaining contact. One was the IOE in London, both for its general position as the 'premiere Institute in the field' and for particular individuals who worked there, such as Bernstein and Young (CCCS Education group 1978). It noted that the University of Aston's Department of Educational Inquiry was important as a 'developing department' that was greatly expanding its research, although it apparently had only limited contact with schools and teachers (CCCS Education group 1978). It also established connections with the new Open University course E353, Education and the State (Johnson 1979).

This group took responsibility for key publications on education including perhaps CCCS's best known work in this area, *Unpopular Education* (CCCS Education group 1981). *Unpopular Education* itself was characteristic of the shared, teamwork style of CCCS in general, embodying its vision of interdisciplinarity. The education group as a whole took collective responsibility for the authorship of this work, to which five members had contributed in different ways (Steve Baron, Dan Finn, Neil Grant, Michael Green and Richard Johnson). This also led to weaknesses and lacunae in its overall analysis (Johnson 1985; Johnson interview 2013) as well as a certain diffuseness in its organisation. There were three parts to the book. The first was on the making of social democracy and education, developing a theoretical framework for the book and examining Labour Party education policies from the 1920s to the 1960s. The second part analysed the limits of social democracy in education, a strong critique of the education policies of the 1960s. The third part investigated the breaking of the social democratic settlement in the 1970s and the failure to defend the gains that had been made. It concluded that while the contest between the 'unpopular education' of social democracy and the 'capitalist schooling' of the Conservatives had been lost, the contest between capitalism and discipline on the one hand and socialism and education on the other had not yet been joined.

Unpopular Education was a significant contribution to the educational debate that attracted wide attention but contained a number of flaws. Its broad, interdisciplinary approach meant that it failed to satisfy specialists in a particular approach or discipline such as the historian Harold Silver, who concluded an extended critique of the book with a summary verdict: 'Its examination of liberal radical policies and strategies is not history. The book has messages for sociologists and political scientists, but it is not sociology or political science' (Silver 1981, p. 299). As Johnson remarks in retrospect, '[I]t's probably quite a fractured book, while certainly we took responsibility for different bits in the end, to get it done' (Johnson interview 2013). Part of its difficulty was that it took several years to be produced, so that a work that was originally intended to be critical of the efforts of a struggling Labour government was published well after the election of a Conservative government. By the time it was completed, as Johnson himself pointed out, 'There was a need to defend education from Conservative restructuring' (CCCS Education group 1985). The original motive for the book, to analyse the unpopularity of education, had actually helped to undermine arguments for further expansion, and so Johnson argued that there was now a need to find 'a middle way, an optimism about and justification for education, but an education in new forms' (CCCS Education group 1985). After the publication of *Unpopular Education*, several members left the group, but it re-formed to prepare later publications that were critical of the Conservative government's policies in education prior to the Education Reform Act of 1988, formulated to respond to what it called 'a need to defend education from Conservative restructuring' (CCCS Education group 1985).

CCCS had little involvement with the University of Birmingham's education department, despite its earlier aspirations to liaise with a broad educational community and even though it was physically based almost next door to the department on the university campus. It made some contributions to the Post Graduate Certificate of Education teacher education programme, and some members of the education department such as the historians of education Richard Szreter and Roy Lowe attended CCCS seminars, but beyond this there was little interaction. This was partly due to the aim of CCCS's education group to construct a critique of the major educational schools of research and policy making in formulating an alternative Marxist theory, programme and practice (CCCS Education group 1976a). Green contended that '[e]ducation professors weren't keen to encourage us' (Wright 2001, p. 339). According to Green, because universities were organised as cost centres, individuals generally preferred to stay in their own group rather than to collaborate with others. This tendency was exacerbated in the case of education, in Green's view, because education was increasingly a 'tortuously complex subject in this country' (Wright 2001, p. 342), treated as a 'specialised topic' rather than as 'part of our general intellectual picture' (Wright 2001, p. 343).

It was on this basis that CCCS retained its own collective practices. In September 1979, for example, it reflected that '[o]ur work is already politicised to an extent rare in academic departments – unthinkable there indeed' (CCCS 1979). It sought to build on this and to develop a 'broad socialist-feminist orientation' with an ambitious and fundamentally political long-term strategy:

> The Centre 'project' is to work *inside* a 'dominant' intellectual institution (which has a formative role for the 'organic' intellectuals of the society and in

the production and distribution of knowledge); to insist on holding upon a critical space inside in which some 'really useful knowledge' can be produced; to challenge the dominant intellectual orthodoxies and moes of intellectual work; to try to polarise the intellectual field in 'our' direction.

(CCCS 1979)

In practice, therefore, the vision of interdisciplinarity in CCCS's education group led it to be somewhat detached from the established field of educational studies and research, although contacts were established with individual members of the Open University, the IOE and the universities of Leicester and Aston (CCCS 1978). In the longer term, CCCS did have some influence on particular ideas and institutions, especially in the sociology of education, through its books, such as Paul Willis's widely praised *Learning to Labour* (Willis 1977), as well as its edited collections, conferences, contributions to debates and its many former students (Johnson 1983; Johnson interview 2013; Steedman 1989). Its accounts of popular culture were also represented in some education courses such as that of the Open University (see for example Open University 1982), where its ideas were especially congruent with new work such as *Schooling and Capitalism* (Dale 1976).

Moreover, according to Johnson, although it had many allies both inside and beyond the university, CCCS was to some extent 'quite inward-looking because it was extremely over-ambitious, so there wasn't time to dialogue much. You know, people had to come to us, and they did but. . . . I suppose we went to conferences and all that but I think in the university we felt a bit isolated as well' (Johnson interview 2013). Another academic with earlier connections to the University of Birmingham recalls that, although CCCS's seminars had always been worthwhile to attend and he had benefited from them, he had not engaged with them as much as he might have (Wally interview). This isolation became increasingly dangerous in the 1980s in spite of its programme being highly popular with students at both undergraduate and postgraduate levels. The politics of the 1980s under the Conservative government of Margaret Thatcher did not favour radical interdisciplinary centres, and the traditional disciplinary departmental structures reimposed themselves. CCCS itself retreated into the relative 'security of departmental status', justifying this move with the argument that '[t]here really is no substitute for this in the context of a Redbrick University like Birmingham' (CCCS 1986). Key members of CCCS reflected that the Centre was given relatively little formal institutional recognition, resources or support:

> . . . much more often, now, because we are, genuinely, way outside the main tendencies of work in a heavily departmental, traditional, single-honours Arts Faculty in a heavily centralized technical-scientific university; also because we are a post-graduate department in a basically undergraduate Faculty (although the very lack of attention and structure in postgraduate work has, paradoxically, given us more space to work in . . .).

(CCCS 1979)

The education subgroup also lamented that the Centre remained 'under-funded, a shoe-string organisation, in almost every dimension, a circumstance which still astounds visitors, who expect to find at least upwards of a dozen full-time lecturers and researchers, video-banks and archives etc etc' (CCCS Education Group 1979). In the end, one witness recalled, CCCS was too threatening to the university and too confrontational (Wally interview). Yet there were also positive lessons to be learned. Another interviewee took the view that CCCS's model of interdisciplinarity could be developed more in education 'if we understand it and actually take time, if we take time to understand it and put the effort into making it work' (Gillian interview). These tensions contributed to CCCS's growing vulnerability within the university and its eventual closure. It pointed out in its own defence in 1986 that it was a unique and internationally significant body, 'the only Centre of postgraduate work in Cultural Studies and also the place where this interdisciplinary approach was first developed' (CCCS 1986). Yet there were growing pressures on individuals as well as on the Centre as a whole, continuing to live in what it had described so presciently in 1971 as a 'no-man's land between fields' (CCCS 1971a) that made it increasingly difficult to maintain CCCS's separate and autonomous existence. Its director openly admitted, 'We certainly cannot sustain the project in its present form for another ten or twenty years' (CCCS 1987). In 1993, Johnson himself took early retirement and left Birmingham, and less than a decade later CCCS was abruptly and controversially closed.

At a national level, too, the freedom that had been available for CCCS as a political initiative seemed by the 1990s to have significantly diminished. The Education Reform Act of 1988 consolidated the extensive educational reforms of the Conservative government. It introduced for the first time a National Curriculum in primary and secondary schools with legal force, based mainly on traditional subject divisions on disciplinary lines. The direct powers to be exercised by the State were strengthened at all levels, including for higher education. The prospects for the future were being fundamentally changed and with them the scope for fresh developments in educational studies and research.

Conclusions

Overall, CCCS provides a model of interdisciplinarity as an intellectual project and social practice, as well as a prime example of the social organisation of interdisciplinarity in humanities and social sciences in British higher education. The model of interdisciplinarity located in CCCS was more explicit and also fuller socially, in terms of the extent of the collegiality among its staff and students and politically in its methods and theories than in the more orthodox circles of educational studies and research. It avowed an interdisciplinary rather than a multidisciplinary set of ideals and practices. There were some links between CCCS and educational studies, both within the University of Birmingham and outside and also with teachers' groups, but overall these were limited and not developed fully, reflecting the constraints of centres and departments in an academic context in developing avowedly interdisciplinary and transdisciplinary approaches to knowledge production. The CCCS's own early aspirations of a transdisciplinary kind were rarely matched in its later practices despite occasional sorties into political and social activism.

At the same time, it should not be forgotten that CCCS's work also had significant disciplinary bases, and indeed that disciplinarity and interdisciplinarity had a synergistic relationship, for example in the intellectual and political outlook of Richard Johnson. This continued to be an oppositional project against the orthodox idea that the past should be viewed only in its own context and as steps leading up to the present that effectively disassociated it from current problems and events. He maintained, rather, that 'historical reconstruction is a powerful force in the present, that all politics involves the production of consciousness of the past, and that history is important for showing the contingent character of contemporary realities' (Johnson 1983b).

Finally, the failure of CCCS to survive as a distinct and independent unit highlights the challenges facing interdisciplinary projects in British higher education, particularly relating to humanities and the social sciences. Wider social and political factors at a national level increasingly shaped the characteristics of knowledge formations in universities, while deeper cultural and epistemological issues remained largely unaddressed.

8

CRISIS AND COLLABORATION

Introduction

In her key work *Interdisciplinarity: History, Theory and Practice*, the American author Julie Thompson Klein suggests that there are 'interdisciplinary individuals' who are especially suited to interdisciplinary activities (Klein 1990, Conclusion). She associates this interdisciplinarity in particular with being at an advanced career stage, possessing specific character traits and cultivating certain abilities. As she observes, nevertheless, there are relatively few 'interdisciplinary autobiographies and biographies' by which to assess this kind of process on an individual basis (Klein 1990, p. 184). Through advances in life history work such as those of Ivor Goodson and Pat Sikes, we now have theories and models by which to understand career histories in their broader social and historical contexts (see for example Goodson 2003, 2013; Goodson and Sikes 2001). We also have recent research on academic careers in the field of education and specifically on 'transnational lives' and the 'understories' of European education over the past generation (for example Angervall and Gustaffson 2014; Lawn 2013, 2014). This chapter will trace the role of disciplinarity in the careers of selected individuals associated with the sociology of education and with the disciplines of history, philosophy, economics and psychology – broadly speaking, disciplinary individuals. It seeks to understand how far their attachment to a key discipline led them to assert a dominant role across educational studies and research or whether it served to support a continuing trend towards fragmentation and compartmentalisation in the field as a whole.

The career trajectories studied in this chapter are drawn from a sample of forty interviews with academics in different areas of educational studies and research that formed part of the project for this present work. They are presented in terms of types of approach and how far they are aligned to disciplinarity. In doing so, their testimonies add to our social histories of educational studies and research, for they provide insights from their own personal and professional standpoints of their experiences in a changing social and political context over the past forty years.

This broader context, since the 1980s, has involved a continuing growth in the direct role of the State in higher education and specifically in research, seen for example in the Research Assessment Exercise (RAE) (since 2014 the Research Excellence Framework [REF]). It has also witnessed a growth in the international dimension of higher education, as well as technological changes in the conduct of research. Educational research has been profoundly affected by policy changes in teacher education and has been subject to a range of criticisms of its quality and relevance. These wider contextual changes, no less than personal experiences, have helped to inform and guide the representations, or maps of educational studies and research that are visualised by academics in this field.

Educational research in crisis?

From the 1970s onwards, the State began to intervene openly and vigorously in different aspects of UK higher education, just as in schooling and in education more broadly, in order to achieve politically and socially defined standards or targets. Under the 1988 Education Reform Act, the Universities Grants Committee was superseded by a new Universities Funding Council (UFC). The binary divide that had existed since the 1960s between the new polytechnics on the one hand and the universities on the other was removed in 1992 through the Further and Higher Education Act. This created a unitary system of universities, although one that remained highly differentiated in terms of the resources allocated to different institutions and in the scope provided for teaching and research. In 1997, the former civil servant Lord Dearing reviewed the purposes, shape, structure and funding of higher education, recommending in his report a shift from grants for undergraduate students to tuition fees paid for through government loans at low interest, in the context of an increasing proportion of young people reaching and participating in higher education (Dearing 1997).

Particular reforms had a direct bearing on the nature of educational studies and research. In the area of teacher education, for example, from the early 1970s onwards, doubts were expressed as to the position of the disciplines in courses of teacher education in universities. Lord James, charged with the task of reviewing teacher education and training as chair of a DES committee, commented privately that while a study of psychology was important for the understanding of learning and child development, '[m]uch of what is done is clearly dominated by a desire to make "education" a respectable academic discipline, in the worst sense of those three words' (James 1971). In introducing issues raised by the James Report at the start of 1972, he acknowledged doubts as to what was meant by the study of education, for example questioning whether the history of education should be included in the study of education rather than of history: 'We can study the history of education – but this is a special part of history' (James 1972; see also DES 1972).

In an increasingly politically charged context of education reform, plans were developed from the early 1980s to lay down national rules for the content of teacher training courses, specifically with the creation of the Council for the Accreditation of Teacher Education (CATE) in 1983 and the publication of Circular 3/84, which set out criteria for courses of training. The enforcement of this by the education secretary of the time, Sir Keith Joseph, posed a threat in the view of one commentator, Peter Wilby, to the provision of educational theory and the disciplines in university training courses: 'What one assumes he wants less of – though this is not spelt out – is educational theory. As Joseph sees it, teachers need simply to know their subjects and how to put them over. Everything else in teacher training – the psychology, philosophy, history, psychology of education – is so much hot air' (Wilby 1983). These reforms were driven by a view, supported by Margaret Thatcher's Conservative government, that the university education departments were partly responsible for low standards in schools, due in particular to the progressive and Marxist theories supposedly held by the academics in these departments. Sheila Lawlor, director of the Centre of Policy Studies, encapsulated this neoliberal critique with an influential pamphlet, *Teachers Mistaught*, published in 1990 (Lawlor 1990).

The thrust of these changes in teacher education was strengthened by Kenneth Clarke as education secretary from 1990. Clarke put in place a further review of teacher training, concluding that there should be a substantial increase in school-based teacher training at the expense of the training courses in the universities. In January 1992, he announced that he wanted 80 percent of teacher training to take place in schools. As one journalist commented, 'In the world inhabited by Mr Clarke, the right-wing think tanks and the tabloid leader-writers, teacher training colleges and university departments of education are staffed by lecturers responsible for the woolly-minded "child-centred" theories which allegedly account for the low standards in so many schools' (Hugill 1992). A senior education academic, Professor Richard Pring of the University of Oxford, was quoted as protesting that '[w]e haven't taught the history, psychology, philosophy or sociology of education for at least 15 years. All our work is practically based. To pretend otherwise is absolute eyewash – a myth' (Hugill 1992). Indeed, Oxford had already developed a pioneering scheme in which trainees spent two-thirds of their time in the classroom, in a partnership arrangement. After the 1992 general election, narrowly won by the Conservative Party, Clarke's aims were consolidated through the setting up of the Teacher Training Agency (TTA) under the 1994 Education Act. Under these reforms, which destabilised not only university teacher training courses but the departments in which they were based and posed a direct threat to the broader tenets and disciplinary-based approaches associated with educational studies, there ensued an uneasy relationship between the University Departments of Education (UDEs) and successive governments, whether Conservative or Labour (McCulloch in press; Teaching and Development Agency 2006).

In the domain of university research, as with schools and teacher education, national policy pressures towards ensuring higher standards and accountability led to new structures and challenges. From 1986, a new national system for assessing the quality of research in all university subjects was created in the form of

the Research Assessment Exercise (RAE). This established a periodic examination through special peer review panels of the research conducted in all university
departments, leading to grades being allocated, unofficial league tables of research
quality and a direct link to funding allocations to universities based on the quality
of research in different departments. Again, this led to particular pressures in the
field of education. In part, this was because a large number of staff members of
UDEs were involved principally in teacher training activities, leaving them with little or no time or scope, where they had aptitude and desire, for research. In addition,
Education tended in practice to be assessed as applied research, which was rated less
highly in successive RAE exercises than the pure disciplinary research of the social
sciences and humanities. These factors combined with the effect that many education departments were allocated very limited funding for research.

Indeed, educational research was widely criticised during the 1990s both for a
lack of quality when judged as a university subject and for a lack of relevance to
the practical work of schools and teachers. Criticisms of quality and relevance often
coalesced to form a discourse that was hostile to educational research itself and that
created a view that educational research was in a form of crisis. High on the list of
complaints about educational research, too, was an argument that an emphasis on
theory was inappropriate for an applied subject such as education and in particular
that approaches to education based on the academic disciplines were ineffective or
misguided.

One example of such criticism was by Professor David Hargreaves of the University of Cambridge, himself well known for his earlier sociological and ethnographic contributions to research on schools (for instance Hargreaves 1967). In
1996, Hargreaves presented the first of what was intended to be an annual series
of TTA lectures in which he argued that the £50–£60 million per year currently
being spent on educational research was poor value for money in terms of improving the quality of education provided in schools (Hargreaves 1996). He complained
that teachers lacked an agreed knowledge base and therefore a shared technical language, largely because the 'so-called foundation disciplines of education –
psychology, sociology, philosophy and history', had failed to create a guide to the
solution of practical problems (Hargreaves 1996, p. 2). Hargreaves also compared
educational research to medical research, suggesting that whereas medical research
was broadly cumulative in building systematically on earlier work, this was not
the case in educational research, and so there was no coherent or agreed body of
knowledge in this area.

Another strong critique came from Chris Woodhead, the chief inspector for
schools, and who had established a reputation as a prominent critic of educational
standards. In a speech at the Royal Geographical Society in 1997, for example,
Woodhead castigated the 'blindingly obvious statements' dressed up in 'a language
that is, frankly, impenetrable' but that was at the same time 'explicitly hostile' to
government policy whether Conservative or Labour (Woodhead 1997, p. 5). Later
that year, Woodhead commissioned an enquiry into educational research, claiming
that '[m]illions in taxpayers' money is spent on producing unintelligible reports into

issues with no practical relevance. . . . We must look for value for money' (*Sunday Times* 1997). The enquiry was to be led by Dr James Tooley of Manchester University, a philosopher of education who was director of the Institute of Economic Affairs, a right-wing think tank (*Times Educational Supplement* 1997), before moving to the University of Newcastle in 1998. Researchers speaking on behalf of BERA, such as Roger Murphy of Nottingham University and Tony Edwards from the University of Newcastle, insisted that these criticisms were ill-founded and prejudiced but could do nothing to prevent the enquiry from going forward (*Times Higher Education Supplement* 1997).

Tooley's eventual report, published in 1998, marked the culmination of this public critique. It focused on four leading British journals in educational research – the *British Educational Research Journal, British Journal of Educational Studies, British Journal of Sociology of Education* and *Oxford Review of Education* – and analysed 41 articles by British authors published in these. On the basis of this exercise, it found what it described as evidence of partisanship in research, flawed methodology and 'academic Chinese whispers' in non-empirical research. In general, moreover, it declared, 'The picture emerged of researchers doing their research largely in a vacuum, unnoticed and unchecked by anyone else' (Ofsted 1998, p. 6). Woodhead responded by endorsing Tooley's findings, asserting that educational research was 'dross' for which universities should not receive funding and that only work that would be useful for training teachers and formulating government policy should receive a share of the educational research budget of £60 million (*The Times* 1998).

Somewhat overshadowed by Tooley's report, another report produced by the Institute of Employment Studies in the summer of 1998 focused on the organisation as opposed to the quality of educational research. This addressed the supposed isolation of researchers and the incoherence of their findings by calling for a national framework of educational research that would promote collaboration and help to build on previous research in significant areas. It proposed also that a National Education Research Forum (NERF) should be established (IES 1998). This new agency was soon created, endorsed by the government, with the aim of coordinating overall research strategy and promoting evidence-based policy (Budge 1998).

Another key initiative also emerged at this time with strong potential to respond to such criticisms and chart a way forward for educational research. This was the Teaching and Learning Research Programme (TLRP), sponsored by the Economic and Social Research Council (ESRC). It was the largest ever education research programme to be established in the UK, with an initial budget of £11.5 million, mainly drawn from money originally allocated to the outcomes of the RAE, that grew to £26 million. The principal idea of the programme was to invite proposals and commission large inter-institutional projects aiming at improving teaching and learning, thus encouraging researchers to work in cognate groups rather than as individuals, and at directing their attention towards improving rather than simply understanding education and its outcomes. It was anticipated that this would also promote interdisciplinarity, since researchers from different backgrounds and approaches would be involved in teams designed to solve a common problem. In particular, a TLRP–Technology Enhanced Learning theme was established to focus on the topic of interdisciplinarity, conducted by the Open University. Teachers would also benefit from the findings of large empirical evidence-based research. As Andrew Pollard, the inaugural director of the TLRP programme, pointed out, this was an unprecedented initiative to improve learning outcomes through educational research (Pollard 2003).

New agendas?

Thus, the political context changed radically during the 1980s and 1990s and led to new challenges to the study of education as a university subject and to educational research, with a more active and more hostile involvement on the part of the State and the creation of new national agencies to reorient the field. Meanwhile, however, the societies, journals and conferences that had been established during the 1960s and 1970s continued and often prospered, with many academics choosing to identify themselves with these networks and groups. In many ways they became entrenched still further in their separate disciplinary bases as a result of external challenge. Further disciplinary activity leading to conferences and new journals also arose during this period, especially from the sociology of education.

In the case of the sociology of education, there were particular grounds for optimism. In the 1980s and 1990s, new institutional forums arose that were related to the sociology of education as a disciplinary community. One new forum for debate from 1978 onwards was the Westhill Sociology of Education conference, held annually at Westhill College, Birmingham. It was intended to use the device of a regular conference to raise and discuss ideas, present current research and establish contacts, thus creating an informal network that would in time become a disciplinary community. Papers presented at these conferences were revised and published in edited collections dealing with particular themes such as schooling and classrooms, teaching, the curriculum, deviance, gender, race and class (see Barton and Meighan 1978, 1979; Barton, Meighan and Walker 1980; Barton and Walker 1983; Walker and Barton 1983). These conferences were significant in terms of providing an organisational focus and a regular meeting place for sociologists of education in the absence of a formal society. Another set of workshops, held on a regular basis at Whitelands College in London, also began to develop a closely related discussion around qualitative methodology in education, which was again dominated by sociological concerns (for instance Burgess 1984, 1985). A further conference venue then became established at St Hilda's College, University of Oxford, with a regular conference on ethnography and education, which led to a new journal being created in this area in 2006 under the editorship of Geoff Troman (*Ethnography and Education* 2006; Walford 2011).

A number of other new journals were also products of this disciplinary activity. The *British Journal of Sociology of Education* (*BJSE*) was launched in 1980, edited by Len Barton. This was envisaged explicitly as 'a forum for the consolidation and development of debate' (*BJSE* 1980, p. 3), which would 'try to initiate themes and discussions and ventilate controversies, all to the benefit of the discipline' (*BJSE* 1980, p. 4). The editorial board of the new journal included representatives of a range of theoretical perspectives and methods. In terms of its readership, meanwhile, the journal aspired to 'consider the needs of both education and sociologists', since, as it commented, although the needs of these two constituencies might not always diverge, and they had much common ground, 'it would be foolish to pretend that they are always identical' (*BJSE* 1980, p. 5). A further journal, *Gender and Education*, was launched in 1989, in this case leading to the establishment of a new society, the Gender and Education Association, at a meeting at the University of North London, with annual conferences following on from this. Another journal, *International Studies in Sociology of Education*, was launched in 1991, again emerging from the Westhill network, which had now relocated to the University of Sheffield with Len Barton.

A related journal, the *Journal of Education Policy*, was published from 1986. This arose from the growth of interest in policy issues that had been stimulated by State activity in this area and was not specifically disciplinary in its approach. However, one of its founding editors, Stephen Ball, was himself a leading sociologist of education (see for example Ball 1981, 2006), and the new journal became, in part at least, a vehicle for what became known as 'policy sociology' (Ball 1990a, 1990b). The other founding editor of *Journal of Education Policy*, Ivor Goodson, was a sociologically oriented historian of education who made a significant contribution especially in the 1980s and 1990s though his active promotion of 'curriculum history'. This took a specifically disciplinary approach to the study of the curriculum, rooted in social history, while drawing on interactionist studies and the sociology of knowledge (Goodson 1985). His book *School Subjects and Curriculum Change* (Goodson 1983) documented the close relationship between high-status academic knowledge on the one hand and patterns of resource allocation and associated work and career prospects. A series of over twenty books under the general theme of Studies in Curriculum History, with Goodson as series editor, developed a range of new work in different national contexts. On a larger plane, Goodson also promoted the field as a whole as a joint director with Malcolm Clarkson of an independent academic publisher in educational studies and research, Falmer Press. This small publishing firm produced nearly 500 books in this field between 1977 and 2009 and, at its peak during the 1990s, was publishing an average of well over twenty new books each year on a wide range of topics, stimulating further research and providing opportunities for fresh work to be published. Falmer Press was eventually taken over by a large academic publisher, Routledge, which was also responsible for publishing a very high proportion of academic journals and books in education.

At the same time, new opportunities were also emerging internationally. Regular and fast air travel and new technology made it easier to communicate and collaborate on a global scale and encouraged the development of transnational organisations including new societies, conferences and journals. For example, in 1985 a small conference held in Leuven, Belgium, led to the formation of the

European Association for Research in Learning and Instruction (EARLI). This association launched an official journal, *Learning and Instruction*, in 1991 and increased its membership from 400 in 1991 to 1,000 in 1999 and to over 2,000 by 2009. Also, in 1994 the European Educational Research Association (EERA) was established, with an annual European Conference in Educational Research (ECER) and its own journal, the *European Educational Research Journal (EERJ)* from 2002. The European Union also provided new opportunities for large-scale research funding, as well as collaboration in international research projects. Besides such large formal institutions, too, many smaller and more specialised groups could come together, often on a disciplinary basis. One such was the International Standing Conference for the History of Education (ISCHE), initially planned by the British historian of education Brian Simon and others in the late 1970s and by the early twenty-first century holding annual conferences for historians of education around the world in Australia, the United States, Mexico and elsewhere, as well as in a wide range of venues around Europe. The 2014 ISCHE conference, held in London for the first time, attracted 550 delegates from over 60 countries.

Overall, then, while there were many challenges to educational studies and research towards the end of the twentieth century, as the national State moved in to take more active control of the university sector, there were also opportunities to find space for new developments in this area. Often these were provided beyond or outside the formal departmental structures of the universities, through the societies, journals and conferences that had in many cases been established before the State had begun to intervene. It was these that offered on the one hand an infrastructure for new and expanding approaches and on the other a sanctuary for areas of work that might otherwise have been lost. In the process, these developments provided a new context for disciplinary collaborations, and it is in the experiences of those actively involved in such work over this time that we can most readily see these relationships in operation.

Sub-sub-sectors of sociology

The sociology of education had been consolidated as a distinct area of study and research in the 1960s and in the 1980s and 1990s was becoming a dominant feature and focus of activity. In 1982, the sociologist of education Olive Banks could affirm that, from the 1950s onwards, 'both sociology itself and the sociology of education as one of its branches established themselves firmly in the British educational scene' (Banks 1982, p. 18). Banks also detected indications that differences among sociologists of education were becoming less visible, with 'not only a desire for greater unity but a move away from positions which, in their extreme form, at least, are certainly quite irreconcilable' (Banks 1982, p. 28). Yet this did not necessarily mean that it became a unified, still less a coherent sub-discipline or sub-field over this time. Indeed, in the 1980s and 1990s, there was clear evidence of fragmentation into smaller groups as a range of activities led into different directions and gave rise to newly emerging divisions.

These growing tensions were observed in retrospect by a number of senior academics in educational studies and research interviewed by the present authors for this volume in the academic year of 2012–13. Of the forty individuals who were interviewed for this purpose, ten, here anonymised with fictionalised first names although retaining gender types, identified themselves as being closely related to sociology, with most though not all of these describing themselves as sociologists or sociologists of education. Six of these were men, while four were women; seven were near the end of their careers or were retired, and all had achieved professorial status in their careers. Overall, they had direct experience of a wide range of university departments of education, societies, conferences and journals in the field since the 1970s. It was this personal and professional experience that served to highlight underlying sources of friction in and around the sociology of education. They each had access to academic networks, and these coincided to some extent but also manifested significant differences.

Most of these respondents had some sociological training at undergraduate, postgraduate or doctoral level. Four of them had a sociology undergraduate degree, and all of these had gone on to take a doctoral degree in an area of sociology related to education. Each of these expressed a particularly strong affiliation to the discipline of sociology. Alan, for example, commented: 'I've always looked at education from a broadly sociological point of view and I've always felt that I was part of the sociological community as much as the educational community' (Alan, interview). Even more strongly, Jeff declared his primary link to sociology rather than to education: 'I see myself primarily as a sociologist, a sociologist of education rather than an educationalist, whatever that might be' (Jeff, interview). Gillian also stressed her sociological roots: 'I describe myself first and foremost as being a sociologist who happens to be in education but I'm interested in key issues around education' (Gillian, interview). Nick, who had followed his undergraduate sociology course with a master's degree and then a doctorate in the sociology of education, also emphasised a strong commitment to sociological perspectives that could then be applied to education:

> [S]ince that initial sociology course gave me that conceptual framework for understanding those issues, I've applied them to education as a field and I've used that as a framework for understanding my own life and that of my family . . . Of course, because it pops up anywhere . . ., the underpinning of my analysis of practice is sociologically informed.
>
> *(Nick, interview)*

Only one of the professors, Felicity, had taken an education undergraduate degree, in her case a four-year bachelor of education course, but she had followed this with a doctorate in the sociology of education and reflected that 'I suppose you would classify me as fairly straightforward as a sociologist of education, so I have a lot of links with the mainstream field of sociology' (Felicity, interview).

The other respondents came from a range of undergraduate backgrounds in history, politics, economics, psychology and English. Most of these had postgraduate or doctoral training in sociology and also identified with sociology as a discipline, although in some cases with a measure of ambivalence and a suggestion of more interdisciplinary sympathies. One, William, affirmed that he was a sociologist but working in the area of education (William, interview). Others were less certain. Kevin, for example, suggested that his primary discipline was 'Sociology, I think' and added that 'the reason I hesitate is my interest in sociology stems from issues in education' (Kevin, interview). Another, Edward, acknowledged that his closest reference point was sociology but insisted that 'I don't have an ology, I'm trying to find an answer to a practical question in education' (Edward, interview). Ursula confessed that she had 'never been that comfortable with describing myself as a sociologist, partly because of my undergraduate background and the fact that a lot of the ideas that I draw on, I draw back from my English literature and criticism background rather than coming to them through sociology . . . although I might then convey a more sociological application' (Ursula, interview). Only one of the respondents had neither an undergraduate nor a postgraduate training in sociology, and she described herself as a 'self-educated sociologist' who had further formal study 'on my plans for the time when I've got a bit more time' (Cynthia, interview).

Most of these respondents affirmed that sociology had become the dominant discipline in educational studies and research compared with the history, philosophy and the psychology of education. According to Felicity, for instance, 'sociology, without doubt, has colonised the study of education at the expense certainly of psychology, certainly of history of education . . ., probably with the exception of economics of education' (Felicity, interview). However, some did raise doubts about the extent of this dominance, and one went so far as to argue that psychology remained the most influential approach, just as it had been earlier in the twentieth century. According to William, psychology continued to dominate the field of education: 'I think there's been a psychologising of education. And I think, in the psychologising of education, philosophy of education, history of education, sociology of education, have been marginalised . . . since the 2000s, but maybe even a bit before then.' In addition, William suggested, the emphasis on school improvement and school effectiveness in education policies in the 1990s encouraged 'a very individualised, almost neoliberal, discourse that is about putting pressure on teachers and schools to transform themselves and in the process transform society'. On this view, sociological perspectives provided a counter-view to the 'individualising' of education. The 'atheoretical, apolitical way of seeing processes and practices in education', the underlying approaches based on psychology and school improvement, had ignored 'a whole lot of social inequalities that are almost put on the backburner' (William, interview).

At the same time that sociology came to occupy a key position in educational studies and research, significant differences developed among those who aligned themselves with the discipline of sociology. In part this was reflected in the range of activities that were often in competition with and even in opposition to one another. Networks emerged around particular people and institutions and were distinctive not simply in disciplinary terms but also in relation to methods and ideologies. One such method was that of ethnography, which had led to the St Hilda's Oxford ethnography conference. One of our interviewees, Jeff, identified very strongly with this development and saw it as being particularly significant. Jeff commented: 'I still see myself as an ethnographer . . . but there were a whole bunch of people all of whom are now luminaries in education in different ways' (Jeff, interview). Jeff recalled that each of the conferences had its own theme but was 'very open in the sense of people were encouraged to give papers'. He continued:

> And it was a very, very supportive context. You gave a paper – I think they were circulated if possible – you'd do a presentation and then there was a discussion. There was lots of time for every paper. And the discussion tended to be very supportive, the whole culture and tenor was one of a supportive relationship. . . . And it was very formative in that sense, both in terms of ideas, methods, possibilities and an intellectual community, again a network, which for a long time was very, very strong and it led on to all sorts of other activities – publishing, research – and many of these relationships still exist for me in one way or another.
>
> *(Jeff, interview)*

This conveys a vivid description of an intellectual network at an everyday level, providing support and further development for its members.

By contrast, another of our interviewees, Alan, had rather different memories of the ethnography conferences. Alan recalled that 'initially most of the other people in my little sociology of education community didn't go to BERA because in the 70s BERA was dominated by people like [name] and co who were interested in more or less psychological research on learning and so on'. They went instead to St Hilda's, but, Alan suggests, it was 'taken over by various people' and 'so the character changed somewhat'. Unlike Jeff, who emphasises the supportive nature of this conference, Alan remembers an antagonistic dimension: 'It wasn't friendly in its early years: I remember [. . .] absolutely savaging one of my colleagues at one of our meetings.' As a network, he adds, 'it was a mixture of people but it was very much geared around quite a thriving little world in the 1970s and saw itself as separate from BERA'. Moreover, according to Alan:

> It was a mixture of people but it was very much geared around a broadly interactionist approach to sociology of education. . . . And it was separate from BERA to a large extent in that it didn't take over a specifically educational orientation, so it wasn't really about how to improve learning or that kind of stuff. It was – in fact, it was antagonistic to that kind of orientation really. It wasn't particularly politically oriented at that time, either.
>
> *(Alan, interview)*

In general, according to Alan, 'There was a lot of activity, it was quite differentiated in terms of the orientation that people had. I mean, there was some overlap as well but there were quite sharp differences, actually, in membership' (Alan, interview). This view suggests that the networks in and around the sociology of education represented a tendency towards fragmentation in the sub-discipline, amounting in some cases to factionalism.

Jeff also recalled this process of fragmentation taking place from the 1980s onwards. With the Westhill conferences and the launching of the *BJSE* in the early 1980s, he suggests, apart from membership, the sociology of education 'had all of the accoutrements of a society', with a conference, regular publications and a journal: 'And that was a focus of publishing work and, again, forging and producing changes and reflecting conflicts within the community. So there was a real sense of there being a research community in sociology of education' (Jeff, interview). However, according to one, this relative unity began to dissolve amid the increasing pressures of the late 1980s and 1990s:

> But then, of course, in the late 80s it began to dissipate and it began to fragment as people moved off into sub-sub-sectors. So, rather than being sociology of education they became feminists or anti-racists or . . . school ethnographers, or one subset moved off into becoming school-effectiveness researchers . . . and management theorists as well . . . school management. From the late 70s through the 80s most of these people were focused around the sociology of education but then went off in all sorts of different directions, new societies were founded, new journals were founded and new communities and networks, or sub-communities and networks.
>
> *(One, interview)*

On this account, it appears that the policy reforms of the late 1980s and 1990s may have had the effect of exacerbating internal tensions within and around the sociology of education, leading to greater fragmentation.

There were several aspects involved in such disputes. One revolved around rival research methods, in particular between qualitative and quantitative approaches. These themselves reflected arguments about the value of positivist and empirical research based on large data sets, as opposed to theoretical discussions of culture. For example, Felicity recalled the 'cultural turn' in the sociology of education in which, as she comments, 'we all started deconstructing everything and problematizing the categories and . . . started talking about what sex you are, what gender you are and what race you are'. Indeed, she concludes, 'So the whole way in which we define the field has changed rapidly and in the height of it, we looked back on those people who counted things as positivist fascists. . . .' (Felicity, interview).

Another area of contention was about whether the sociology of education should attempt to contribute to the improvement of education rather than confining itself to critiques. Ursula, for example, argued that it was important to 'become more relevant again to practitioners and policy makers' and especially, as she proposed, '[t]o stop with the endless critique and start thinking a bit more constructively about what practitioners and policy makers need to try – perhaps to try to recognise that actually people out there are trying really hard and they don't always need to be sneered at, they could sometimes need to be supported' (Ursula, interview).

In addition, there were ideological dimensions to these differences. For example, Basil Bernstein, who had become the inaugural Karl Mannheim Professor at the IOE in 1977, was not always regarded wholly sympathetically by other sociologists of education. One, Kevin, observes that while Bernstein was the key academic influence, Kevin himself was not part of what he describes as the Bernstein 'mafia', which, he ventures to suggest, 'do form a fairly hermetically sealed, self-referential group' (Kevin, interview).

A further tendency that contributed to fragmentation of the sub-discipline in the 1990s was the departure of some academics who had formerly been involved in the sociology of education into groups that focused on particular issues such as gender and ethnicity in relation to education. One, for example, identified with issues around race and gender. Paradoxically in a way, this led her to engage more closely with the British Sociological Association than with BERA because, she suggested, the BSA was more likely to address these issues than was a BERA conference, which she saw as 'a predominantly white, middle class, male group', while the BSA was 'much more diverse' (interview).

Speckled birds

Besides those mainly associated with sociology, we also interviewed 21 senior academics in educational studies and research who aligned themselves with other disciplines: six with history (including with Richard Johnson at Birmingham), five with philosophy, four with economics and six with psychology. These also noted continuing disciplinary activity taking place in the 1990s and early 2000s, especially in the societies and centres and through the journals. They also reflected a growing trend towards fragmentation and compartmentalisation within and around the disciplines over this time.

The six individuals interviewed who described themselves as historians were all senior figures, based in a range of institutions, four of them either at the end of their careers or retired, five men and one woman. They came from different educational backgrounds, but five had doctorates in history (the other in English), and these five also had undergraduate qualifications mainly or in part in history. One, Arthur, described his approach as being 'history with a social purpose . . ., engaged historical scholarship', which he associated with the radical social historians Christopher Hill and E.P.Thompson (Arthur, interview).

None of the historians we met had been principally involved with BERA, and some had never been to a BERA conference. On the other hand, at least three had been closely involved in the History of Education Society and attended its conferences nearly every year. Annette, for example, had never attended a BERA conference but had attended both the History of Education Society (HES) conferences and the conferences of the Women's History Network since the early 1990s: '[T]here was opportunity for networking and I think it's the networking that brings you together with people that you've read, people whose work you've read' (Annette, interview). Similarly, Ben acknowledged that 'to me, the History of Education Society was a fascinating kind of network of people who were driven to study history from one motive or another' (Ben, interview).

William, too, had been involved in the Historical Association and the History of Education Society, rather than BERA, as he recalled, because 'I already knew by this time, late 70s, that if I turned up at a History of Ed conference I was, one, surrounded by people I knew, you know, some of whom I related to really well and some less well; and that it was also a place where there would be a really interesting raft of scholars from overseas' (William, interview). The pressures facing education departments and more specifically the history of education seem to have been significant in helping to encourage this movement towards the History of Education Society. As William contended, 'I'd been fighting my corner at [name of affiliation] and probably hadn't always felt that, as historians, [we] got the recognition that we might have merited. . . . And I'm, throughout this period, thinking, look, we've got a great learned society, we're doing our stuff, give us a bit of recognition' (William, interview). Moreover, according to William:

> This sounds more than personal to me, I think. Isn't it the nature of an academic society, a network, to have colleagues who are speaking the same language, who are comfortable, who build on each other's work and that might be made even stronger by the sense of being, in a sense, alienated or estranged from their own departments and want somewhere as a refuge, almost, from all that?
>
> *(William, interview)*

Thus, at the same time that the history of education as a discipline was being driven out of teacher education courses, its position was being consolidated as a research network in the History of Education Society and in the regular conferences and its journal, *History of Education*, as well as increasing international connections.

Some sub-disciplinary tensions also played themselves out around the HES. Richard Johnson had not viewed the HES as sufficiently adventurous intellectually to lead radical new developments in this area. According to Ben also, in the 1980s the HES was a 'largely, sort of, conservative society', although 'it was beginning to open up and become aware of broader trends in cultural history' (Ben, interview). It was also giving greater attention to issues of social class, especially under the influence of Brian Simon, and increasingly associating itself with new approaches to gender. On the other hand, as he observes:

> [W]e've all got our intellectual and disciplinary interests but . . . we've also got mouths to feed and jobs to have and retain. And the problem for historians of education, I think – and it's a problem that's simply been growing over the whole period that I've been in teacher education – is that we had a secure footing, because we were a recognised discipline that contributed to theory,

which was a necessary part of the teacher's professional preparation. And that secure footing has disappeared.

(Ben, interview)

This institutional pressure also encouraged a trend in the sub-discipline away from its earlier interests in early modern and nineteenth-century history of education and towards an emphasis on more recent history that could more plausibly inform an understanding of contemporary educational policies (see also McCulloch 2011).

In relation to the philosophy of education, too, our respondents who associated themselves with philosophy could also claim specialist grounding and an affinity for philosophy rather than education. These five philosophers had all gained doctorates in philosophy or more particularly in the philosophy of education, as well as having a grounding in philosophy at the undergraduate level. They were four males and one female, with two either at the end of their careers or in retirement. Three were involved in BERA conferences, two less so. One, Bill, explains his preference for philosophical writings over education in rather colourful terms: 'But if you look at my library at home, you'll find a modest number of educational books and a large number of books on philosophy, theory, culture, history, because I find a great deal of educational writing pretty ghastly . . . moribund, technicist, neurotic, self-absorbed, myopic and generally pretty badly written' (Bill, interview). He adds: 'I don't mean to be too critical because I think people work under tremendous pressure and people come into education . . . already conditioned by their normative attachments. And it's very hard for them to break free from those. But we do need to be more analytic' (Bill, interview). Bill claimed that the disciplines of education had 'almost disappeared' but that 'the challenge is to recuperate some of the best thinking' (Bill, interview). For Bill, it was the 'analytical disposition' in a broad sense that mattered most in this rather than whether it came from philosophy, sociology or psychology.

Another philosopher, Tom, argues that teacher education in the early 1990s had lost a sense of theory in favour of an emphasis on competencies, which became standards:

So it was at that time that textbooks became much more pragmatic, tips for teachers, that type of thing. And it was also at that time that you ended up with a situation where people going into education didn't really understand what education was. They weren't really having a discussion about the meaning of education or its purpose, they were simply there to make sure that kids passed an exam or that they could teach seven-year-olds or twelve-year-olds history in the most efficient manner possible. Totally instrumental and data-driven.

(Tom, interview)

This echoed the view of historians of education that education had become to some extent hollowed out as a field because of the loss of philosophy, history and disciplinary knowledge.

The economics of education was, by contrast, an example of a sub-discipline that had become much sought after in educational policy circles. We interviewed four senior academics who described themselves as economists of education, two males and two females, one of whom was at the end of their career. All of these were thoroughly grounded in economics at the undergraduate and doctoral levels. One, Susan, acknowledged that she came from 'a fairly firm discipline base' in economics, although she now had shifted her academic identity and saw herself as 'an educationist who comes from an economics background'. She now published in both education and economics, which presented different challenges, not so much in terms of discipline but because of methods; 'you start to have not only disciplinary boundaries but you have method boundaries' (Susan, interview). Susan's chosen method is quantitative in its approach, and according to her there had been insufficient recognition of this approach in education. Unlike in the US, for example, where there was a stronger quantitative tradition in education:

> [Title] is increasingly publishing quantitative articles but it's still a big uphill battle. And in my personal opinion, some of the pieces published in [title], you know, wouldn't make it into a good economics journal, for example, in terms of their method, which means that you get the skew on the rankings [of journals].
>
> *(Susan, interview)*

Another economist, David, also regarded himself as an educationalist, although he also expressed some criticisms of educational studies and research. He suggested that economists of education would most often network at the conferences of the Royal Economics Society rather than at BERA, partly because of 'quality issues' and also because he was interested in a particular style of research that was rarely represented in the education field:

> I'm interested in people who can showcase fantastic, large-scale, really robust quantitative projects, and that's not just using administrative data, it's people who are doing really large-scale, interesting primary survey collection including like, you know, psychologists, for example. And I just don't see enough of that when I go to BERA. I see a lot of people doing small-scale conceptual work that's interesting but it's quite a long way removed from the stuff that can influence the kind of research I want to do.
>
> *(David, interview)*

As with Susan, David saw key differences between education journals and economics journals, in that economics journals were 'incredibly hierarchical so it's absolutely clear to everybody where the best and the worst are' (David, interview). Education might be rebalanced in favour of quantitative research, but 'we're always going to be limited in the extent to which we can do it because the kind of people who are going to research education are going to be the kind of people who are interested in education' (David, interview). This meant that it was difficult to publish his work in education journals. David concluded:'I think it's hard to sit in a discipline [education] that isn't quantitative at all. It's hard for us to get published in [title], we are still a minority activity within the discipline as a whole' (David, interview).

Finally, there were six interviewees who regarded themselves as being associated with psychology. These were all of professorial standing, two of them at the end of their careers or in retirement, three men and three women in all. All had some psychological background at undergraduate level except for one (whose undergraduate background was in physics), and all had completed PhDs in psychology, although these varied in terms of developmental, clinical and educational psychology. Two were involved in BERA, while four had gone to a BERA conference only very rarely, two of them never.

One, Larry, observed that his early career, having been appointed to his department in 1976, 'certainly locates me very firmly within psychology'. At that time, as he recalls, 'it was still quite common for people to be appointed in the traditional disciplines that fed education, so most departments/faculties/schools of education would want psychologists, sociologists, philosophers, even the odd historian, someone in economics of education if they were particularly big, I suspect' (Larry, interview). Larry affirms that he had not wished to be in a psychology department where he would do 'pure psychology for the sake of doing pure psychology', but:

> . . . was always likely to be happier either in a post that came with some expectation that you were going to have an applied aspect to your work or to be in a department, and there are other departments of course of applied psychology, which I might have got involved in, of education which at that time you could be quite readily engaged in as a psychologist with an interest in education.
>
> *(Larry, interview)*

In terms of their disciplinary allegiances, also, the interviewees tended to emphasise the particular type of psychology that they related to. One, Amy, pointed out that developmental psychology was not always closely related to education and that some developmental psychologists preferred to dissociate themselves from it. Indeed, Amy claimed that there was no such thing as the psychology of education; instead, she suggested, 'there's the way psychologists can ask questions that have implications for education or the way that education can produce challenges that are good questions for psychologists to address' (Amy, interview). On the other hand, another psychologist, Nathan, preferred not to think of his work in terms of disciplines:'I just do it.' According to Nathan, 'I think it's often driven by an issue to which one wants to get an understanding of it . . ., whatever works, really. . . . And whatever seems to fit really. So I've never really been very conscious of academic disciplines except when reflecting on the thing in a much more removed sort of way' (Nathan, interview).

Among all the disciplinary groups, as we have seen, there was some sense that the specific group to which respondents belonged was now in the minority in relation to the field as a whole or even in terminal decline. This was the case even for sociology, which overall was recognised as having become the strongest group. Psychology, as we have seen in the earlier chapters of the current book, was for several decades acknowledged to be the dominant discipline in a field that was largely shaped by the disciplines. So, it is striking that at least some of the psychologists interviewed for the current study saw their own work as being outside the mainstream of educational studies and research. Two of them, as previously noted, had never been to a BERA conference. One of these, Amy, even suggested that 'I've never been to a BERA conference and I wouldn't really see myself as perhaps even being welcome at a BERA conference' (Amy, interview). More generally, Amy reflected, psychology had been 'demonised' in educational circles because of earlier work on intelligence testing and issues around eugenics, and so 'I think psychologists who've been successful in education departments have often shed their psychology baggage or cards, in very subtle ways' (Amy, interview). Another, who has had a stronger role in BERA, maintains that it is only the 'common language' in relation to research methodology that has kept her in the field of education: 'I don't really feel like I have a specialism and I don't have an expertise in education, really. I'm a bit of a . . ., I don't know what I am – I'm still just a speckled bird. The methodology is what I always fall back on, that's my main primary interest' (Sophie, interview).

At the same time, the psychology respondents often registered a view that they were not connected in a positive way with their parent discipline either. Partly, as with the economists, this related to compromises that had to be made in preparing and presenting their work of publication in psychology journals as opposed to education journals. Psychology journals had a higher impact factor than educational journals, and impact and citations were generally regarded as more important in psychology submissions for the RAE than they were for education submissions (Wendy, interview). It was also linked to the organisational arrangements of the BPS, which has a very small section in educational psychology and another section in developmental psychology.

Conclusions

There is ample evidence here, then, then disciplinary activity continued to be significant in educational studies and research at the end of the twentieth century and that the newly dominant discipline, sociology, was itself divided into sub-disciplinary groups and factions that limited its capacity to provide a united or coherent outlook, still less clear leadership for the field as a whole. The nature of these networks sometimes promoted fragmentation and even factionalism within the discipline rather than cross-disciplinary endeavour, while in some they strengthened the notion of a disciplinary-based network. In the early twenty-first century, there continued to be many attempts across educational studies and research to adopt a more integrated and interdisciplinary approach. The question remained whether the challenges confronting the field would allow it to resist a countervailing trend towards fragmentation and compartmentalisation.

9

CROSSING PATHS?

Educational studies and research in the twenty-first century

In the early twenty-first century, the relationship between the academic disciplines and interdisciplinary approaches to teaching and research returned to the prominent position in debates over higher education that it had occupied in the 1960s and 1970s, forty years before. The issues involved were broadly similar in both periods, although the emphasis in the new century across higher education tended to be on consolidation and competition rather than on growth and opportunity. In this chapter, we examine the themes developed around interdisciplinarity in teaching and learning in higher education in these first two decades of the century before reviewing the changing context of educational studies and research and the prospects for interdisciplinarity in this area.

Interdisciplinarity in the twenty-first century

Higher education policy in the UK in the early twenty-first century, initially under the Labour governments of Tony Blair and then Gordon Brown until 2010, continued to favour an increased concentration of resources in research around key priority areas. According to the 2003 white paper *The Future of Higher Education*, for example, the current performance and productivity of UK universities were excellent, but the Government could not 'stand still' in the face of increasing international competition (DfES 2003, p. 24). Significant new investments were being made in university research, but, to be fully effective, research needed to be organised through greater collaboration 'among institutions and across traditional disciplines' (DfES 2003, p. 28). This would lead to a concentration of resources in key areas of research, which was applauded for its likely beneficial outcomes: 'Concentration brings real benefits, including better infrastructure (funding excellent equipment and good libraries), better opportunities for interdisciplinary research, and the benefits for both staff and students which flow from discussing their research and collaborating in projects' (DfES 2003, p. 28). The older model of lone scholars working on their own in the university library was frowned upon, and it was proposed that larger groups of researchers either in one subject or in related subjects performed particularly well, 'at least in the natural and social sciences'. The humanities were not mentioned. Overall, it continued, collaboration was to be encouraged, although it was not to be 'imposed top-down', and there was no 'blueprint' for particular forms of collaboration. Instead, as it affirmed, it was more appropriate to encourage different forms of collaboration to 'grow organically over time' (DfES 2003, p. 29).

More than a decade later, David Cameron's Conservative government returned to this theme, albeit only in the final section of its own *Higher Education White Paper of 2016*. This also affirmed that the UK had a world leading reputation in research and innovation but that this success could not be taken for granted and the system could be even more effective through greater collaboration. As it argued, 'The challenges facing the world are complex, and increasingly require multi- or interdisciplinary approaches' (DfBIS 2016, p. 68). It therefore endorsed a recent report by Sir Paul Nurse to consider how Research Councils could help to support research most effectively. A new body, UK Research and Innovation (UKRI), would bring together the seven different funding councils for research to allow 'a greater focus on cross-cutting issues that are outside the core remits of the current funding bodies, such as multi- and inter-disciplinary research, enabling the system to respond rapidly and effectively to current and future challenges' (DfBIS 2016, p. 69).

Unlike the reports of the 1970s, this policy discourse took little account of the institutional and cultural constraints of universities, such as the entrenched nature of university departments, that effectively constrained interdisciplinary activities. It also linked a trend towards interdisciplinarity with the accountability of university research to national priorities, or what critics described as an 'audit culture' (Holmwood 2010). Nevertheless, it provided a favourable context for further support for interdisciplinarity to be forthcoming from different quarters. In relation to research, the head of policy at the Higher Education Funding Council for England (HEFCE) recognised the importance of disciplinary diversity and suggested that combining a broad range of disciplines improved the impact of research, while recognising that there were concerns that the Research Excellence Framework (REF) provided a barrier to work that spanned disciplinary boundaries (Hill 2015). This followed a report conducted by Elsevier for the UK's four funding bodies and the Medical Research Council that showed UK interdisciplinary research activity growing in intensity, in line with a global trend (Elsevier 2015). The Higher Education Academy (HEA) argued strongly that interdisciplinarity was 'the new zeitgeist' for higher education and that '[r]ecognition of the need for interdisciplinary research to address global, societal challenges is accelerating' (HEA 2015, p. v). However, in terms of teaching in higher education, it complained that while this 'evolving landscape' had generated new demands for 'global citizens' and 'future employees who have the skills to work in multi-professional teams and adopt holistic approaches to complex problems', the dominant structures were still maintained on a 'conventional, academic basis' (HEA 2015, p. v). It noted also that while most universities were committed to interdisciplinary approaches, individual academics and programme directors tended to be less enthusiastic in this regard. In this situation, it recommended more co-teaching, interactive methods and programme-level strategies.

Internationally, too, there were signs of fresh interest in interdisciplinarity among official agencies. In Denmark, for example, the Danish Business Research Academy (DBRA) and Danish Forum for Business Education (DFBE) brought out a joint report in 2008 calling for 'thinking across disciplines' (DEA/FBE 2008). In the US, the National Academies of Science published another report, *Facilitating Interdisciplinary Research* (NAS 2015). The science periodical *Nature* published a special issue in September 2015 on the theme of interdisciplinarity, insisting in its editorial that interdisciplinary science must break down the barriers between fields to build common ground. It suggested that interdisciplinary science comprised 'a synthesis of different approaches into something unique' and might be compared to 'the wine and underwear shop, not the hypermarket' (*Nature* 2015). In May 2016, the Global Research Council held a meeting in New Delhi of research funders around the world, hosted by Research Councils UK and the Indian Science and Engineering Board, which issued a new report supporting interdisciplinary research. The key principles of interdisciplinarity that it upheld in particular were research excellence, a diverse approach, research infrastructures, creating a robust and supportive environment, review and evaluation, capacity building and management and career development (Global Research Council 2016).

This new wave of advocacy for interdisciplinarity found ready proponents in the UK. In Durham University, for example, Veronica Strang, an anthropologist, teamed up with Tom McLeish, a physicist, to issue a comprehensive practical guide to evaluating interdisciplinary research. Interdisciplinarity, they argued, 'serves to reunite the academy and strengthen its collective intellectual foundations' (Durham University 2015, p. 6). A formal review of the REF by Lord Stern in 2016 emphasised the need for interdisciplinary approaches to be given much greater attention (HEFCE 2016a), and this was duly supported in the consultation for the next REF in 2021 published in November 2016 (HEFCE 2016b).

One of the most interesting of these fresh calls for interdisciplinary approaches was a report commissioned by the British Academy entitled *Crossing Paths*. This report, produced by a working group led by Professor David Soskice, insisted that there was a 'deep need to take active steps to promote interdisciplinarity' (BA 2016, p. 5). It accepted that universities were organised mainly on disciplinary lines, as were research councils, most leading journals and publishers and indeed the BA itself (BA 2016, p. 5). However, it urged, while maintaining vigorous disciplines, interdisciplinary research was 'central to academic innovation, leading to new subdisciplines both within and across existing disciplines' (BA 2016, p. 5). In order to promote this, it proposed that panels of established academics should be set up to evaluate interdisciplinary research and training, that universities should enable their experienced and interdisciplinary researchers to guide projects and institutions and that universities should consider providing centres for interdisciplinary research to enable researchers to work together across departments.

It was in this broader context, in which higher education was again being encouraged to promote interdisciplinarity, that educational studies and research sought to develop during this period. Yet the pressures that this field of study were subjected to were rather more specific and pressing. These were the issues that had become highly familiar during the previous century: a continued lack of status within the academy and criticisms of both the research and the teacher training base.

A contested field

Many of the established characteristics of educational studies and research persisted into the new century. Nonetheless, they persisted in a rapidly changing social and political context, which increasingly raised questions about the position of this field of study in a university setting. University-based teacher education came under growing pressure from government policies, which in turn threatened to destabilise the university education departments in which teacher education was based. Educational research as measured by the regular RAEs (HEFCE 2001; HEFCE 2009), followed by the REF of 2014 (HEFCE 2015), was adjudged at its best to be as strong as in any other social science subject in the UK but had a relatively high percentage of low-scoring 'outputs' (published works selected for the exercise) and a gradually decreasing number of active researchers being included. The most successful education submissions to the RAE/REF tended to be those that emphasised social science methods and critical engagement with the disciplines rather than issues of teaching and learning or the school subjects. These included in particular the IOE, Oxford and Cardiff University. The IOE had become one of the leading education departments in the world, and in 2014 it merged with University College London, bringing to an end its unique position as a standalone specialist institution while cultivating links with a wide range of subject areas in its new context. At Cardiff, education was associated with the social sciences in a large combined school. In the 2008 RAE, Cardiff did not submit an education submission and decided instead to submit its researchers in this area to sociology. Wales was left with little credit or funding in educational research until Cardiff again entered an education submission in the 2014 REF (Cardiff University 2015). In Scotland, while the universities of Edinburgh, Glasgow and increasingly Stirling included substantial research of high quality, overall funding for educational research remained low and the profile of education in the academy continued to be precarious.

The Conservative–Liberal coalition government formed by David Cameron as prime minister from 2010 to 2015 posed new challenges to university education departments. Michael Gove, the secretary of state for education, supported an increased amount of teacher training taking place in schools rather than in a university setting, and his policy of introducing academies and free schools permitted teachers in the classroom in such institutions with no training at all. The education White Paper published in November 2010, *The Importance of Teaching* (DfE 2010), was anticipated in advance of its publication as a means by which 'Gove serves notice on teacher training'. It would, it was predicted, lead to the 'biggest upheaval in decades' (*TES* 2010a). The White Paper announced that DfE funding for ITT would in future be confined only to graduates who had at least a Second Class degree, in order to help improve the quality of teachers and teaching and to raise the status of the profession. New routes into teaching for able young people would also be developed and extended, in particular Teach First, which recruited graduates who would not have considered teaching to train for a short period before being placed in schools as paid trainees. At the same time, Armed Forces leavers would also be encouraged to become teachers, through a Troops for Teachers programme to sponsor service leavers to train as teachers. There would be stronger incentives for the best graduates to come into teaching, especially in shortage subjects. Teacher education itself would also be reformed and diversified by improving and extending school-based routes into teaching rather than relying on courses based in higher education (DfE 2010; see also McCulloch in press). Critics warned that these changes might lead to very severe budget cuts and in some cases to closure of university education departments (*TES* 2010b).

At the same time, the DfE continued to become increasingly active in educational research, especially through the disbursement and promotion of funding for research projects of particular types. In April 2011, following a selection process, it provided a grant of £125 million for the Sutton Trust and Impetus Trust to establish and endow a new charity, the Education Endowment Foundation (EEF). This provided a 'toolkit' as an accessible summary of educational research, with evidence on the impact of different teaching approaches and interventions on pupil attainment (EEF (2015). The popular science author Ben Goldacre was also invited by the DfE to examine how to improve the use of evidence in schools and responded in March 2013 with a ringing endorsement of randomised controlled trials, which the EEF quickly supported (Goldacre 2013a, 2013b).

Another area of educational research in which the State intervened actively at this time was that of character education. In December 2014, Nicky Morgan, who had taken over from Michael Gove as secretary of state for education earlier in the year, announced a new fund to improve character education in England, with the ultimate aim of England becoming a global leader in the field. This provided a £3.5 million grant scheme for character education projects in schools (DfE 2014). Moreover, a further £1 million was allocated to expand research into the most effective ways in which character could be taught, an amount that would be matched by the EEF. The Jubilee Centre for Character and Virtues at the University of Birmingham, established in 2012 with the support of funding from the Templeton Foundation based in the US, was a strong advocate of character education.

In Scotland, a significant development was the Applied Educational Research Scheme (AERS), funded by the Scottish Funding Council and the Scottish Executive Education Department. This provided about £2 million from 2004 to 2007 for the universities of Edinburgh, Stirling and Strathclyde, which operated collaboratively as a consortium, coordinated by Professor Stephen Baron of the University of Strathclyde with close links to the ESRC's TLRP. SCRE, once such a prominent body in the national and international field, became a centre within the Faculty of Education of the University of Glasgow in 2002, slowly fading from view. The Centre for Educational Sociology at the University of Edinburgh, originally founded in 1972 as part of the Department of Sociology, belonged from 1998 to its Education Department (Humes 2007; Powell 2012).

Amid these instances of change and decline, the longstanding societies and journals created in the second half of the twentieth century were also a source of stability in the field. New organisations were created to address current concerns, for example the Institute of Effective Education at the University of York, established in 2011 and directed by Bette Chambers, committed to more effective uses of educational research. Nevertheless, in a number of cases, the institutions of educational studies and research were now able to mark anniversaries that recognised how long they had survived, adapted and indeed often flourished in unpropitious times. The SCSE, founded in 1951, changed its title on its fiftieth anniversary in 2001 to the Society for Educational Studies (SES) to denote a broadened composition and a makeover of its Standing Conference to become an annual seminar. In 2011, it was able to celebrate its sixtieth anniversary, followed by the *BJES* in 2012 (Davison 2012). BERA, SERA and *BERJ* also passed their fortieth anniversaries in 2014 as the Philosophy of Education Society and the History of Education Society, and their associated journals approached their respective half-centuries (see for example PESGB 2016).

At the same time, there was a discernible fragmentation or splintering of the field into specialist groups linked with particular topics, methods and sub-disciplines. In 2016, BERA supported 33 special interest groups (SIGs) as shown in Figure 9.1.

Each of these SIGs received funding and support to conduct its own events for members. These activities were designed to stimulate interest and increase membership, and yet they also suggested a diversification of the field into a large number of specialisms. To this extent, the anxieties of Ed Stones at the founding of BERA in 1974 that the Association might promote 'indiscriminate spawning' of specialist interests appeared to have been borne out. In the 1960s, the field had been parcelled into four disciplinary categories linked together through the philosophical rationales of Paul Hirst and Richard Peters. By the early years of the twenty-first century, the disciplinary basis of educational research had been widely criticised and to some extent undermined, only to be superseded by a much larger number of categories and the challenge of retaining a fully integrated rationale.

This process of diversification was also reflected in the description of the field provided for education submissions to the Research Excellence Framework. This was outlined in the way shown in Figure 9.2.

In the outline, research in education was defined as 'multidisciplinary' with a 'diversity of content and methodology'. Its 'disciplinary traditions' included but were not confined to the four 'foundation' disciplines of history, philosophy, psychology and sociology, together with nine others: anthropology, applied linguistics, economics, geography, humanities, mathematics, statistics, political science

Alternative Education
Arts Based Educational Research
Comparative and International Education
Children and Childhoods
Creativity in Education
Curriculum, Assessment and Pedagogy
Early Childhood Education and Care
Educational Effectiveness and Improvement
Educational Leadership
Educational Research and Educational Policy-making
Educational Technology
Higher Education
History
Inclusive Education
Independent Researchers' Forum
Literacy and Language
Mathematics in Education
Neuroscience and Education
Philosophy of Education
Physical Education and Sports Pedagogy
Post-compulsory and Lifelong Learning
Postgraduate Forum
Practitioner Research
Race, Ethnicity and Education
Religious and Moral Education
Research Methodology in Education
Science Education
Sexualities
Social Justice
Social Theory and Education
Socio-cultural and Cultural-historical Activity Theory
Teacher Education and Development
Youth Studies and Informal Education

FIGURE 9.1 BERA special interest groups (2016)

and science. This did not appear to encourage breadth, still less interdisciplinary approaches to educational or related social problems.

Hence, educational studies and research in the early twenty-first century were confronted by a number of competing pressures. Growing State activity in the field, supported by large amounts of funding, reflected agitation for greater accountability and direct relevance to professional and public concerns and also focused attention in particular areas. Well established societies, conferences and journals continued to support academic research and studies based mainly in higher education. At the same time, a tendency to develop increasing specialisation within these institutions ran against initiatives to promote interdisciplinarity in the field or to articulate its overall purposes and mission.

Unit of Assessment 25: Education 26. Descriptor: Research in education is multidisciplinary and is closely related to a range of other disciplines with which it shares common interests, methods and approaches. This diversity of content and methodology requires the sub-panel to be flexible in setting out the boundaries of work relevant to the REF. 27. The UOA may be broadly described as being concerned with research in the areas identified in the following illustrative lists:

- Research which addresses education systems, issues, processes, provision and outcomes in relation to sectors, such as: early years, primary, secondary, further, higher, medical, workplace, adult and continuing education. It also includes teacher, healthcare and other forms of professional education, vocational training, and informal, community and lifelong learning.
- Research which addresses substantive areas, such as: curriculum, pedagogy, assessment, language, teaching and learning; children, young people, student and adult learners; parents, families and communities; culture, economy and society; teacher training, professionalism and continuing professional development (CPD); special and inclusive education; participation, rights and equity issues; technology-enhanced learning; education policy; the organisation, governance, management, effectiveness and improvement of educational institutions; education, training, workplaces, industry and the labour market; comparative, international and development education.
- Research which employs a range of theoretical frameworks and methodologies drawn from disciplinary traditions, including, but not limited to: anthropology, applied linguistics, economics, geography, history, humanities, mathematics, statistics, philosophy, political science, psychology, science and sociology. Research in the field of education deploys a range of qualitative and quantitative methodologies with structured, exploratory and participatory research designs. These include, but are not limited to: surveys, experiments and controlled trials; ethnography, interview and narrative enquiry; action research and case study; evaluation research; critical theory and documentary analysis; analytic synthesis and systematic review.

FIGURE 9.2 Criteria for education submissions (REF 01.2012)

Educationists and interdisciplinarity

These developing traits of the field were keenly observed also by the senior academics interviewed as part of this project. Eight of the forty education academics interviewed for this purpose defined themselves broadly as educationists rather than primarily as specialists in a particular area or discipline. All of this group of eight (four men and four women) were of professorial level: four had recently retired and could recall developments in the field dating back to the 1950s and 1960s; two were at the end of their careers in post, and two were in mid-career. They came from a range of academic backgrounds. Only two originally had had interests in education as undergraduates, the other six having begun with history and international relations, history, geography, English, economics and physics respectively. All had gravitated towards education in their postgraduate study, all except one possessing doctorates in education. All were regular attenders at BERA conferences and, in the cases of the three who had the experience of being based in Scotland, also at SERA conferences.

In terms of defining their own positions in the field, one of these educationists, John, commented:

> [I]f people said what is your discipline, I would say, well, I haven't really got one, or, if you pushed me, I'm probably a sociologist more than others. But I really see myself as an educationist, somebody who ... was interested in educational issues and problems and who would bring whatever resources I could find to bear on them.
>
> *(John, interview)*

He added that his reticence to claim sociology as his discipline was due to a lack of thorough grounding and qualifications in the subject: 'I was more a sociologist than anything else but, probably, because I'd never done a sociology degree . . . never did read the great sociologists in the original . . . but more of an educationist than a single discipline person.' His own contribution, he suggested, was broadly about 'teaching in schools' and bringing a 'critical and analytical eye' to related issues.

Similarly, another respondent, Sarah, affirmed that she regarded herself first and foremost as an educationist: 'I would say it is education first and I think that derives from my experience as a classroom teacher.' Interests and direct experience in school teaching, for these interviewees, seem to encourage a broad identification with education as opposed to a specialist approach. A further respondent, Brenda, who also defined herself as an educationist rather than as a specialist in a particular area, argued that it was possible to have education itself as a specialism. For her, such a definition depended on one's own context and colleagues, the nature of the professional and academic networks involved:

> I think it's about your institutional allegiance and which conversations you want to be in, which journals you want to write in, where you want your work to be considered most significantly, so you choose your community and you define yourself in relation to that. I think what matters, for me, is around the work that we can do related to educational institutions and the people who work in them. And I don't really mind how people come at that.
>
> *(John, interview)*

Sarah also noted that her own expertise was 'more towards practice and school-related knowledge, policy-related knowledge'.

Some criticisms were voiced among these generalists about certain aspects of work based in the different disciplines. Paul had the strongest critique in that he proposed that educational studies were framed too much in terms of the disciplines because of the higher academic status generally associated with these, whereas it might have achieved more by promoting itself as a 'practical' community rather than as a 'theoretical' community. In this sense, he suggested, education differed from the community of medicine within the academy:

> [W]e actually got our status through theorising, through social sciences, not through practical things. So, unlike the medical community, that happily, for

historical reasons, has been able to coexist within the academy as a practical community as well as a theoretical community, we actually chose the more theoretical route, which I believe has always left us running to catch up because we've never made it into the mainstream disciplines. There's a few people that have done that but, generally speaking, we've not done that.

(John, interview)

This view was one that related the problems of educational studies and research to their location within a hierarchy of academic knowledge, suggesting that over the longer term, the field had suffered by moving in the wrong direction to defend its position in the academy. Another respondent, Harry, noted that although he was himself interested in sociology and social theory, some writings in social theory failed to engage with practice and policy-making communities 'in ways which are intelligible'. According to Harry:

> I've just been looking at the proceedings for a conference I've been asked to chair a couple of sessions at and most of the abstracts seem to be written in Greek, as far as I can see. You know, social theory for me is fabulous in that it illuminates and explains but if we're writing in language that's unintelligible to the average person then, you know, we're not doing ourselves any favours, we're cutting ourselves off.

(Harry, interview)

Another, Margaret, expressed reservations about the 'showmanship' that she found 'off-putting' of some theorists who regarded themselves as 'a sort of God almighty'. These were frank observations that highlighted some of the tensions in and around educational studies and research.

On the other hand, none of these educationists opposed the application of the disciplines in educational studies and research, and indeed they often stressed the importance of maintaining healthy disciplines. For example, Veronica insisted that interdisciplinary activities should not be fostered 'at the expense of others who want disciplinary focus'. Indeed, she asserted, 'I think we should have room for both and both have got value'. She noted a need for more researchers with strong skills in quantitative research and that many departments of education had become weak on the history of education. With regard to the latter, indeed, she found it 'shocking' that 'the people you're teaching don't know the most rudimentary things about the history of education', such as how and why independent schools had arisen:

> [T]hey hadn't thought about the history or politics of education, which is a kind of sine qua non for somebody of our age, probably, in the way we were educated, you couldn't not see education as in the political sphere and involving historical change. But sometimes students have been encouraged to see teaching apolitically and ahistorically, as a set of instrumental practices, because of the ways they've been educated themselves.

(Veronica, interview)

These reflections again located changes in educational studies, in this case particularly with student teachers, within a medium-term shift in the broader educational, social and political context.

Enthusiasm for the disciplines among these educationists was often framed in terms of combining the disciplines in an interactive way rather than leaving them or the individuals who belonged to them to operate on their own. Errol, for example, observed that he had once come across a large university where there were fifteen specialists in one of the education foundations who rarely if ever met to discuss their discipline. These, he averred, were 'excellent people but scattered about within a topic- and project-based organisation'. By contrast, he argued, the study of education required 'a multi-dimensional structure that brings together staff with common disciplinary backgrounds and interests on a regular basis, and at the same time facilitates interaction with colleagues whose disciplines also contribute to action-oriented projects and programmes'. He lamented what he regarded as 'the scarcity of cross-citation in the literature of education and the social sciences' and commented: 'There's no real crossover, even in the discussion of issues where contributions from several different disciplines would facilitate the emergence of fresh insights and effective policies and outcomes.' Harry was more positive about the current possibilities for 'crossover', for instance in working with a philosopher whose ideas he did not fully understand, commenting that 'because we have a common interest in education, we can work together . . ., it's interdisciplinary in the sense that actually any substantive field of study in education, I think, has to draw upon a range of perspectives of a different disciplinary nature'. John also voiced this preference for a combination of disciplines with an interdisciplinary outlook or purpose. As he put it, 'I'm afraid I want to have my cake and eat it.' Sociological research was 'incredibly important', while he also accepted that 'you can only understand . . . today's problems through adopting in part a historical perspective'. This kind of interaction, according to John, was also more possible from his experience in Scottish universities rather than in most English universities because of their different traditions.

Some of these educationist respondents, furthermore, described their own work as interdisciplinary in nature. For example, Paul located himself within the study of pedagogy, which he described as 'definitely interdisciplinary' and his own contribution as interdisciplinary 'in the sense that it's focused on pedagogy across a range of subjects and teaching contexts and so forth'. Indeed, in this sense, he insisted, 'all the major issues that affect the education community are interdisciplinary'. John also affirmed that 'I think I do tend to operate as an interdisciplinary type of person'. By this, he meant 'synthesising across disciplines and drawing out professional relevance for teachers who are wanting to improve their practice'. He saw interdisciplinary studies as being very important in education due to a need to be professionally relevant but also because 'they do tend to reveal some distinctive insights that you can't get in a single discipline'.

The contributions of academic educators such as Lawrence Stenhouse and Donald McIntyre, with broad interests in issues of learning and teaching, were regarded as providing models of interdisciplinary work. Margaret admired the 'polymath' ideas of McIntyre and his awareness of issues in educational psychology, philosophy, mathematics and science that he engaged with in his research on teachers and teaching. Paul recalled Stenhouse's work on the Humanities Curriculum Project in the late 1960s, emphasising that he 'certainly stood up for the notion of education research and people who were doing the task of teaching working . . . very closely together'. John also singled out Gerald Grace's approach to critical policy scholarship in relation to teachers and urban education as a key influence, describing this as interdisciplinary, 'even though he's a sociologist first and foremost with a strong historical element'.

It is fair to emphasise the legacy of educationists such as Stenhouse and McIntyre and also the many colleagues who followed their work in the new century such as Sally Brown, Jean Rudduck and John Elliott. Stenhouse had died in 1982 and McIntyre in 2007, but their ideas continued to be celebrated and invoked, not only in the names of buildings at the universities of East Anglia and Cambridge but in their broad conceptions of education related to teaching and learning. There was here an interdisciplinary vision of educational studies and research as practical and applied enquiry drawing eclectically across a wide range of disciplines in the social sciences.

The dilemmas of interdisciplinarity

More broadly, it was the obstacles in the way of combining forces that appeared to be most prominent. Problems included broad political and economic issues, but internal divisions also seemed difficult to overcome. Even where disciplinary distinctions were not directly involved, compartmentalisation and fragmentation became increasingly pronounced, and it was pessimism about the prospects of working together that was evident rather than optimism.

This pessimism was in some cases linked to a negative view about wider social and political trends that were held to be undermining the potential contribution of educational studies and research. According to Arthur, for example, a 'broad neoliberal agenda' supporting the privatisation of education was hostile to critical studies in education. Tim also pointed to what he regarded as a 'narrowing of what counts as valid and worthwhile research', with a failure to ask 'big questions'. This, he argued, was partly due to governments discouraging big questions because of the relatively short electoral timeframe: 'They're not interested in research that has large headlines, they're not interested in the footnotes, and they want something that they can publicise and do a publicity puff about before the next election.' Nevertheless, in most cases, it was fragmentation within the field itself that was held to be primarily responsible for a failure to develop an interdisciplinary approach. Different kinds of fragmentation were highlighted. Intellectual incompatibilities appeared to discourage a common outlook even within the same department. Institutional barriers evidently presented a further set of obstacles.

For a number of respondents, it was difficult to work closely with individuals with different kinds of backgrounds and training across their own departments.

One economist, Lynn, recalled that in her first department in the 1970s, inter-disciplinarity had been regarded as a desirable goal: 'You were to abandon your discipline background; interdisciplinarity was a great mish-mash but somehow it was valued intellectually above all these artificial divisions of disciplines' (Lynn, interview). She did not approve of this and preferred to work within her own particular area. Larry, a psychologist, was anxious that an interdisciplinary approach might 'lose that notion of discipline and everything gets a bit softer and fuzzier'. According to Larry, this presented a risk, especially as 'educational research is often criticised in that kind of way as being a bit fluffy' (Larry, interview). Jeff, a soci-ologist, regarded education, as a field, as 'a kind of diaspora of different disciplines and all sorts of ad hoc collectivities of people based around issues or perspectives or problems'. He was often not able to engage with many of these colleagues on an intellectual or academic basis. In his first department, again in the 1970s, as he recounts, 'there were people there with whom it was very difficult to have a sen-sible academic conversation because we didn't share the same language, we didn't share the same history and background, we didn't read the same things, we didn't use the same concepts'. In his current department, also, this continued to be the case, as he notes that 'there are certainly groups of people whom I find very alien and I'm sure they find me very alien as well in terms of our personal projects but also in terms of what they conceive of being useful and sensible' (Jeff, interview). This meant in his view that there was little that could be described as 'educational theory' to bring colleagues together in a common cause. On the other hand, he could draw on ideas from outside his department in political and social theory and also in psychosocial studies.

Harold, a psychologist, also claimed that his experience of large inter-institutional ESRC projects reflected the difficulty of working with colleagues from different backgrounds and difficulties. From his point of view, 'The issue was that around the table, in trying to run this project, we were coming to it with fundamentally differ-ent approaches.' They held project meetings lasting for two days with some strong characters who saw problems from their own disciplinary positions and experi-ences. Harold argued that interdisciplinarity was an obstacle in that the perspectives of the researchers were not complementary but existed in parallel universes. This being the case, he concluded, it would be very difficult to cultivate interdisciplinar-ity across an education department (Harold, interview).

The character of the range of approaches within an education department was also a source of informal fragmentation. Some respondents saw it as particularly difficult for psychologists to find common ground with sociologists and vice versa, although these have been overall the two dominant disciplines in educational stud-ies and research. One economist, David, noted that economists are comfortable working with psychologists, partly because their methods are fairly similar but also because of a similar theoretical base. David argued that 'they have a theoreti-cal underpinning to their research that's based on the idea of individual behav-iour and understanding individual behaviour'. In relation to sociologists, he could understand those who were interested in individual agency such as rational choice theorists but not those who did not focus on individuals. Thus, he supported 'bringing people together like that who sit within different disciplines of education but are actually quite similar to each other in what they are trying to do' (David, interview). Harold also argued that psychology and sociology were incompatible: 'The value systems of sociology and psychology are essentially contradictory in terms of the underlying theory. They concern notions that are almost opposite on different dimensions, creating conceptual fireworks, non-overlapping' (Harold, interview).

This kind of fragmentation within departments was frustrating to some respondents who held to an interdisciplinary ideal. Edward, for instance, commented that 'I, as an education researcher, don't have to link up with someone in the sociology department to be interdisciplinary.' In his view, 'the research is better the more we pull things together'. In examining issues about attainment or poverty, 'You must consider politics, school clustering, the nature of pedagogy, the nature of housing, health issues, all of that'. Yet, he reflected, he was 'almost entirely isolated' in taking this approach within his own department (Edward, interview). As Felicity put it, 'the silos are still pretty clear' (Felicity, interview).

Others placed greater emphasis on restrictions imposed by the structures of higher education. For example, Ursula attributed these problems at least in part to the divisions between university departments. She acknowledged the signals emanating from the ESRC and her own institution about the need for greater interdisciplinarity. However, she suggested, 'apart from the odd token gesture, it never seems to me that very much is done about that'. She felt that this was because of the departmental structure of the university:

> I was talking to a policymaker about this just recently when they were asking me do I know someone in another department and I was trying to explain why I didn't, and how segmented life is in English universities and you don't tend to meet people unless you happen to be on the same senior committee or something like that.
>
> *(Ursula, interview)*

She added that 'although there's constant reference to this need, very little tends to be done to facilitate that'. Moreover, she argued, the persistently low status of educational studies and research within the university exacerbated this problem because it was 'constantly . . . slightly denigrated and doesn't quite fit in with other disciplines' (Ursula, interview).

Beyond these university institutions, the structure of the REF attracted criticisms of a similar kind. With up to four published outputs being expected for each academic submitted to the REF, there was a view that interdisciplinary research would not be given high grades in the exercise. One respondent, Wendy, suggested that 'as much as we argue cross-disciplinary stuff is great, very little of it goes into the higher journals'. She was interested in looking to the 'borders' of her area of study but had decided that for the purposes of the REF, she needed to publish four papers in journals within her discipline before she could safely do so. Wendy continued:

> So the problem with moving to the boundaries is it's fine once I have my four papers but until then . . . and the other thing is I don't know how short the next cycle [for the REF] is going to be, so those four need to come out first. . . . And I think that's how a lot of academics treat it, I need to get those four . . . and then I [can do what I want]. . . . But I'm not sure that helps British academia.
>
> *(Wendy, interview)*

On the other hand, as the editor of a leading journal, Wendy was also trying to introduce annual reviews and special issues that might encourage such work.

At another level, some respondents suggested that the established conferences and societies might do more to encourage interdisciplinary research. Gillian regarded the field of education as compartmentalised and suggested that conferences such as BERA reflected this. Her own research interests were in two discrete areas, and it was rare for these to be discussed together at conferences: 'And so you rarely have those cross-conversations because of the way in which things are positioned separately, although we're all interested and we have a common goal in education and we're all interested in that field of education. But I do think that things are very much more compartmentalised.' She suggested that ESRC seminar series were able to support these 'cross-conversations' more effectively from her own experience.

> Because at the beginning we sat down and we let each person have a say and we listened to what each person thought and we had probably about three or four meetings to make sure we each understood the other and what we were hoping to achieve. So it was that cross-dialogue which was actually very important to that being successful.
>
> *(Gillian, interview)*

At the same time, she added:

> But also that you can disagree with someone and understand that their interests may not be the same as yours but it doesn't prevent you from actually having a common and a coherent voice in terms of what you're trying to achieve and also the messages that you're trying to convey. So it is possible to have that cross-dialogue and that cross-working.
>
> *(Gillian, interview)*

Gillian concluded that this kind of opportunity for discussion had the potential to generate a greater common understanding around many issues; 'when you do have these discussions you very often find that your ideas are not that dissimilar to someone else's but because we've not had the conversation you don't know that'.

Tom was also critical of larger conferences such as BERA, which he described as 'a tower of Babel now where people are not really communicating with each other with any language that I think was there beforehand'. He argued that the language of the four key disciplines had been replaced by greater diversity and fragmentation with little coherence: 'It lacks an R.S. Peters to bring it together as a coherent whole.' He protested: 'There're too many subjects, too many themes that educationists are trying to address and they're not addressing them adequately.' According to Tom, this meant in turn that it was not possible to present a united front with a core philosophy, either to policy makers or to the academic community. For Tom, as with a number of other respondents, Peters continued to resonate with his ideas. While Stenhouse provided a model of interdisciplinarity as practical theory, Peters embodied a moral theory, perhaps not in his drawing and quartering of the field, but in the way he conceived and mapped education as a whole.

Conclusions

In the early years of the twenty-first century, interdisciplinarity became a fashionable theme in higher education and a frequent target for government and funding agencies. Educational studies and research largely failed to engage with this agenda in practice despite the wide range of teaching and research interests involved in university education departments that were potentially available to address it and take it forward. This was overall a measure of the particular struggles of the field. Its teacher training base was endangered, while its research continued to be subjected to criticism alongside the growing threat of the State and the rise of non-university agencies. Its societies, journals and conferences continued to be a source of stability and strength. Nevertheless, as a field it was contested between different factions and interests and provided a home for a number of competing groups, a 'tower of Babel'.

In these circumstances, a number of leading figures warned of impending changes. John Gardner of Queen's University Belfast argued in his presidential address for BERA in 2010 that educational researchers should stop 'sticking their heads in the sand' and continued: 'Would the general public notice if there was no educational research? As president of BERA, I'm not sure they would' (Gardner 2011; *THE* 2011). A former BERA president, John Furlong of the University of Oxford, asserted that if education was to survive as a university-based study, it must show the value of allowing teachers to engage critically with evidence and demonstrate its practical relevance (Furlong 2013b). Furlong and Lawn, in a detailed study of the disciplines of education, concluded, 'If theoretical, disciplinary-based knowledge was uncertain and if key aspects of professional knowledge were by definition *implicit*, then the traditional contribution of the disciplines to understanding in the field of education became increasingly open to question' (Lawn and

Furlong 2011, p. 8). One university provider of teacher education, Michael Day at Roehampton University, anticipated that many centres of teacher education would be closed in favour of a smaller group of university departments (*THE* 2013). Its pioneers had preached unity in a common cause. Its champions had often mapped out a means of developing a partnership that would bring with it respectability and success in the wider academy. Now, as it fought for survival in an often hostile environment, it sought once again to come to terms with its long-term challenges.

10
CONCLUSIONS

The broad field of educational studies and research has a very rich history and a strong and positive story to tell. It has made an enormous contribution over the past century to our understanding of education not only in our own society but in many different societies around the world. Its range has been extensive indeed, as it has included for example the many concepts of education, the management and leadership of an expanding education system, different levels of schooling and higher education as they have become established and grown, a large number of subject areas, the understanding of individual development at different stages and inequalities in education of many kinds. Many highly distinguished researchers have spent their careers studying the many aspects of education in greater depth, creating a large literature base and a set of theoretical understandings and empirically based appraisals that continue to be built on today.

Despite this record of substantial achievements, it is also a field that has suffered from persistently low status and a poor reputation across the academy, often undermined by criticisms of both its quality and its relevance. These criticisms are a further dimension of the social history of educational studies and research. In England at least, they stem in large part from its origins in teacher training, which contributed to a general lack of acceptance as an academic discipline. At the same time, its base in the academy and aspirations for respectability as a social science encouraged a critique that it was too far remote from the everyday concerns of teachers and classrooms to be of practical value. Over the long term, exponents of the field struggled on both of these fronts with its borders in dispute to establish a secure territory.

Educational studies and research experienced a relatively early phase of rapid development in Scotland in the first decades of the twentieth century, but in the UK as a whole the field developed late compared with the United States and continental Europe. In order to establish itself, it was supported by cognate learned societies, notably the British Psychological Society and the British Association for the Advancement of Science, and then by overseas funding. The emergence of the Institute of Education within the University of London in the 1930s created an institutional focus and a model for the further development of the field around the country. Public funding of educational research was not allowed until the 1944 Education Act and remained low until the 1960s.

This field of study has developed in the context of the UK largely within a university setting, itself a sector that has changed rapidly from an elite set of institutions at the start of the twentieth century to a much larger and highly diverse and differentiated category catering for a much wider proportion of the population. This base in the universities has often cultivated a critical and independent outlook, orientated towards examining schools, curricula and other educational phenomena from the elevated vantage point of higher education. Teachers, schools, local education authorities and charities have all made significant contributions whether as the authors or as the recipients of research, as part of and alongside this sustained and increasing investment on the part of the academy.

Until the 1960s and 1970s, this growing field was not directly regulated by the State or the central education department, which generally avoided becoming actively involved in details of the school curriculum and even more so in the university sector. From this point it began to have a more direct influence, partly through funding support for students and research, also based on more detailed regulation of teacher education, and in part also in the pursuit of an integrated national education policy. By the twenty-first century, this active intervention had become established to the extent that the State was now a key partner and sponsor of educational research in the universities, with the power and increasingly the inclination to direct resources and support in particular directions. This included a challenge to the previously accepted role of the universities and a sponsoring of alternative providers, especially in the schools.

It was in the period after the Second World War, one of educational expansion and economic growth, that the general infrastructure of educational studies and research became established through first SCSE and then BERA. The characteristic conferences, academic societies and journals also originated mainly in this period from the 1950s to the 1970s. In many ways the field also reached the peak of public acceptance and support in the period between the 1944 Education Act and the economic and political difficulties of the late 1970s. It was able to operate in the context of a growing university sector and expanding education system, with additional support from the influx of public funding from the 1960s. After this period, with the growth of direct State involvement and more critical attitudes to teacher education and educational research, the institutions of educational studies and research were obliged to adapt to a much changed political and social context.

These changing educational, social, political and economic developments thus shaped and structured the field of educational studies and research in a powerful way, providing the general contours for this social history. Yet we must look to the relationships and institutions created by the teachers, scholars and researchers who have inhabited the field to fully understand the dynamics involved. These included university departments and centres but also journals, texts, conferences and academic societies. These played a full part in the life of the academy, even if they were not always fully accepted by it, and in so doing they defined their field and indeed themselves. There is scope for a great deal of further research on the social and historical experiences of this broader university project – the journals, societies, centres, conferences and other spaces and places in the field. Increased comparative, international, transnational and cross-cultural awareness is also likely to extend still further our understanding of this distinctive field of study.

The field of education grew so rapidly and so broadly that it was soon very difficult to provide an account of it that could provide what Collingwood, in the 1920s, described as a *speculum mentis* (Collingwood 1924). It was in these circumstances that the disciplines of education established themselves, as different ways of conceptualising and addressing the problems of education. Psychology rose first, before the Second World War. From the 1960s, sociology became probably the foremost single discipline. History and philosophy both developed potent rationales and communities in their own right. In the 1960s, even as they presented independent worldviews, there were attempts to help them work together in a common pursuit. Philosophers like Peters and Hirst, historians such as Simon, and curriculum specialists led by Lawton could still conceive of the whole, even if it was necessarily partitioned into convenient sections. The four-disciplines approach then fell apart, in its most basic form, especially as its limitations for practice became evident. This did not establish a single dominant orthodoxy, however, but rather a multitude of competing interests based on topics and problems as well as academic disciplines and represented by a number of different groups.

Thus, the development of educational studies and research needs to be understood historically but not teleologically. This field of study has not evolved gradually to become a single discipline or idea of the good. It has been contested throughout the past century between different approaches and interests, between the practicalities of today and the theories of tomorrow, between the ideals of individuality and those of social improvement. Such contests have been played out within a broader context that has often tipped the balance in different directions within and around this unstable coalition.

And it is here, finally, that we can begin to understand how interdisciplinarity has impinged on this field over the longer term. Interdisciplinarity helped to inspire the two great successive waves of development and innovation in educational studies and research that have taken place since the Second World War: the first associated with SCSE in the 1950s, the second with BERA in the 1970s. Both proved only temporary in their effects, and ultimately the contests within the field encouraged pluridisciplinarity, or multidisciplinarity, more than it did interdisciplinarity. This pattern persisted into the twenty-first century. It contrasted vividly with the authentically interdisciplinary practices evident in a cognate centre, CCCS at the University of Birmingham, as was demonstrated in Chapter 7. Yet educational studies and research also retained scope for visions of interdisciplinarity to inspire and underpin a number of key initiatives at national, local and institutional levels. Also, this interplay was not a simple dichotomy between the disciplinary and interdisciplinary. There was, rather, a symbiosis between these ideals; they were opposite sides of the same coin. Within the multidisciplinary conference, journal or text, interdisciplinary arguments could still resonate. Communities of the sub-disciplines in a society or centre could generate broad initiatives in which a particular discipline might take the lead but in the interests of a broader goal.

This was strikingly the case also for many of the key individuals in the field. Whereas Julie Thompson Klein has emphasised the importance of 'interdisciplinary individuals' as ideal types who represent interdisciplinarity rather than other approaches (Klein 1990), we have found in the current work that many of the figures who preached interdisciplinarity were themselves leaders of their disciplines. Clarke was a sociologist, Oliver a psychologist, Peters a philosopher, Simon a historian, and others such as Tibble, Baron, Taylor, Stenhouse, Rudduck, McIntyre and Brown also had specialist interests. The key for these perhaps was that they built upon their own disciplinary or particular expertise to forge a practical or theoretical partnership of the field *en tout*. This was also true of the radically different interdisciplinary project of CCCS, led by the sociologist Stuart Hall and the historian Richard Johnson.

Nevertheless, in general we can conclude from the account provided in this book that the initiatives to promote interdisciplinarity in educational studies and research have been limited and partial in their longer-term effects. This may have serious implications, as it means a dispersal of effort, an incoherence of approach and a lack of unity in maintaining the interests of the field as a whole. Dispersal of effort appears wasteful especially at a time of straitened resources. Incoherence risks a failure to conceptualise and articulate shared values and ideals across the field. Lack of unity may harm the prospects of defending the field against rival interests in higher education and in public policy and debate.

In more positive terms, renewed efforts at collaboration across the field may yield fruitful outcomes. If, as is often argued, an interdisciplinary approach requires healthy disciplines, achieving a more fully interdisciplinary outlook for educational studies and research may require refreshed and increasingly active contributions from the sub-disciplines in the interests of the whole. Fresh vigour around broad themes and issues may encourage a stronger and more effective field and even potentially a third wave of interdisciplinary innovation following those of the postwar years. This, after all, is the vision that Fred Clarke once entertained and fought to attain in the early decades of the twentieth century: 'a whole, which while being concrete and diversified, is also a unity' (Clarke 1923, p. 11). Might there still be scope for such an ideal in the new realities of the twenty-first century world?

BIBLIOGRAPHY

1. Primary unpublished sources

ATCDE papers, Modern Records Centre, University of Warwick

ATCDE (1965) Memorandum, 'Ad hoc committee on research', 29 October (ATCDE papers, Modern Records Centre, University of Warwick, 176/CD/AT/3/T141).

Valentine, C.W. (1941) 'Statistical articles in the *British Journal of Educational Psychology*: Memorandum for the directors of the Journal and the Council of the British Psychological Society', February (ATCDE papers, Modern Records Centre, University of Warwick, 176/CD/AT/3/T247).

Australian Council for Educational Research

Clarke, F. (1935a) Letter to K.S. Cunningham, 14 February (ACER papers).

Clarke, F. (1936) Letter to F.Tate, 21 June (ACER papers).

BERA papers, MRC, University of Warwick

BERA (1974) Minutes of inaugural meeting, 6 April (BERA papers, 368/10/4).

Entwistle, N. (1973) Letter to K.B. Start, 3 May (BERA papers, 268/10/1).

Forrester, D.M. (1973) Letter to E. Stones, 16 May (BERA papers, 268/10/1).

Postlethwaite, N. (1973a) Memo, 'Establishment of a European Educational Research Association', 15 May (BERA papers, 268/10/1).

Postlethwaite, N. (1973b) letter to E. Stones, 11 October (BERA papers, 268/10/1).

Ross, A. (1974a) Letter to E. Stones, 14 January (BERA papers, 268/10/3).

Ross, A. (1974b) Letter to E. Stones, 21 January (BERA papers, 268/10/3).

Start, K.B. (1973) Letter to W.B. Dockrell, N.J. Entwistle, G. Miller, 9 April (BERA papers 268/10/1).

Stones, E. (1974) Letter to A. Ross, 18 January (BERA papers, 268/10/3).

Whitfield, R.C. (1973) Letter to Professor W.Taylor, 19 October (BERA papers, 268/10/1).

Carnegie Corporation, New York

Carnegie Corporation (1933) Meeting with Fred Clarke and others, 19 January (CC papers).
Clarke, F. (1934) Letter to F. Keppel, 30 November (Carnegie Corporation papers).
Clarke, F. (1935b) Letter to F. Keppel, 23 May (Carnegie Corporation papers).
Clarke, F. (1935c) Letter to F. Keppel, 13 June (Carnegie Corporation papers)
Deller, E. (1931) Letter to F. Keppel, 20 November (Carnegie Corporation papers).
Kandel, I. (1932) Letter to F. Keppel, 5 July (Carnegie Corporation papers).
Nunn, P. (1934) Letter to F. Keppel, 28 May (Carnegie Corporation papers).

CCCS papers, Cadbury Research Library, University of Birmingham

CCCS

CCCS (1964) Annual report (Richard Johnson papers, Cadbury Research Library University of Birmingham, Box 14)
CCCS (1965) Annual report (Johnson papers, Box 14).
CCCS (1966) Annual report (Johnson papers, Box 14).
CCCS (1971a) Annual report (Johnson papers, Box 14).
CCCS (1971b) *Working Papers in Cultural Studies.* Birmingham: CCCS.
CCCS (1974) Annual report (Johnson papers, Box 14).
CCCS (1975) Memorandum, 'Centre sub-groups 1975–76' (Johnson papers, Box 7).
CCCS (1976a) Annual report (Johnson papers, Box 14).
CCCS (1976b) Memorandum, 22 July (Johnson papers, Box 7).
CCCS (1978) Annual report (Johnson papers, Box 14).
CCCS (1979) Notes, 'The Centre, 1978–79' (Michael Green papers, Box 1).
CCCS (1986) Annual report (Johnson papers, Box 14).
CCCS (1987) Annual report (Johnson papers, Box 14).

Michael Green papers

CCCS Education group (1979) Note, 'Our priorities', May (Michael Green papers, Cadbury Research Library, University of Birmingham, Box 1).

Richard Johnson papers

CCCS Education group (1976a) Spring term programme, 15 January (Johnson papers, Box 7).
CCCS Education group (1976b) Report of meetings held on 18 May, 25 May (Johnson papers, Box 7).
CCCS Education group (1977) Report of education presentation (Johnson papers, Box 7).
CCCS Education group (1978) Report of education presentation (Johnson papers, Box 7).
CCCS Education Group (1985) note, 15 October (Johnson papers, Box 7.)
Green, N. (1975) memo, 'Ideas re CCCS programme'.
'A note on the Education group: Confessions of an optimist', 7 July (Johnson papers, Box 7).
Johnson, R. (1976a) Memorandum, 'Popular struggles and State education, 1880s–1930s' (Johnson papers, Box 8).

Johnson, R. (1976b) 'A note on the Education group', 29 September (Johnson papers, Box 7).

Johnson, R. (1983) Letter to D. Wardle, 9 February (Johnson papers, Box 15).

Johnson, R. (1985) My politics of education, October (Johnson papers, Box 7, Education group file).

Johnson, R. (1989) Paper to London Association of Teachers of English, Under new management: Cultural studies, education and the 1988 Act, 11 March (Johnson papers, Box 15).

Steedman, C. (1989) Letter to R. Johnson, 15 August (Johnson papers, Box 15).

Eric James papers, University of York

James, E. (1971) Notes on teacher education and training, March (James papers, University of York, JAM/3/1/1).

James, E. (1972) Notes on James Report (James papers, University of York, JAM/2/1/1).

Ministry of Education papers, National Archives, Kew

Embling, J.F. (1963) Note to J.P. Carswell, 19 April (Ministry of Education papers, National; Archive, Kew, ED.23/1111).

Parliamentary and Scientific Committee papers, London

Parliamentary and Scientific Committee (1961) Memorandum, 'Research in education', 7 July (Parliamentary and Scientific Committee papers, London).

SERA papers, University of Strathclyde

SERA (1975) Minutes of 1st ADM, Stirling University, 31 January (SERA archive, T-SERA/3).

SERA (1994) Executive committee, note by John Nisbet, 14 June (SERA archive, University of Strathclyde, T-SERA/2).

Wilkinson, E., and Morrison, E. (1976) Memo, 'The case for and against a formal line between SERA and SES', 27 January (SERA papers, T-SERA/3).

UCL Institute of Education

George Baron staff file

Baron, G. (1956) Letter to G.B. Jeffery, 3 August (George Baron staff file, IOE).

Baron, G. (n.d./1963?) Memo, 'Notes on the study of educational administration' (George Baron staff file, IOE).

Elvin, L. (1962) Reference for George Baron, 21 November (George Baron staff file, IOE).

Elvin, L. (1966) Letter to Lord Murray, 3 March (George Baron staff file, IOE).

Basil Bernstein staff file

Halsey, A.H. (1963) Letter to L. Elvin, 7 November (Basil Bernstein staff file, IOE, IE/SFR/B/3).

Fred Clarke papers

BAAS (1939a) Committee on research in education, 2nd meeting, 29 March, minute 3 (Institute of Education papers, Fred Clarke personal file, IE/FC/2/2).

Clarke, F. (1935d) Report on tour (1935) (Fred Clarke papers, Institute of Education London, FC/1/59).

Clarke, F. (1939a) Memo, 'The present position of educational research in England' (Clarke papers, FC/3/15, IOE).

Clarke, F. (1939b) Letter to Richard Oliver, 26 July (Clarke papers, FC/2/2, IOE).

Committee on research in education (1939) Draft report (Clarke papers, IOE, FC/2/2, IOE).

Mannheim, K. (1939) Note to Clarke, 4 November (Clarke papers, file 47, IOE).

Nunn, P. (1930) Memo, 'The University department of education', 22 February (Fred Clarke papers, Institute of Education, University of London, FC/1/34).

Nunn, P. (1937) Note to Clarke, 5 January (Clarke papers, file 38, IOE).

Oliver, R.A.C. (1939) Letter to Fred Clarke, 20 July (Institute of Education papers, Fred Clarke personal file, IE/FC/2/2).4

Department of Curriculum Studies

Department of Curriculum Studies (DCS) (1981) Note on departmental visitation, February (DSC papers, IOE).

IOE DCS Department of Curriculum Studies lecture programme, 1978–79 (readings and questions omitted) (DCS 1978).

Lawton, D. (1974) Memorandum, 'Curriculum Studies Department and interdepartmental cooperation', February (DSC papers, IOE, 1973–83 file).

IOE papers

Carr-Saunders, A.V. (1953) Letter to G.B. Jeffery, 4 February (IOE papers, IE/5FR/C/1).

Elvin, L. (1953) Letter to G.B. Jeffery, 18 January (IOE papers, IE/SFR/C/1).

Ginsberg, M. (1952) Letter to G.B. Jeffery, 5 May (IOE papers, IE/SFR/C/1).

Jeffery, G.B. (1952) Letter to A. Carr-Saunders, 8 July (IOE papers, IE/SFR/C/1).

Jeffery, G.B. (1953) Letter to L. Elvin, 16 February (IOE papers, IE/SFR/C/1).

Judges, A.V. (1952a) Letter to G.B. Jeffery, 2 May (IOE papers, IE/SFR/C/2).

Judges, A.V. (1952b) Letter to G.B. Jeffery, 30 May (IOE papers, IE/SFR/C/1).

Lauwerys, J. (1952) Letter to G.B. Jeffery, 17 June (IOE papers, IE/SFR/C/1).

Read, M. (1952) Letter to G.B. Jeffery, 5 May (IOE papers, IE/SFR/C/1).

Vernon, P. (1952) Letter to G.B. Jeffery, 5 May (IOE papers, IE/SFR/C/I).

Wootton, B. (1952) Letter to G.B. Jeffery, 9 May (IOE papers, IE/SFR/C/1).

Brian Simon papers

Simon, B. (1974) Memorandum to vice-chancellor, Leicester University, 'Some reflections on the School of Education', 24 February (Simon papers, IOE, DC/SIM/5/3/2).

Simon, B. (n.d./1990s) note, 'University and the School of Education, 1950–1980' (Simon papers, IOE, DC/SIM/4/5/2/30).

Interviews

40 anonymised semi-structured interviews with Education academics, 2012–13 (labelled by gender and by areas/discipline: economics, history, philosophy, psychology, sociology, general).

2. Published sources

Abbott, A. (2002) 'The disciplines and the future', in S. Brint (ed), *The Future of the City of Intellect*, Stanford, CA: Stanford University Press, pp. 206–230.

Adams, J. (1902/1980) 'Training of teachers', in P. Gordon (ed), *The Study of Education: Inaugural Lectures*, vol. 1: *Early and Modern*. London: Woburn Press, pp. 43–53.

Adams, J. (1922) *Modern Developments in Educational Practice*. London: London University Press.

Aldrich, R. (2002) *The Institute of Education 1902–2002: A Centenary History*. London: University of London.

Allen, A. (2011) 'Michael Young's *The Rise of the Meritocracy*: A philosophical critique', *BJES*, 59/4, pp. 367–382.

Anderson, A., and Valente, J. (eds) (2002) *Disciplinarity at the Fin de Siecle*. Princeton, NJ: Princeton University Press.

Andrews, R. (2005) 'The place of systematic reviews in educational research', *BJES*, 53/4, pp. 399–416.

Angervall, P., and Gustaffson, J. (2014) 'The making of careers in academia: Split career networks in education science', *European Educational Research Journal*, 13/6, pp. 601–615.

Armytage, W.H.G. (1954/1980) 'The role of an education department in a modern university', in P. Gordon (ed), *The Study of Education: Inaugural Lectures*, Vol. 1: *Early and Modern*. London: Woburn Press, pp. 160–179.

Armytage, W.H.G. (1956) 'Some sources for the history of technical education in England–part one', *BJES*, 5/1, pp. 72–79.

Armytage, W.H.G. (1957a) 'Some sources for the history of technical education in England-part two', *BJES*, 5/2, pp. 159–165.

Armytage, W.H.G. (1957b) 'Some sources for the history of technical education in England-part three', *BJES*, 6/1, pp. 64–73.

Armytage, W.H.G. (1967) *The American Influence on English Education*. London: Routledge and Kegan Paul.

Armytage, W.H.G. (1968) *The French Influence on English Education*. London: Routledge and Kegan Paul.

Armytage, W.H.G. (1969a) *The German Influence on English Education*. London: Routledge and Kegan Paul.

Armytage, W.H.G. (1969b) *The Russian Influence on English Education*. London: Routledge and Kegan Paul.

Aronova, E. (2014) 'Big science and "Big Science Studies" in the United States and the Soviet Union during the cold war', in N. Oreskes and J. Krige (eds), *Science and Technology in the Global Cold War*. Cambridge, MA: MIT Press, pp. 390–430.

Arthur, J., Davison, J., and Pring, R. (eds) (2012) *Education Matters: Sixty Years of the British Journal of Educational Studies*. London: Routledge.

Arundale, R.L. (1968) 'St. Deiniol's residential library, Hawarden, Deeside, Flintshire: Index of Pamphlets on Education', *BJES*, 16/2, pp. 179–195.

Avis, J. (2003) 'Work-based knowledge, evidence-informed practice and education', *BJES*, 51/4, pp. 369–389.

Bailey, R. (2001) 'Overcoming veriphobia – Learning to love truth again', *BJES*, 49/2, pp. 159–172.

Bain, A. (1877) 'Education as a science', *Mind: A Quarterly Review of Psychology and Philosophy*, 2/5, pp. 1–21.

Ball, S. (1981) *Beachside Comprehensive: A Case-Study of Secondary Schooling*. Cambridge: Cambridge University Press.

Ball, S. (1990a) *Politics and Policy-Making in Education: Explorations in Policy Sociology*. London: Routledge.

Ball, S. (1990b) 'The sociological implications of the Education Reform Act', *British Journal of Sociology of Education*, 11/4, pp. 485–491.

Ball, S. (1993) 'Education policy, power relations and teachers' work', *BJES*, 41/2, pp. 106–121.

Ball, S. (2006) *Education Policy and Social Class: The Selected Works of Stephen J. Ball*. London: Routledge.

Baltic Association of Historians of Pedagogy (ed) (2009) *History of Education and Pedagogical Thought in the Baltic Countries Up to 1990: An Overview*. Riga, Latvia: RaKa.

Baltic Association of Historians of Pedagogy (ed) (2010) *History of Pedagogy and Educational Sciences in the Baltic Countries from 1940 to 1990: An Overview*. Riga, Latvia: RaKa.

Banks, O. (1955) *Parity and Prestige in English Secondary Education: A Study in Educational Sociology*. London: Routledge.

Banks, O. (1968) *The Sociology of Education*. London: Batsford.

Banks, O. (1982) 'The sociology of education, 1952–1982', *BJES*, 30/1, pp. 18–31.

Barnard, H.C. (1954) 'Some sources for French educational history to 1789', *BJES*, 2/2, pp. 166–169.

Barnard, H.C. (1958) 'Some sources for French educational history during the Revolution and the Napoleonic Period', *BJES*, 7/1, pp. 56–63.

Baron G. (1969) 'The study of educational administration in England', in G. Baron and W. Taylor (eds), *Educational Administration and the Social Sciences*. London: Athlone Press, pp. 3–17.

Baron, G., and Taylor, W. (eds) (1969) *Educational Administration and the Social Sciences*. London: Athlone Press.

Bartlett, D., and Burton, D. (eds) (2006/2016) *Introduction to Education Studies*. 4th edition: Thousand Oaks, CA: Sage.

Bartlett, L. (1992) 'National curriculum in Australia – An instrument of corporate federalism', *BJES*, 40/3, pp. 218–238.

Barton, L., and Meighan, R. (eds) (1978) *Sociological Interpretations of Schooling and Classrooms: A Re-Appraisal*. Driffield, UK: Nafferton Books.

Barton, L., and Meighan, R. (eds) (1979) *Schools, Pupils and Deviance*. Driffield, UK: Nafferton Books.

Barton, L., Meighan, R., and Walker, R. (eds) (1980) *Schooling, Ideology and the Curriculum*. London: Falmer Press.

Barton, L., and Walker, R. (eds) (1983) *Gender, Class and Education*. London: Falmer Press.

Beales, A.C.F. (1954) 'Some sources for Spanish educational history: Part one—To the end of the Monarchy in 1931', *BJES*, 3, pp. 59–71.

Beales, A.C.F. (1955) 'Some sources for Spanish educational history: Part two—Developments since 1931', *BJES*, 3, pp. 155–166.

Becher, T., and Parry, S. (2005) 'The endurance of the disciplines', in I. Bleiklie and M. Henkel (eds), *Governing Knowledge: A Study of Continuity and Change in Higher Education*. Dordrecht: Springer, pp. 133–144.

Bell, R.E. (1983) 'The education departments in the Scottish universities', in W. Humes and H. Paterson (eds), *Scottish Culture and Scottish Education, 1880–1980*. Edinburgh: John Donald Publishers, pp. 151–174.

Berger, G. (1977) 'Introduction', in SRHE (ed), *Interdisciplinarity*, pp. 3–7. London: Author.

Bernstein, B. (1965) 'Some relations between sociology and the Education course', presentation to DES Hull conference, March 1964.

Best, J.W. (1959) *Research in Education*. Englewood Cliffs, NJ: Prentice Hall.

Biesta, G. (2011) 'Disciplines and theory in the academic study of education: A comparative analysis of the Anglo-American and Continental construction of the field', *Pedagogy, Culture and Society*, 19/2, pp. 175–192.

Billett, S. (2008) 'Learning throughout working life: A relational interdependence between personal and social agency', *BJES*, 56/1, pp. 39–58.

BJES (1952), 'Notes and news: The *British Journal of Educational Studies*', 1/1, pp. 67–69.

BJES (1953), 'The Standing Conference on Studies in Education', 1/2, pp. 191–192.

BJES (1954), 'Notes and news: The Standing Conference', 2/2, pp. 170–71.

BJES (1955) 'Notes and news: The Standing Conference', 3/2, pp. 168–170.

BJES (1956), 'Notes and news: The standing conference', 4/2, pp. 165–169.

BJES (1957), 'Notes and news: The standing conference', 5/2, pp. 166–167.

BJES (1969), 'Notes and news: The standing conference', 17/2, pp. 209–217.

BJSE (1980), 'Editorial', 1/1, pp. 3–5.

BJES (1982), 'Editorial', 30/1, pp. 5–6.

Black, E.L. (1962) 'The marking of G.C.E. scripts', *BJES*, 11/1, pp. 61–71.

Black, H.D., and Dockrell, W.B. (1980) *Diagnostic Assessment in Secondary Schools: A Teacher's Handbook*. London: Hodder & Stoughton.

Blackwell, A.M. (1950) *A List of Researches in Education and Educational Psychology*. London: Newnes Educational Publishing, *NFER*.

Blackwell, A.M (1958) *Lists of Researches in Education and Educational Psychology: Presented for Higher Degrees in the United Kingdom, Northern Ireland and the Irish Republic in the Years 1956 and 1957*. London: Newnes Educational, NFER.

Blei, D.M., Ng, A.Y., and Jordan, M.I. (2003) 'Latent dirichlet allocation', *Journal of Machine Learning Research*, 3, pp. 993–1022.

Blin-Stoyle, R. (ed) (1986) *The Sussex Opportunity: A New University and the Future*. New York: Harvester Press.

Blishen, E. (1963) *Education Today: The Existing Opportunities*. London: BBC Publications.

Blyth, W.A.B. (1977) 'Integrated study and educational research: Some observations on the British scene', *BJES*, 25/2, p. 109.

Blyth, W.A.B. (1982) 'Response and autonomy in the study of education: A personal account of three decades', *British Journal of Educational Studies*, 30/1, pp. 7–17.

Board of Education (1944) *The Supply, Recruitment and Training of Teachers and Youth Leaders* (McNair Report). London: HMSO.

Bone, T.R. (1982) 'Educational administration', *BJES*, 30/1, pp. 32–42.

Boreham, N. (2004) 'A theory of collective competence: Challenging the neo-liberal individualisation of performance at work', *BJES*, 52/1, pp. 5–17.

Bourdieu, P. (1986/1987) 'The forms of capital', in J. Richardson (ed), *Handbook of Theory and Research for the Sociology of Education*. New York: Greenwood Press (republished in A.H. Halsey, Hugh Lauder, Phillip Brown, and Amy Stuart Wells (eds), *Education: Culture, Economy, and Society*. Oxford: Oxford University Press, pp. 46–58.

Bowles, S., and Gintis, H. (1976) *Schooling in Capitalist America: Educational Reform and the Contradictions of Economic Life*. New York: Basic Books.

Bowyer-Bower, T.A. (1954) 'A pioneer of army education: The Royal Military Asylum, Chelsea, 1801–1821', *BJES*, 2/2, pp. 122–132.

Bowyer-Bower, T.A. (1955) 'Some sources for the history of education in the British army during the 19th century', *BJES*, 4/1, pp. 71–77.

Brehaut, W. (1973) 'British research in education – Some aspects of its development', in H.J. Butcher and H.B. Pont (eds), *Educational Research in Britain 3*. London: University of London Press, pp. 1–18.

Briggs, A. (1972) 'The study of the history of education', *History of Education*, 1/1, pp. 5–23.

Briggs, A. (1986) 'The years of plenty, 1961–1976', in J. Blin-Stoyle (ed), *The Sussex Opportunity*. New York: Harvester Press, pp. 1–21.

Briggs, A. (2004) 'History and the social sciences', in W. Ruegg (ed), *A History of the University in Oxford*. vol. 3, Universities in the Nineteenth and Early Twentieth Centuries. Cambridge: Cambridge University Press, pp. 459–491.

Brighton McGowan, M. (1986) 'A challenge for the humanities', in J. Blin-Stoyle (ed), *The Sussex Opportunity*. New York: Harvester Press., pp. 66–78.

Brim, O. (1958) *Sociology and the Field of Education*. New York: Russell Sage Foundation.

British Academy. (2016) *Crossing Paths*. London: British Academy.

Brownell, W.A. (1963) 'Educational research in the decade ahead', *California Journal of Educational Research*, 14/2, p. 58.

Bryce, T., and Humes, W. (eds) (1999) *Scottish Education*. Edinburgh: Edinburgh University Press.

Bryce, T., and Humes, W. (eds) (2003) *Scottish Education: Post Devolution*. Edinburgh: Edinburgh University Press.

Bryce, T., and Humes, W. (eds) (2008) *Scottish Education: Beyond Devolution*. Edinburgh: Edinburgh University Press.

Bryce, T., Humes, W., Gillies, D.(eds) (2013) *Scottish Education: Referendum*. Edinburgh: Edinburgh University Press.

Bryce, T., Humes, W., Gillies, D., and Kennedy, A. (eds) (2013) *Scottish Education: Fourth Edition, Referendum*. Edinburgh: Edinburgh University Press.

Burgess, R. (ed) (1984) *The Research Process in Educational Settings: Ten Case Studies*. London: Falmer Press.

Burgess, R. (ed) (1985) *Field Methods in the Study of Education*. London: Falmer Press.

Burgess, R. (1995) *Howard Becker on Education*. Maidenhead: Open University Press.

Burke, P. (2012) *The Social History of Knowledge*, vol. II: From the *Cyclopedie* to Wikipedia, Cambridge: Polity.

Burt, C. (1959) 'The examination at eleven plus', *BJES*, 7/2, pp. 99–117.

Burt, C., and Pear, T.H. (1964) 'Obituary notice', *British Journal of Psychology*, 55/4, pp. 385–390.

Butcher, H.J. (ed) (1968) *Educational Research in Britain*. London: University of London Press.

Butcher, H.J. (ed) (1970) *Educational Research in Britain 2*. London: University of London Press.

Butcher, H.J. (ed) (1973) *Educational Research in Britain 3*. London: University of London Press.

Butler, P. (1983) *Politics and Law Making in Special Education*. Exeter: Exeter Research Group.

Carolan, B. (2008) 'The structure of educational research: The role of multivocality in promoting cohesion in an article interlock network', *Social Networks*, 30, pp. 69–82.

Carr, D. (1991) 'Education and values', *BJES*, 39/3, pp. 244–259.

Carr, W. (2006) 'Education without theory', *BJES*, 54/2, pp. 136–159.

CCCS. (1971) *Working Papers in Cultural Studies*. Birmingham: CCCS.

CCCS. (1977) *On Ideology*. London, Paris: Hutchinson OECD.

CCCS. (1980) *Culture, Media, Language*. London: Hutchinson.

CCCS education group. (1981) *Unpopular Education: Schooling and Social Democracy in England since 1944*. London: Hutchinson.

CERI. (1972) *Interdisciplinarity: Problems of Teaching and Research in Universities*. Paris: OECD.

Chambers, P. (1971) 'The study of education in the colleges: Harking back!', in J.W. Tibble (ed), *The Future of Teacher Education*. London: Routledge and Kegan Paul, pp. 68–80.

Christie, F., and Maton, K. (2011) 'Why disciplinarity?', in F. Christie and K. Maton (eds), *Disciplinarity: Functional Linguistic and Sociological Perspectives*. London: Continuum, pp. 1–9.

Clarke, A.M. (1982) 'Psychology and education', *BJES*, 30/1, pp. 43–56.

Clarke, C. (2006) 'Sir Fred Clarke: A reappraisal of his early years 1880–1911', *Education Research and Perspectives*, 33/1, pp. 33–61.

Clarke, F. (1918/1923) 'The study of education', in F. Clarke (ed), *Essays in the Politics of Education*. Oxford: Oxford University Press, pp. 132–144.

Clarke, F. (1923) *Essays in the Politics of Education*. Oxford: Oxford University Press.

Clarke, F. (1940) *Education and Social Change: An English Interpretation*. London: Sheldon Books.

Clarke, F. (1943) *The Study of Education in England*. Oxford: Oxford University Press.

Clarke, J., Critcher, C., Johnson, R. (eds) (1979) *Working Class Culture: Studies in History and Theory*. London: Hutchinson in association with CCCS.

Cohen, L., Thomas, J., and Manion, L. (1982) *Educational Research and Development in Britain 1970–1980*. Berkshire: NFER-Nelson.

Collingwood, R.G. (1924/2013) *Speculum Mentis: Or the Map of Knowledge*. London: Ghosh Press.

Collins, P. (1979) 'The origins of the British Association's Education Section', *BJES*, 27/3, pp. 232–244.

Committee on Higher Education. (1963) *Higher Education* (Robbins Report). London: HMSO.

Connolly, P. (2006) 'Keeping a sense of proportion but losing all perspective: A critique of Gorard's notion of the "politician's error"', *BJES*, 54/1, pp. 73–88.

Culbertson, J.A., and Hencley, S.P. (1963) *Educational Research: New Perspectives*. Danville, IL: Interstate Printers & Publishers.

Cunningham, R. (ed) (1997) *Interdisciplinarity and the Organisation of Knowledge in Europe*. Luxembourg: European Communities.

Curtis, W., Murphy, M., and Shields, S. (2013) *Research and Education*. Abingdon: Routledge.

Cutler, T., and Waine, B. (2000) 'Mutual benefits or managerial control? The role of appraisal in performance related pay for teachers', *BJES*, 48/2, pp. 170–182.

Dale, R. (ed) (1976) *Schooling and Capitalism: A Sociological Reader*. London: Routledge and Kegan Paul.

Davies, P. (1999) 'What is evidence-based education?', *BJES*, 47/2, pp. 108–121.

Davison, J. (2012) 'Sixty years of the Society For Educational Studies', in J. Arthur, J. Davison, and R. Pring (eds), *Education Matters: Sixty Years of the* British Journal of Educational Studies. Abingdon: Routledge, pp. viii–xii.

Dawson, H. (1968) *On the Outskirts of Hope: Educating Youth from Poverty Areas*. New York: McGraw-Hill.

DEA/FBE (2008) *Thinking across Disciplines: Interdisciplinarity in Research and Education*, August. Copenhagen: Author.

Dearden, R.F. (1968) *The Philosophy of Primary Education*. London: Routledge and Kegan Paul.

Dearden, R.F. (1974) 'Education and ethics of belief', *BJES*, 22/1, pp. 5–17.

Dearden, R.F. (1982) 'Philosophy of education, 1952–82', *BJES*, 30/1, pp. 57–71.

Dearing, R. (1997) *Higher Education in the Learning Society*. London: Stationery Office.

Deem, R. (1994) 'Free marketeers or good citizens – Educational policy and lay participation in the administration of schools', *BJES*, 42/1, pp. 23–37.

Dixon, K. (1968) 'On teaching moral procedures', *BJES*, 16/1, pp. 17–29.

DES. (1965) *Conference on the Course in Education in the Education of Teachers, Held at Hull University, 16–21 March 1964*. London: Author.

DES. (1972) *Teacher Education and Training* (James Report). London: HMSO.

DfBIS. (2016) *Success as a Knowledge Economy: Teaching Excellence, Social Mobility and Student Choice*. London: Higher Education White Paper, Stationery Office.

DfE. (2010) *The Importance of Teaching*. London: Education White Paper, Stationery Office.

DfES (2003) *The Future of Higher Education*. London: Higher Education White Paper, Stationery Office.

Elam, S. (1995) *How America views its schools: the PDK/Gallup polls, 1969–1994*. Arlington, VA: Phi Delta Kappa Educational Foundation.

Elliott, J. (1987) 'Educational theory, practical philosophy and action research', *BJES*, 35/2, pp. 149–169.

Elliott, J., and Norris, N. (eds) (2012) *Curriculum, Pedagogy and Educational Research: The Work of Lawrence Stenhouse*. London: Routledge.

Elsevier. (2015) *A Review of the UK's Interdisciplinary Research Using a Citation-Based Approach*. Amsterdam: Author.

Elvin, L. (1987) *Encounters with Education*. London: Institute of Education, University of London.

Ethnography and Education (2006), 'Editorial', 1/1, pp. 1–2.

Ferguson, J. (1981) *Christianity, Society and Education: Robert Raikes, Past, Present and Future*. London: SPCK.

Field, D. (1970) *Change in Art Education*. New York: Routledge & Kegan Paul.

Finlayson, D. (1973) 'Towards a socio-psychological view of school achievement', *BJES*, 21/3, pp. 290–306.

Fleming, C.M. (1946) *Research and the Basic Curriculum: A Brief Guide to the Findings of Research in Their Relevance to the Teaching of the Basic Subjects*. London: University of London Press.

Floud, J., and Halsey, A.H. (eds) (1956) *Social Class and Educational Opportunity*. London: Heinemann.

Friedmann, F.G. (1971) *Youth and Society*. Basingstoke: Palgrave Macmillan.

Frodeman, R. (ed) (2010) *The Oxford Handbook of Interdisciplinarity*. Oxford: Oxford University Press.

Furlong, J. (2013a) *Education – An Anatomy of the Discipline: Rescuing the University Project?* London: Routledge.

Furlong, J. (2013b) 'In pursuit of the truth', *THE*, 2 May

Furlong, J., and Lawn, M. (ed) (2011) *Disciplines of Education: Their Role in the Future of Education Research*. London: Routledge.

Gallie, W.B. (1960) *A New University: A.D. Lindsay and the Keele Experiment*. Keele: Melandrium Books, Keele.

Gardiner, D., O'Donoghue, T., and O'Neill, M. (2011) *Constructing the Field of Education as a Liberal Art and Teacher Preparation at Five Western Australian Universities: An Historical Analysis*. New York: Edwin Mellen Press.

Gardner, J. (2011) 'Educational research: What (a) to do about impact!', *BERJ*, 37/4, pp. 543–561.

Gibbons, M., Limoges, C., Nowotny, H., Schwartzman, S., Scott, P., and Trow, M. (1994) *The New Production of Knowledge: The Dynamics of Science and Research in Contemporary Societies*. London: Sage.

Gibson, M. (2007) *Culture and Power: A History of Cultural Studies*. Oxford: Berg.

Glatter, R. (2004) 'Professor George Baron, 1911–2003', *Educational Management, Administration and Leadership*, 32/3, pp. 355–359.

Goldacre, B. (2013a) Report, 'Building evidence into education'.

Goldacre, B. (2013b) 'Teachers need to devise the research agenda', *The Guardian*, 18 March

Goodson, I. (1983) *School Subjects and Curriculum Change*. London: Croom Helm.

Goodson, I. (1985) 'Towards curriculum history', in I. Goodson (ed), *Social Histories of the Secondary Curriculum: Subjects for Study*. London: Falmer Press, pp. 1–9.

Goodson, I. (2003) *Professional Knowledge, Professional Lives: Studies in Education and Change*. Maidenhead: Open University Press.

Goodson, I. (2013) *Developing Narrative Theory: Life Histories and Personal Representation*. London: Routledge.

Goodson, I., and Sikes, P. (2001) *Life History Research in Educational Settings: Learning from Lives*. Maidenhead: Open University Press.

Gorard, S. (1999) 'Keeping a sense of proportion: The 'politician's error' in analysing school outcomes', *BJES*, 47/4, pp. 235–246.

Gorard, S. (2002) 'Political control: A way forward for educational research', *BJES*, 50/3, pp. 378–389.

Gorard, S. (2005) 'Revisiting a 90-year-old debate: The advantages of the mean deviation', *BJES*, 53/4, pp. 417–430.

Gordon, P. (1966) 'Some sources for the history of the Endowed Schools Commission, 1869–1900', *BJES*, 14/1, pp. 59–73.

Gordon, P. (ed) (1980a) *The Study of Education: Inaugural Lectures*, vol. 1: *Early and Modern*. London: Woburn Press.

Gordon, P. (ed) (1980b) *The Study of Education: Inaugural Lectures*, vol. 2: *The Last Decade*. London: Woburn Press.

Gordon, P. (1980c) 'Introduction', in P. Gordon (ed), *The Study of Education*, vol. 1: *Early and Modern*. London: Woburn Press, pp. ix–xxiii.

Gordon, P. (ed) (1988) *The Study of Education: Inaugural Lectures*, vol. 3: *The Changing Scene*. London: Woburn Press.

Gordon, P. (1990) 'The university professor of education', in J.B. Thomas (ed), *British Universities and Teacher Education: A Century of Change*. London: Falmer Press, pp. 163–179.

Gordon, P. (ed) (1995) *The Study of Education: Inaugural Lectures*, vol. 4: *End of an Era?*. London: Woburn Press.

Gosden, P. (1982) 'The educational system of England and Wales since 1952', *BJES*, 30/1, pp. 108–121.

Gosden, P. (1992) *The North of England Education Conference, 1902–1992*. Leeds: University of Leeds.

Graff, H. (2015) *Undisciplining Knowledge: Interdisciplinarity in the Twentieth Century*. Baltimore: Johns Hopkins University Press.

Greaves, J., and Grant, W. (2010) 'Crossing the interdisciplinary divide: Political science and biological science', *Political Studies*, 58, pp. 320–339.

Green, A. (1993) *Educational Provision, Educational Attainment and the Needs of Industry: A Review of Research for Germany, France, Japan, the USA and Britain*. London: Institute of Education, University of London and National Institute of Economic and Social Research.

Greenaway, H. (1973) 'The work of the Society for Research in Higher Education', in H.J. Butcher and H.B. Pont (eds), *Educational Research in Britain* 3. London: University of London Press, pp. 328–344.

Griffiths, J. (2003) *NFER: The First Fifty Years 1946–1996*. London: NFER.

Hall, S. (1971) 'Introduction', in *Working Papers in Cultural Studies* 1. Birmingham: University of Birmingham, pp. 1–10.

Hall, S. (1980) 'Cultural studies and the centre', in CCCS (ed), *Culture, Media, Language*. London: Hutchinson, pp. 15–47.

Halsey, A., Floud, J., and Anderson, C. (eds) (1961) *Education, Economy, and Society: A Reader in the Sociology of Education*. New York: Free Press of Glencoe.

Halsey, A.H., Lauder, H., Brown, P., Stuart, A. (1997) *Education: Culture, Economy, Society*. Oxford: Oxford University Press.

Hamilton, D. (2002) '"Noisy, fallible and biased though it be" – (On the vagaries of educational research)', *BJES*, 50/1, pp. 144–164.

Hammersley, M. (2001) 'Interpreting achievement gaps: Some comments on a dispute', *BJES*, 49/3, pp. 285–298.

Hare, W.F. (1968) 'Correspondence: On teaching moral procedures: A reply', *BJES*, 16/2, pp. 200–202.

Hargreaves, D. (1967) *Social Relations in a Secondary School*. London: RKP.

Hargreaves, D. (1996) *Teaching as a Research-Based Profession: Possibilities and Prospects*. London: TTA Annual lecture.

Hartley, J. (2007) *A Short History of Cultural Studies*. London: Sage.

Hearnshaw, L.S. (1964) *A Short History of British Psychology, 1840–1940*. London: Methuen.

HEFCE (2016a) *Landscape Review of Interdisciplinary Research in the UK*, September, www.hefce.ac.uk/media/HEFCE.2014/Content/Pubs/Independentresearch/2016/Two.reports.on.interdisciplinary.research/Landscape%20review%20of%20UK%20interdisciplinary%20research.pdf.

HEFCE (2016b) *Consultation document for 2021 REF*, November.

Henderson, J.L. (1960) 'Some sources for the study of German education', *BJES*, 9/1, pp. 48–56.

Higher Education Academy (HEA) (2015) *Interdisciplinary Provision in Higher Education: Current and Future Challenges*. Edinburgh: Author.

Hill, D. (2006) 'New Labour's education policy', in Kassem, D., Mufti, E., and Robinson, J. (eds) (2006) *Education Studies: Issues and Critical Perspectives*. Maidenhead: Open University Press pp. 73–86.

Hill, S. (2015) 'The diversity dividend: Why interdisciplinarity strengthens research', *The Guardian*, 7 August.

Hirst, P. (ed) (1983a) *Educational Theory and Its Foundation Disciplines*. London: Routledge and Kegan Paul.

Hirst, P. (1983b) 'Educational theory', in P. Hirst (ed), *Educational Theory and Its Foundation Disciplines*. London: Routledge and Kegan Paul, pp. 3–29.

Hirst, P., and Peters, R. (1966) *The Logic of Education*. London: Routledge and Kegan Paul.

Hobsbawm, E. (1997) *On History*. London: Weidenfeld and Nicolson.

Hofstetter, R. (2012) 'Educational sciences: Evolutions of a pluridisciplinary discipline at the crossroads of other disciplinary and professional fields (20th century)', *BJES*, 60/4, pp. 317–335.

Hofstetter, R., and Schneuwly, B. (2002) 'Institutionalisation of educational sciences and the dynamics of their development', *European Educational Research Journal*, 1/1, pp. 3–26.

Hofstetter, R., and Schneuwly, B. (2004) 'Introduction: Educational sciences in dynamic and hybrid institutionalisation', *Paedagogica Historica*, 40/5, pp. 569–589.

Hoggart, R. (1957) *The Uses of Literacy*. London: Chatto and Windus.

Hoggart, R. (1963) *Schools of English and Contemporary Society: An Inaugural Lecture*. Birmingham: University of Birmingham.

Holloway, D.G. (1977) 'The structure of the four-year degree courses at Keele', in SRHE (ed), *Interdisciplinarity*. London: SRHE, pp. 17–19.

Holmwood, J. (2010) 'Sociology's misfortune: Disciplinarity, interdisciplinarity and the impact of audit culture', *British Journal of Sociology*, 61/4, pp. 639–658.

Hopkins, E. (1969) 'A charity school in the nineteenth century: Old Swinford Hospital school, 1815–1914', *BJES*, 17/2, pp. 177–192.

House of Commons Debates (1962) Debate on educational research, 19 April, vol. 658, columns 723–751.

Houston, R. (1982) 'The literacy myth? Illiteracy in Scotland 1630–1760', *Past and Present*, 96, pp. 81–102.

Hudson, L. (1966) *Contrary Imaginations*. New York: Penguin.

Hudson, L. (1968) *Frames of Mind*. London: Methuen.

Hugill, B. (1992) 'Why Mr Clarke has got it all wrong', *The Observer*, 5 January.

Humes, W. (2007) 'The infrastructure of educational research in Scotland', *European Educational Research Journal*, 6, pp. 71–86.

Illich, I. (1971) *Deschooling Society*. London: Calder and Boyars.

Ives, E. (2000) *The First Civic University: Birmingham 1880–1980: An Introductory History*. Birmingham: Birmingham University Press.

Jacobs, J.A. (2013) *In Defense of Disciplines: Interdisciplinarity and Specialization in the Research University*. Chicago: University of Chicago Press..

Jeffery, T. (1978) *Mass-Observation: A Short History*. Birmingham: Centre for Contemporary Cultural Studies, University of Birmingham.

Jensen, G.E. (1965) *Educational Sociology: An Approach to Its Development as a Practical Field of Study*. New York: Center for applied research in education.

Johnson, R. (1979) '"Really useful knowledge": Radical education and working-class culture, 1790–1848', in J. Clarke, C. Critcher, and R. Johnson (eds), *Working Class Culture: Studies in History and Theory*. London: Hutchinson, pp. 75–102.

Johnson, R. (1983) 'Correcting the grammar – What are cultural studies?', *CCCS Stencilled Occasional Paper*, SP no. 74.

Johnson, R. (1989) 'Thatcherism and English education: Breaking the mould, or confirming the pattern?' *History of Education*, 18/2, pp. 91–121.

Johnson, R. (2001) 'Historical returns: Transdisciplinarity, cultural studies and history', *European Journal of Cultural Studies*, 4/3, pp. 261–288.

Jones, D. (2001) *School of Education 1946–1996*. Leicester: University of Leicester.

Journal of Curriculum Studies (1969), 'Editorial', 1/2.

Judges, A.V. (1952) 'The late Sir Fred Clarke', *BJES*, 1/1, pp. 67–68.

Judges, A.V. (ed) (1955) *Looking Forward in Education*. London: Faber and Faber.

Karabel, J., and Halsey, A.H. (eds) (1977a) *Power and Ideology in Education*. New York: Oxford University Press.

Karabel, J., and Halsey, A.H. (1977b) 'Educational research: A review and an interpretation', in J. Karabel and A.H. Halsey (eds), *Power and Ideology in Education*. New York: Oxford University Press, pp. 1–85.

Kassem, D., Mufti, E., and Robinson, J. (ed) (2006) *Education Studies: Issues and Critical Perspectives*. Maidenhead: Open University Press.

Kennedy, K. (1989) 'National initiatives in curriculum – The Australian context', *BJES*, 37/2, pp. 111–124.

Kerr, J.F. (1959) 'Some sources for the history of the teaching of science in England', *BJES*, 7/2, pp. 149–160.

Kerr, J.F. (ed) (1968a) *Changing the Curriculum*. London: University of London Press.

Kerr, J.F. (1968b) 'The problem of curriculum reform', in J.F. Kerr (ed), *Changing the Curriculum*. London: University of London Press, pp. 13–38.

King, A.R., and Brownell, J.A. (1966) *The Curriculum and the Disciplines of Knowledge: A Theory of Curriculum Practice*. London: John Wiley and sons.

Klein, J.T. (1990) *Interdisciplinarity: History, Theory, and Practice*. Detroit, MI: Wayne State University Press.

Klein, J.T. (1993) 'Blurring, cracking, and crossing: Permeation and the fracturing of discipline', in E. Messer-Davidson, D.R. Shumway, and D.J. Sylvan (eds), *Knowledges: Historical and Critical Studies in Disciplinarity*. Charlottesville: University Press of Virginia, pp. 185–211.

Klein, J.T. (2010) 'A taxonomy of interdisciplinarity', in R. Frodeman (ed), *Oxford Handbook of Interdisciplinarity*. Oxford: Oxford University Press, pp. 15–30.

Knox, H. (1951) 'The study of education in British universities', *The Universities Review*, 24/1, pp. 34–46.

Korbert, J.M. (2000) *Keele: The First Fifty Years: A Portrait of the University 1950–2000*. Keele: University of Keele.

Ku, H.-Y. (2013) 'Education for liberal democracy: Fred Clarke and the 1944 Education Act', *History of Education*, 42, pp. 578–597.

Labaree, D. (2006) *The Trouble with Ed Schools*. New Haven, CT: Yale University Press.

Lagemann, E. (1989) *The Politics of Knowledge: The Carnegie Corporation, Philanthropy, and Public Policy*. Chicago: Chicago University Press.

Lagemann, E. (1997) 'Contested terrain: A history of education research in the United States, 1890–1990', *Educational Researcher*, 26/9, pp. 5–17.

Lagemann, E. (2001) *An Elusive Science: The Troubling History of Education Research*. Chicago: University of Chicago Press.

Laot, F., and Rogers, R. (eds) (2015) *Les Sciences de l'Education: Emergence d'un Champ de Recherche dans l'Apres-Guerre*. Rennes, France: Presses Universitaires de Rennes.

Larsen, L. (2010) 'Interdisciplinary research: Big science at the table', *Nature*, 468, 23 December, pp. 52–54.

Lauder, H., Brown, P., and Halsey, A.H. (2009) 'Sociology of education. A critical history and prospects for the future', *Oxford Review of Education*, 35/5, pp. 569–585.

Lauwerys, J. (1965) 'The theory of education: Its place in schools of education', presentation to DES Hull conference, March 1964

Lawlor, S. (1990) *Teachers Mistaught: Training in Theories or Education in Subjects?* London: CPS.

Lawn, M. (2013) 'The understories of European education: The contemporary life of experts and professionals', *Sisyphus: Journal of Education*, 1/1, pp. 18–35.

Lawn, M. (2014) 'Transnational lives in European educational research', *European Educational Research Journal*, 13/4, pp. 481–492.

Lawn, M., and Deary, I. (2014) 'The new model school of education: Thomson, Moray House and Teachers College, Columbia', *Paedagogica Historica*, 50/3, pp. 301–319.

Lawn, M., and Deary, I. (2015) 'Inventing a Scottish school of educational research 1920–1950', in R. Anderson, M. Freeman, and L. Paterson (ed), *The Edinburgh History of Education in Scotland*. Edinburgh: Edinburgh University Press, pp. 326–345.

Lawn, M., Deary, I., Bartholomew, D., and Brett, C. (2010) 'Embedding the new science of research: The organised culture of Scottish educational research in the mid-twentieth century', *Paedagogica Historica*, 46/3, pp. 357–381.

Lawn, M., and Furlong, J. (2007) 'The social organisation of education research in England', *European Educational Research Journal*, 6/1, pp. 55–70.

Lawn, M., and Furlong, J. (2011) 'The disciplines of education: Between the ghost and the shadow', in J. Furlong, and M. Lawn (eds), *Disciplines of Education: Their Role in the Future of Educational Research*. London: Routledge, pp. 1–12.

Lawton, D. (1973) *Social Change, Educational Theory and Curriculum Planning*. London: University of London Press.

Lawton, D. (1978/1980) 'The end of the secret garden?', in P. Gordon (ed), *The Study of Education*, vol. 2: *The Last Decade*. London: Woburn Press, pp. 305–325.

Layton, D. (1981) 'The schooling of science in England, 1854–1930', in Roy M. MacLeod and P.D.B. Collins (eds), *The Parliament of Science: The British Association for the Advancement of Science, 1831–1981*. London: Science Reviews, pp. 188–210.

Layton, D., and Lovell, K. (1982) 'The centre for studies in science education at the University of Leeds', *European Journal of Science Education*, 4/2, pp. 216–221.

Lee, R. (2003) *Life and Times of Cultural Studies: The Politics and Transformation of the Structures of Knowledge*. London: Duke University Press.

Lester Smith, W.O. (1950) 'The teacher and the community' (inaugural lecture, IOE, delivered 16 October).

Lovell, K. (1958) *Educational Psychology and Children*. London: University of London Press.

Lovell, K. (1979) 'Developmental psychology', *Educational Review*, 32/2, pp. 103–109.

MacLeod, R., and Collins, P. (1981) (eds) *The Parliament of Science: The British Association for the Advancement of Science, 1831–1981*. London: Science Reviews.

Mallinson, V. (1955) 'Some sources for the history of education in Belgium', *BJES*, 4/1, pp. 62–70.

Martin, S (1977) *Youth Into Industry: A Study of Young People's Attitudes to Work at a Large Midlands Factory*. London: National Youth Bureau.

Martinotti, G. (1997) 'Interdisciplinarity and the social sciences', in R. Cunningham (ed), *Interdisciplinarity and the Organisation of Knowledge in Europe*. Luxembourg: European Communities, pp. 149–176.

Mathers, H. (2005) *Steel City Scholars*. Sheffield: University of Sheffield.

McCulloch, G. (1994) *Educational Reconstruction: The 1944 Education Act and the Twenty-First Century*, London: Woburn Press.

McCulloch, G. (1996) 'Educating the public: Tawney, the *Manchester Guardian* and educational reform', in R. Aldrich (ed), *In History and in Education*. London: Woburn, pp. 116–137.

McCulloch, G. (2002) '"Disciplines contributing to education"? Educational studies and the disciplines', *British Journal of Educational Studies*, 50/1, pp. 100–119.

McCulloch, G. (2004a) *Documentary Research in Education, History and the Social Sciences*. London: Routledge Falmer.

McCulloch, G. (2004b) 'J.A. Green', *Oxford Dictionary of National Biography*. Oxford: Oxford University Press.

McCulloch, G. (2010) 'A people's history of education: Brian Simon, the British Communist Party, and *Studies in the History of Education, 1780–1870*', *History of Education*, 39/4, pp. 437–457.

McCulloch, G. (2011) *The Struggle for the History of Education*. London: Routledge.

McCulloch, G. (2012a) 'Introduction: Disciplinarity, interdisciplinarity and educational studies: Past, present and future', *British Journal of Educational Studies*, 60/4, pp. 295–300.

McCulloch, G. (2012b) 'The Standing Conference on Studies in Education– Sixty years on', *British Journal of Educational Studies*, 60/4, pp. 301–316.

McCulloch, G. (2014a) 'Fred Clarke and the internationalisation of educational studies and research', *Paedagogica Historica*, 50/1–2, pp. 123–137.

McCulloch, G. (2014b) 'Birth of a field: George Baron, educational administration and the social sciences in England, 1946–1978', *Journal of Educational Administration and History*, 46/3, pp. 270–287.

McCulloch, G. (2016) 'British labour party education policy and comprehensive education: From *Learning to Live* to Circular 10/65', *History of Education*, 45/2, pp. 225–245.

McCulloch, G. (in press) 'Politics, ideology and the history of teacher education in England', in M. Ben-Peretz (ed), *The Role of Ideology and Political Movements in Designing Teacher Education Programs*. Lanham, MD: Rowman and Littlefield.

McCulloch, G., Jenkins, E.W., Layton, D. (1985) *Technological Revolution? The Politics of School Science and Technology in England and Wales since 1945*. London: Falmer.

McCulloch, G., Woodin, T., and Cowan, S. (2012) 'The British Conservative Government and the raising of the school leaving age, 1959–1964', *Journal of Education Policy*, 27/2, pp. 509–527.

McDade, D.F. (1982) 'The things that interest mankind: A commentary on 30 years of comparative education', *BJES*, 30/1, pp. 72–84.

McGowan, M. (1986) 'A challenge for the humanities', in R.J. Blin-Stoyle (ed), *The Sussex Opportunity*. New York: Harvester Press, pp. 66–78.

Meikeljohn, J.M.D. (1876/1980) 'Inaugural address', in P. Gordon (ed), *The Study of Education*. London: Woburn Press, pp. 1–42.

Ministry of Education. (1954) *Early Leaving*. London: HMSO.

Ministry of Education. (1959) *15 To 18* (Crowther Report). London: HMSO.

Ministry of Education. (1963a) *Half Our Future* (Newsom Report). London: HMSO.

Ministry of Education. (1963b) *Higher Education* (Robbins Report). London: HMSO.

Mitchell, F.W. (1967) *Sir Fred Clarke: Master-Teacher: 1880–1952* Upper Saddle River, NJ: Prentice Hall Press.

Morrell, J., and Thackray, A. (1984) (eds) *Gentlemen of Science: Early Correspondence of the British Association for the Advancement of Science*. London: Royal Historical Society.

Morris, B. (1952) 'National research centres: 1. The National Foundation for Educational Research in England and Wales', *BJES*, 1/1, pp. 33–38.

Morris, B. (1955) 'Educational research in England and Wales', *International Review of Education*, 1/1, pp. 77–102.

Morris, P., and Chan, K.K. (1997) 'Cross-curricular themes and curriculum reform in Hong Kong: Policy as discourse', *BJES*, 45/3, pp. 248–262.

Moser, C.A. (1958) *Survey Methods in Social Investigation*. London: Heinemann.

Mullainathan, S., and Thaler, R. (2000) 'Behavioural economics', working paper 7948, National Bureau of Economic Research, Cambridge, www.nber.org/papers/w7948, downloaded 13 February 2016.

National Academies of Science. (2015) *Facilitating Interdisciplinary Research*. Washington, DC: National Academies Press

Nature (2015) Editorial, 'Mind meld', 16 September.

NFER (1976) *Register of Educational Research in the United Kingdom 1973–76*. Slough, UK: Author.

NFER (1977) *Register of Educational Research in the United Kingdom, Volume 2 1976–77*. Slough, UK: Author.

NFER (1978) *Register of Educational Research in the United Kingdom, Volume 3 1977–78*. Slough, UK: Author.

NFER (1980) *Register of Educational Research in the United Kingdom, Volume 4 1978–80*. Slough, UK: Author.

Nisbet, J. (1974) 'Educational research: The state of the art' (inaugural BERA presidential address).

Nisbet, J. (2000) 'When the "rot" set in: Education and research, 1960–75', *BERJ*, 26/3, pp. 409–421.

Nisbet, J. (2002) 'Early textbooks in educational research: The birth of a discipline', *European Educational Research Journal*, 1/1, pp. 37–44.

Nisbet, J. (2003) 'A forlorn aspiration?: The story of SHCSE', *Scottish Educational Review*, 35, pp. 60–64.

Nisbet, J. (2005) 'What is educational research? Changing perspectives through the 20th century', *Research Papers in Education*, 20, pp. 25–44.

Nisbet, J. (2009) 'Reflections on being an educational researcher', *Education in the North*, 17/1, pp. 1–4.

Nisbet, S. (1984) 'Does Scotland need SERA?', *Scottish Educational Review*, 16, pp. 127–133.

Norris, N. (2012) 'Lawrence Alexander Stenhouse: an educational life', in J. Elliott and N. Norris (eds), *Curriculum, Pedagogy and Educational Research: The Work of Lawrence Stenhouse*. London: Routledge, pp. 7–48.

Nuffield Foundation (NF). (1975a) *Interdisciplinarity*. London: Author.

Nuffield Foundation (NF). (1975b) *Case-Studies in Interdisciplinarity*, Group 3, London: Author.

Nunn, P. (1920) *Education: Its Data and First Principles*. London: Edward Arnold.

Ohles, J.F. (ed) (1978) *Biographical Dictionary of American Educators, Vol. 1*. Westport, CT: Greenwood Press.

Oliver, R. (1946) *Research in Education*. London: Allen and Unwin.

Oliver, R. (1950–1951). 'Institutes of education'. *Universities Quarterly*, 5/4, pp. 359–365.

Oliver, R. (1951–1952). 'Institutes of education'. *Universities Quarterly*, 6/1, pp. 48–53.

Open University (1982) Popular Culture, Block 7, The state and popular culture, Unit 1, Culture and the state; U203 course team.

Orton, A. (1998) 'Kenneth Lovell 1915–1996', in L. Bills (ed), *Proceedings of the British Society for Research into Learning Mathematics*. London: BSRLM, pp. 1–10.

Ottaway, A.K.C. (1953) *Education and Society: An Introduction to the Sociology of Education*. London: Routledge and Kegan Paul.

Parker, J. (2008) 'Beyond disciplinarity: Humanities and supercomplexity', *London Review of Education*, 6/3, pp. 255–266.

Pearson, R. (1989) 'Foreword', in R. Pearson, J. D. Turner, and G. M. Forrest (ed), *The Psychologist as Educator: The Writings of R.A.C. Oliver*. School of Education, Manchester: University of Manchester, pp. 7–12.

Pearson, R., Turner, J., and Forrest, G. M. (eds) (1989) *The Psychologist as Educator: The Writings of R.A.C. Oliver*. School of Education, Manchester: University of Manchester.

Peel, E. (1956) *The Psychological Basis of Education*. Edinburgh: Oliver and Boyd.

Peel, E. (1960) *The Pupil's Thinking*. London: Oldbourne.

Peel, E. (1971) *The Nature of Adolescent Judgement*. London: Staples.

Percival, A. (1973) *Very Superior Men: Some Early Public School Headmasters and Their Achievements*. London: Knight.

PESGB (2016) PESGB @ 50, www.philosophy-of-education.org/about/pesgb-at-50.html

Peters, A.J. (1964) 'Published sources for the study of contemporary British further education', *BJES*, 13/1, pp. 71–86.

Peters, A.J. (1965) 'Published sources for the study of contemporary British further education (Continued)', *BJES*, 13/2, pp. 170–187.

Peters, R. (1963/1980) 'Education as initiation', inaugural lecture at IOE, in P. Gordon (ed), *The Study of Education: Inaugural Lectures*, vol. 1: *Early and Modern*. London: Woburn Press,, pp. 273–299.

Peters, R. (1965) 'The place of philosophy in the training of teachers', in DES Hull conference, March 1964

Peters, R. (1967) 'In defence of Bingo: A rejoinder', *BJES*, 15/2, pp. 188–194.

Peters, R. (1983) "Philosophy of education', in P. Hirst (ed), *Educational Theory and Its Foundation Disciplines*, London: Routledge and Kegan Paul, pp. 30–61.

Petrie, H. (1976) 'Do you see what I see? The epistemology of interdisciplinary inquiry', *Educational Researcher*, 5/2, pp. 9–14 (also published in *Journal of Aesthetic Education*, 10/1, pp. 29–43).

Pirrie, A. (2001) 'Evidence-based practice in education: The best medicine?', *BJES*, 49/2, pp. 124–136.

Pirrie, A., and Gillies, D. (2012) 'Untimely meditations on the disciplines of education', *BJES*, 60/4, pp. 387–402.

Platt, J. (2003) *The British Sociological Association: A Sociological History*. London: Sociology Press.

Platt, P. (1979) 'Works of Professor E.A. Peel', *Educational Review*, 31/2, pp. 99–102.

Pollard, A. (2003) 'What is and what might be? TLRP strategies and the development of educational research', SERA lecture 2003, www.ser.stir.ac.uk/pdf/264.pdf

Powell, J. (2012) 'The Scottish council for research in education 1928–2003: A short history', *Scottish Educational Review*, 44.2, pp. 60–77.

Priestley, R. (1948) 'Foreword'. *Educational Review*, 1, pp. 1–2.

Pring, R. (2000) 'Editorial: Educational research', *BJES*, 48/1, pp. 1–19.

Pring, R. (2005) 'The development of Curriculum Studies at the Institute of Education', in D. Halpin and P. Walsh (eds), *Educational Commonplaces: Essays to Honour Denis Lawton*. London: IOE, pp. 195–208.

Pritchard, D.G. (1963) 'Some sources for the history of the education of handicapped children in England and Wales', *BJES*, 11/2, pp. 167–176.

Pugh, R.B. (1952) 'Educational records: I sources for the history of English primary schools', *BJES*, 1/1, pp. 43–51.

Quality Assurance Agency (2015) *Benchmark Subject Statement for Education Studies*, February, www.qaa.ac.uk/en/Publications/Documents/SBS-education-studies-15.pdf

Quick, R.H. (1868) *Essays on Educational Reformers*. London: Thoemmes Press.

Radnor, H. (1988) 'GCSE – Does it support equality?', *BJES*, 36/1, pp. 37–48.

RAE (2001) *Education Submissions*, www.rae.ac.uk/2001/submissions/Inst.asp?UoA=68

RAE (2008) *Education Submissions*, www.rae.ac.uk/news/2009/sub.asp

RAE (2014) *Education Submissions*, www.results.rae.ac.uk/Results/ByUoA/25

Ramsey, C.E (1967) *Problems of Youth: A Social Problems Perspective*. Belmont, CA: Dickenson Publishing.

Redford, M. (2013) 'The political administration of Scottish education, 2007–12', in T.G.K. Bryce, W.M. Humes, D. Gillies, A. Kennedy, Donald Gillies, and Aileen Kennedy (eds), *Scottish Education, Referendum*. Edinburgh: Edinburgh University Press.

Reid, L.A. (1952) 'Education and the map of knowledge', *British Journal of Educational Studies*, 1/1, pp. 3–16.

Reid-Smith, E.R. (1965) 'Some sources of information on training college libraries in England and Wales', *BJES*, 14/1, pp. 90–100.

Repko, A. (2008) *Interdisciplinary Research: Process and Theory*. London: Sage.

Research in Education (1969) 'Editorial notes' no 1, May, p. vii.

Richardson, W. (2002) 'Educational studies in the United Kingdom, 1940–2002', *BJES*, 50/1, pp. 3–56.

Robertson, A. (1990) *A Century of Change: The Study of Education at the University of Manchester*. Manchester: School of Education, Manchester University.

Robinson, E. (1968) *The New Polytechnics: The People's Universities*. London: Penguin.

Ruegg, W. (2003) *A History of the University in Europe*, vol. 3, *Universities in the 19th and Early 20th Centuries, 1800–1945*. Cambridge: Cambridge University Press.

Rusk, R.R. (1913) *Introduction to Experimental Education*. New York: Longmans, Green, and Co.

Rusk, R.R. (1952) 'The Scottish council for research in education', *BJES*, 1/1, pp. 39–42.

Rusk, R. (1961) 'Sir John Adams, 1857–1934', *BJES*, 10/1, pp. 49–57.

Sanderson, J.M. (1962) 'The Grammar school and the education of the poor, 1786–1840', *British Journal of Educational Studies*, 11/1, pp. 28–43.

Schools Council Welsh Committee (1968) *Educational Research in Wales*. London: HMSO.

Schriewer, J., and Keiner, E. (1992) 'Communication patterns and intellectual traditions in educational sciences: France and Germany', *Comparative Education Review*, 36/1, pp. 25–51.

Schulman, N. (1993) 'Conditions of their own making: An intellectual history of the Centre for Contemporary Cultural Studies at the University of Birmingham', *Canadian Journal of Communication*, 18/1, http://cjc-online.ca/index.php/journal/article/via/717/623

Schultz, T.W. (1963) *The Economic Value of Education*. New York: Columbia University Press.

Scotland, J. (1982) 'Scottish education, 1952–1982', *BJES*, 30/1, pp. 122–135.

Scottish Education Department (1980) *What Do They Know: A Review of Criterion-Referenced Assessment*. Occasional Papers. London: HMSO.

Seidel, R. (1992) 'The origins of the Lawrence Berkeley laboratory', in P. Galison and B. Henry (eds), *Big Science: The Growth of Large-Scale Research*. Stanford, CA: Stanford University Press, pp. 21–45.

Silver, H. (1981) 'Policy as history and as theory', *British Journal of Sociology of Education*, 2/3, pp. 293–299.

Simon, B (1953) *Intelligence Testing and the Comprehensive School*. London: Lawrence and Wishart.

Simon, B. (1966) 'The history of education', in J.W. Tibble (ed), *The Study of Education*. London: Routledge and Kegan Paul, pp. 91–131.

Simon, B. (1966/1980) 'Education: The new perspective', in P. Gordon (ed), *The Study of Education*, vol. 2. London: Woburn Press, pp. 71–94.

Simon, B. (1978) 'Educational research – Which way?', *Research Intelligence*, 4/1, pp. 2–7.

Simon, B. (1982) 'The history of education in the 1980s', *BJES*, 30/1, pp. 85–96.

Simon, B. (1990) 'The study of education as a university subject', in J.B. Thomas (ed), *British Universities and Teacher Education*. London: Falmer, pp. 125–142.

Simon, B. (1991) *Education and the Social Order, 1940–1990*. London: Lawrence and Wishart.

Simon, B. (1997) *A Life in Education*. London: Lawrence and Wishart.

Simon, J. (1965) *Education and Society in Tudor England*. Cambridge: Cambridge University Press.

Simon, M. (1977) *Youth Into Industry: A Study of Young People's Attitudes to Work at a Large Midlands Factory*. London: National Youth Bureau.

Skilbeck, M. (1982) 'Notes for discussion on curriculum studies: Trends, issues and possible developments', for IOE DCS staff conference, July (DCS papers, IOE).

Smelser, N. (2003) 'On comparative analysis, interdisciplinarity and internationalisation in sociology', *International Sociology*, 18/4, pp. 643–657.

Smeyers, P., and Depaepe, M. (2013) 'Exploring a multitude of spaces in education and educational research', in P. Smeyers, M. Depaepe, and E. Keiner (eds), *Educational Research: The Importance and Effects of Institutional Spaces*. Dordrecht: Springer, pp. 1–10.

Smith, B. (2001) 'Life through a plate glass window', *Times Higher Education*, 10 August.

Smith, H.B. (1913/1980) 'Education as the training of personality', in P. Gordon (ed), *The Study of Education Inaugural Lectures*, vol. 1: *Early and Modern*. London: Woburn Press, pp. 76–97.

Society for Research into Higher Education (SRHE) (ed) (1977) *Interdisciplinarity*. London: SRHE.

Soffer, R. (1987) 'Nation, duty, character and confidence: History at Oxford, 1850–1914', *Historical Journal*, 30/1, pp. 77–104.

Stead, H.G. (1942) *The Education of a Community: To-day and Tomorrow*. Bickley: University of London Press.

Stedman Jones, G. (1972) 'History: the poverty of empiricism', in R. Blackburn (ed), *Ideology in Social Science: Readings in Critical Social Theory*. London: Fontana Press, pp. 96–115.

Stenhouse, L. (1963) 'A cultural approach to the sociology of the curriculum', *Pedagogic Forskning*, Vol 7.1, pp. 120–134.

Stenhouse, L. (1968) 'The Humanities curriculum project', *Journal of Curriculum Studies*, 1/1, pp. 26–33.

Stenhouse, L. (ed) (1980) *Curriculum Research and Development in Action*. London: Heinemann.

Stewart, W.A.C. (1952) 'Karl Mannheim and the sociology of education', *BJES*, 2/1, pp. 99–113.

Stimson, D. (1948) *Scientists and Amateurs: A History of the Royal Society*. New York: Henry Schuwen.

Stones, E. (1985a) 'The development of the British Educational Research Association: A personal view', in M. Shipman (ed), *Educational Research: Principles, Policies and Practices*. London: Falmer Press, pp. 17–26.

Stones, E. (1985b) 'The development of the British Educational Research Association', *BERJ*, 11/2, pp. 85–90.

Sunday Times (1997) Report, 'Woodhead in purge against "PC" research', 31 August.

Sutherland, M.B. (1982) 'Progress and problems in education in Northern Ireland, 1952–1982', *BJES*, 3, pp. 136–149.

Swift, D.F. (1968) 'Social class and educational adaptation', in H.J. Butcher (ed) with H.B. Pont, *Educational Research in Britain*. London: University of London Press.

Swift D.F. (1970) *Basic Readings in the Sociology of Education*. London: Routledge Kegan Paul.

Szreter, R. (1980) 'Landmarks in the institutionalisation of the sociology of education in Britain', *Educational Review*, 32/3, pp. 293–300.

Tate, W.E. (1953a) 'Educational records: II some sources for the history of English grammar schools', *British Journal of Educational Studies*, 1/2, pp. 164–175.

Tate, W.E. (1953b) 'Educational records: II sources for the history of English grammar schools (Continued)', *British Journal of Educational Studies*, 2/1, pp. 67–81.

Tate, W.E. (1954) 'Educational records: II sources for the history of the English grammar schools (Concluded)', *British Journal of Educational Studies*, 2/2, pp. 145–165.

Taylor, W. (1969) *Society and the Education of Teachers*. London: Faber and Faber.

Taylor, W. (1972) 'Retrospect and prospect in educational research', *Educational Research*, 15/1, pp. 3–9.

Teaching and Development Agency. (2006) *Improving Teacher Training Provision in England, 1990–2005: A Political History of the Challenges Faced by the Government in Improving Teacher Training Provision in England: 1990–2005*. London: Author.

Tempest, N.R. (1960) 'Some sources for the history of teacher-training in England and Wales', *BJES*, 9/1, pp. 57–66.

Thaler, R. (2015) *Misbehaving: The Making of Behavioural Economics*. London: Allen Lane.

Thomas, J. (2012) 'Disciplinarity and the organisation of scholarly writing in educational studies in the UK: 1970–2010', *BJES*, 60/4, pp. 357–386.

Thomas, J.B. (1982) 'J.A. Green, educational psychology and the *Journal of Experimental Pedagogy*', *History of Education Society Bulletin*, 29, pp. 41–44.

Thomas, J.B. (ed) (1990) *British Universities and Teacher Education: A Century of Change*. London: Falmer Press.

Thomas, J.B. (1992) 'Birmingham University and teacher training: Day training college to department of education', *History of Education*, 21/3, pp. 307–321.

Thomas, J.B. (2007) 'Psychology of education in the UK: Development in the 1960s', *Educational Studies*, 33/1, pp. 55–63.

Thompson, D.C. (1949) *Training Worker Citizens: An Exposition by Experts of Some Modern Educational Methods Designed to Equip Youth for the Service of Industry and the State*. London: Macdonald & Evans.

Thompson, E.P. (1964) *The Making of the English Working Class*. New York: Pantheon.

Thomsan, D.G. (1949) *Training Worker Citizens: An Exposition by Experts of Some Modern Educational Methods Designed to Equip Youth for the Service of Industry and the State*. London: Macdonald & Evans.

Thoulness, R.H. (1969) *Map of Educational Research: A Survey of Salient Research for Those Engaged in the Practice of Education*. Slough: NFER.

Tibble, J.W. (ed) (1966a) *The Study of Education*. London: Routledge and Kegan Paul.

Tibble, J.W. (1966b) 'The development of the study of education', in J.W. Tibble (ed), *The Study of Education*. London: Routledge and Kegan Paul, pp. 1–28.

Times Educational Supplement (*TES*) (1997) Report, 'Research inquiry sparks row', 12 September.

Times Educational Supplement (*TES*) (2010a) Front paper headline article, 'Gove serves notice on teacher training', 19 November.

Times Educational Supplement (*TES*) (2010b) Report, 'MP warns of 85% university training cuts'.

Times Higher Education Supplement (*THE*) (1997) Report, 'Research inquiry sparks row', 12 September.

Times Higher Education Supplement (*THE*) (2011) Report, 'Researchers told to wake up and small the cogency', 28 July.

Times Higher Education Supplement (*THE*) (2013) Report, 'Hey, torpid teacher training colleges, leave those kids alone', 13 March.

The Times (1997) Report, 'Education research is dross, says Woodhead', 23 July.

Timmins, N. (1995) *The Five Giants: A Biography of the Welfare State*. London: HarperCollins.

Torrance, H. (2011) 'Using assessment to drive the reform of schooling: Time to stop pursuing the chimera?', *BJES*, 59/4, pp. 459–485.

Tropp, A. (1958) 'Some sources for the history of educational periodicals in England', *BJES*, 6/2, pp. 151–163.

Tuckett, A. (2014) *Seriously Useless Learning: The Collected TES Writings of Alan Tuckett*. Leicester, Cardiff: National Institute of Adult Continuing Education.

Turner, C.M. (1969) 'Sociological approaches to the history of education', *BJES*, 17/2, pp. 146–165.

University of Durham (2015) *Evaluating Interdisciplinary Research*, July, Institute of Advanced Study, www.dur.ac.uk/resouias/poublications/StrangandMcLeish.EvaluatingInterdisciplinaryResearch.July2015_2.pdf

Valentine, C.W. (1916) *An Introduction to Experimental Psychology in Relation to Education*. Baltimore: Warwick & York, Inc.

Valentine, C.W. (1930) 'The future of "The Forum of Education"', *Forum of Education*, 8/3, November, pp. 161–162.

Valentine, C.W. (1950) *Psychology and Its Bearing on Education*. New York: Routledge.

Valentine, C.W. (1951) 'The Journal comes of age', *BJEP*, pp. 226–229.

Van Dalen, D.B. (1962) *Understanding Educational Research*. New York: McGraw Hill.

Van Praagh, G. (ed) (1973) *H.E. Armstrong and Science Education*. London: John Murray.

Vernon, P. (1962) 'The contributions to education of Sir Godfrey Thomson', *BJES*, 10/2, pp. 123–138.

Walford, G. (2011) 'The Oxford ethnography conference: A place in history?', *Ethnography and Education*, 6/2, pp. 133–145.

Walker, J.C., and Evers, C.W. (1982) 'Epistemology and justifying the curriculum of educational studies', *BJES*, 30/2, pp. 213–229.

Walker, R., and Barton, L. (eds) (1983) *Race, Class and Education*. London: Falmer Press.

Walkup, V. (ed) (2011) *Exploring Education Studies*. Harlow: Longman.

Wall, W.D. (1979) 'The contribution of E.A. Peel to educational psychology', *Educational Review*, 31/2, pp. 93–98.

Wang, Z. (2009) *In Sputnik's Shadow: The President's Science Advisory Committee and Cold War America*. New Brunswick, NJ: Rutgers University Press.

Ward, S. (ed) (2004) *Education Studies: A Student's Guide*. London: Routledge.

Watts, D.G. (1969) *Environmental Studies*. Routledge & Kegan Paul.

Weingart, P. (2010) 'A short history of knowledge formations', in R. Frodeman (ed), *Oxford Handbook of Interdisciplinarity*. Oxford: Oxford University Press, pp. 3–14.

White, H.D. (2014) 'Scientific and scholarly networks', in John Scott and Peter J. Carrington (eds), *The SAGE Handbook of Social Network Analysis*. New York: Sage, pp. 271–285.

Whyte, W. (2015) *Redbrick: A Social and Architectural History of Britain's Civic Universities*. Oxford: Oxford University Press.

Wilby, P. (1983) 'Teaching: The real dangers', *Sunday Times*, 27 March.

Williams, G. (1982) 'The economics of education: Current debates and prospects', *BJES*, 30/1, pp. 97–107.

Williams, R. (1958) *Culture and Society*. London: Chatto and Windus.

Williams, R. (1961) *The Long Revolution*. London: Chatto and Windus.

Williamson, H. (2004) 'Human rights and education', in S. Ward (ed), *Education Studies: A Student's Guide*. London: Routledge, pp. 57–66.

Willis, P. (1977) *Learning to Labour: How Working Class Kids Get Working Class Jobs*. Ann Arbor, MI: Saxon House.

Willmott, R. (2002) 'Reclaiming metaphysical truth for educational research', *BJES*, 50/3, pp. 339–362.

Wilson, J. (2002) 'Is education a good thing?', *BJES*, 50/3, pp. 327–338.

Wilson, P.S. (1967) 'In defence of Bingo', *BJES*, 15/1, pp. 5–27.

Wiseman, S. (1953) 'Higher degrees in education in British universities', *BJES*, 2/1, pp. 54–66.

Wiseman, S. (1965) 'Educational psychology in the education of teachers', paper presented to DES Hull conference, March 1964.

Woodhall, M. (1970) *Cost-Benefit Analysis in Educational Planning*. Paris: UNESCO.

Woodhead, C. (1997) 'Inspecting schools: The key to raising educational standards', 'The Last Word' lecture at the Royal Geographical Society, 21 January.

Woodin, T., McCulloch, G., and Cowan, S. (2013) *Secondary Education and the Raising of the School Leaving Age: Coming of Age?* New York: Palgrave Macmillan.

Wright, H.K. (2001) 'Michael Green's reflections on personal and institutional development of Cultural Studies in Education at Birmingham (Part II)', *Review of Education, Pedagogy and Cultural Studies*, 23/4, pp. 335–348.

Wrigley, J. (1975) 'Pitfalls in educational research', BERA presidential address.

Yates, A. (ed) (1971) *The Role of Research in Educational Change*. Palo Alta: Pacific Book.

Year Book of Education (1932), London: Evans Brothers Ltd.

Young, M. (ed) (1965) *Innovation and Research in Education*. London: Routledge and Kegan Paul.

Young, M.F.D. (ed) (1971) *Knowledge and Control: New Directions for the Sociology of Education*. London: Collier-Macmillan.

Zembylas, M. (2007) 'Emotional capital and education: Theoretical insights from Bourdieu', *BJES*, 55/4, pp. 443–463.

INDEX

Thoulness, Robert 45, 98
Tibble, J.W. 3, 18, 49, 55–7, 73, 99, 100, 164; Clare, John 100
Times, The 130
Times Educational Supplement 66, 97, 130
Times Higher Education Supplement 130
Tizard, Jack 104
Tooley, James 130
Topic Modelling 67–8, 82
Totterdell, Michael 109
Tout, Thomas 13
Training College Association (TCA) 22–3; *Training College Record* 23
Treasury (UK) 53
Troman, Geoff 131
Turner, C.M. 70
Tyack, David 106

UK Research and Innovation (UKRI) 145
UNESCO: Department of Education 37
Universities Quarterly 67
University College London (UCL) 14, 22
University Department of Education 26, 128–9
University Funding Council 127
University Grants Committee 127
USA 5, 12, 13, 46, 95, 101, 105–6, 120, 133, 161; Eastern seaboard 28; Interdisciplinarity in 8; Response to Sputnik 14

Valentine, C.W. 23, 66, 104
Vernon, Philip 36, 104
VosViewer software 83–4

Wales 19, 49, 54, 71; Schools Council Welsh Committee 53
Walker, Rob 59

Walkup, Vivienne 110
Wall, William 104
Wall Street 29
Walsall 51
Ward, S. 108
Warwick University 120
Watts, D.G. 100
Web of Knowledge 67
Web of Science 68, 83
Weingart, Peter 10
West, E.G. 103
Westhill College 131
Westhill Sociology of Education Conference 131, 137; Network 132
West Midlands College of Education 51
Whitelands College 131
White Paper, *The Importance of Teaching* 147–8; Teach First 148; Troops for Teachers 148
Whitfield, R.C. 60
Wilby, Peter 128
Williams, Raymond 116
Williamson, Heather 108
Wilson, Paul 123
Wiseman, Stephen 54–5, 98
Wolverhampton, University of 109
Women's History Network 138
Woodhall, Maureen 103
Woodhead, Chris 129, 130
Wooton, Barbara 37
Wrigley, Jack 63, 103

Yearbook of Education 94
York, University of (Canada) 13
York, University of (UK) 18; Institute of Effective Education 149
Young, Michael F.D. 58, 105, 120–1; *Knowledge and Control* 58